AF471216

BLASPHEMY

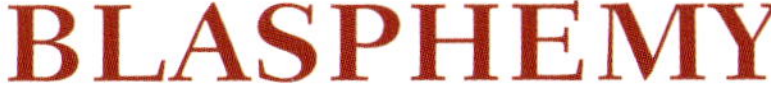

BLASPHEMY

Art That Offends

S Brent Plate

black dog publishing

PREFACE

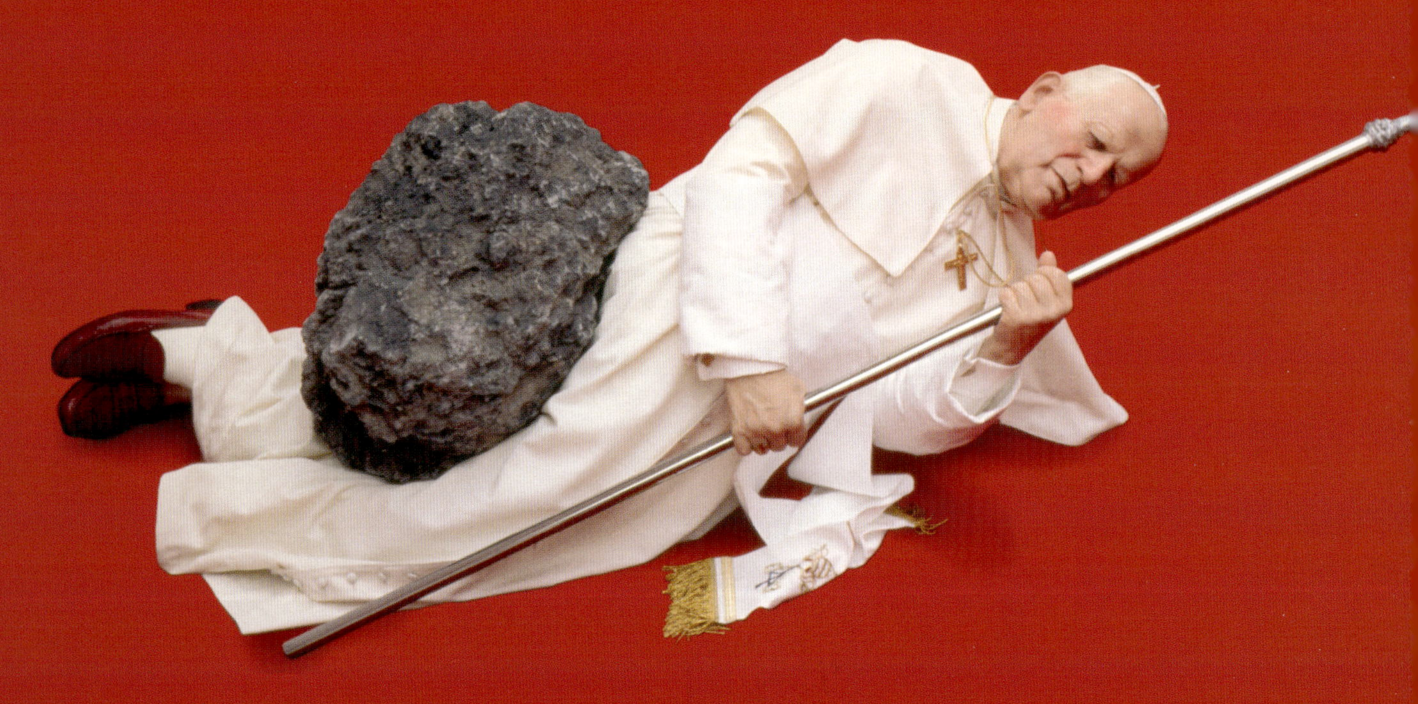

Maurizio Cattelan, *La Nona Ora* (*The Ninth Hour*), 1999, wax, clothing, polyester resin with metallic powder, volcanic rock, carpet, glass, courtesy of Galerie Emmanuel Perrotin, Paris
As lot 317, this controversial sculpture sold at Christie's auction house in May 2001. The catalogue cover depicted the life-like wax figure of Pope John Paul II felled by a meteorite yet still clinging to his crosier, a symbol both of the Pope's authority and Christ's humility.

PREFACE

Since so much history has burned, banned, and banished blasphemous art and artists, this book has limits. In a real way, these limits are often unknown limits: I have no idea what images were considered blasphemous in, say, the eleventh century, since the chances are quite good that they were destroyed by some religio-political authorities. Further research might indicate a handful of works from that time that can be pointed to, but never represented since there is no material remainder of them. We are left here, as in all artistic and religious histories, with the hard materials that recreate history by surviving the storms of time: clay, marble, stone, gold, silver, and even well-made paper or papyrus bound within leather.

And yet there is, of course, plenty of material here to comment upon, to come up with some suggestions, theories, and propositions about blasphemous images and how they function in the lives of religious and secular people in the past and present. And this is what I have attempted to make clear in the following. For all its shortcomings, its elisions of history, I hope this book will provide some working terms for the reader so as to continue conversations on issues vital to contemporary life: censorship, the religious-political divide, the role of technology and mass media, and religious fundamentalism and liberalism.

This book is well illustrated, and I am grateful to be working with the publishers on this project, a relatively small press that believes in the power of both image *and* word. In spite of their great efforts, part of what has become so intriguing is the fact that, even with a commitment to reproduce images, and with a vast array of electronic technologies and some funding, it is not possible here to reproduce all the images that were desired. In the process of assembling this book there has been a real uneasiness on the part of artists to be included in a book on blasphemy. Along the way we've run into cartoonists from central Europe who have been through enough already and want no more inclusion in anything that suggests blasphemy; painters who want to know exactly how their work will be included and retain veto power to reproduce their artworks if the words surrounding them do not come off correctly; and curators of photographs and other works who seemingly fear for their very lives. This book includes representations by artists who have actually been killed for the images they've created. All of this is serious stuff and I've tried to be respectful of all sides in the matters at hand.

I personally do not consider any of the works contained here to be blasphemous in and of themselves. My interest is to emphasise the contexts in which images come to be called blasphemous, sacrilegious, idolatrous, obscene, or immoral. And I challenge the reader to understand the context in which these various images are discussed and condemned. Many, though not all, of the illustrations seen in these pages have indeed been accused of blasphemy and part of my attempt here is to indicate the reasons why anyone would consider these images to be blasphemous. People hold particular persons, places, times, and things to be sacred and it is important to understand when, where, why, and how this occurs. On the other hand, many of the illustrations included here are intended as *counterarguments* to the charges of blasphemy and they serve to set the larger context for the issues raised. Just because an image is included here does not mean I suggest it to be a blasphemous image.

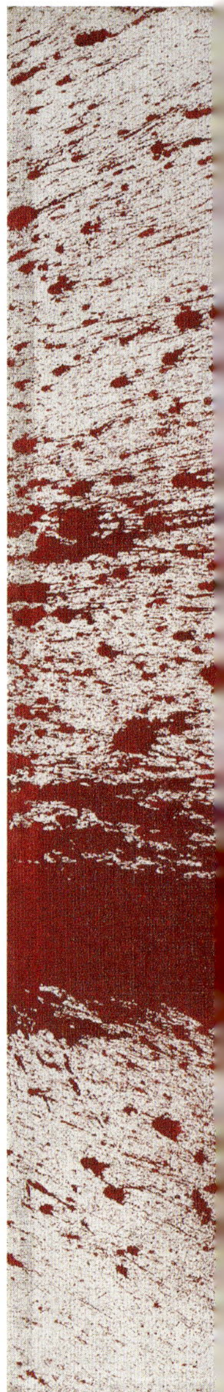

Those in biggest need of acknowledgement include the exceptional work of Madeleine Boyd, Finella Halligan and Helen Frosi who have been working on permissions and much additional research on most of the images seen here. Duncan McCorquodale, for initially suggesting this topic and setting me on an unexpected course enquiry; and Catherine Grant, Oriana Fox, Amy Sackville, and Safiya Waley for following up. My student research assistant, Megan Ammann, whose work led me to new areas; Allen Roberts, for emailed conversations about the limits of what to include in such a book; David Morgan, for initial thoughts on the topic; Diane Apostolos-Cappadona, for passing on quotes, thoughts, and support for the project; Simon Halliday for teaching me more about the subject than I ever thought possible; and along the way Doug Adams, Timothy Beal, Stefano Carboni, Maryam Ekhtiar, Paul Gehl, Tod Linafelt, Darren JN Middleton, Jack Renard, and members of Tel Mac, have all offered good assistance. Any responsibility for what is included and excluded here is, of course, my own. Finally, it is Sabina Elli and Edna Melisa that I must thank most for the seamless life that they provide me with.

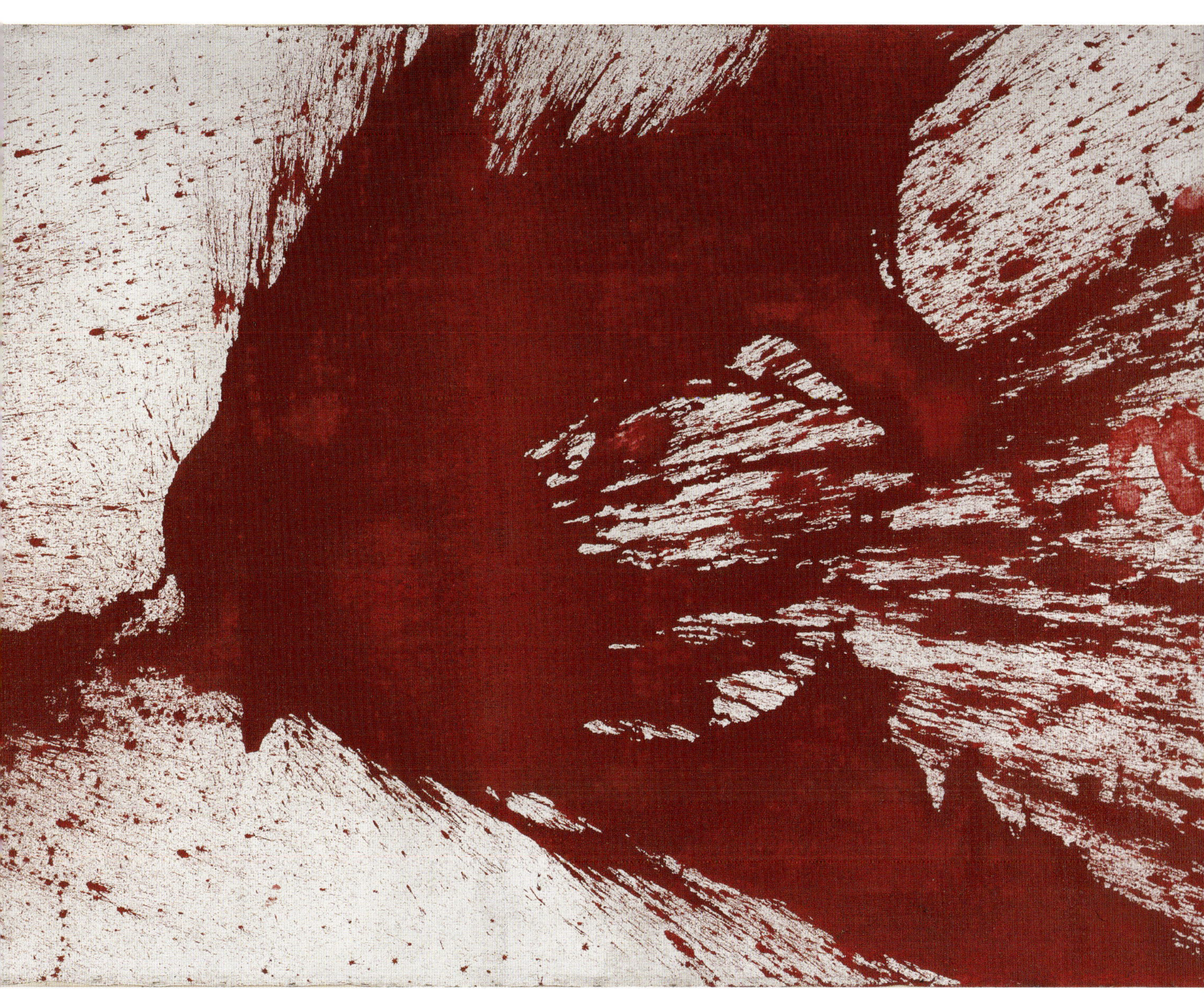

Herman Nitsch, *Splatter Painting*, 1983, oil and acrylic on canvas, courtesy of Saatchi Gallery, London

Celebrated as the 'Pope of Viennese Aktionism', Nitsch's *Splatter* paintings embody the artist's preoccupation with pagan and Christian symbolism and ritual. The series references the imagery of holy relics and evokes thoughts of blood, violence and martyrdom.

THE POWER OF OFFENSIVE IMAGES

Introduction

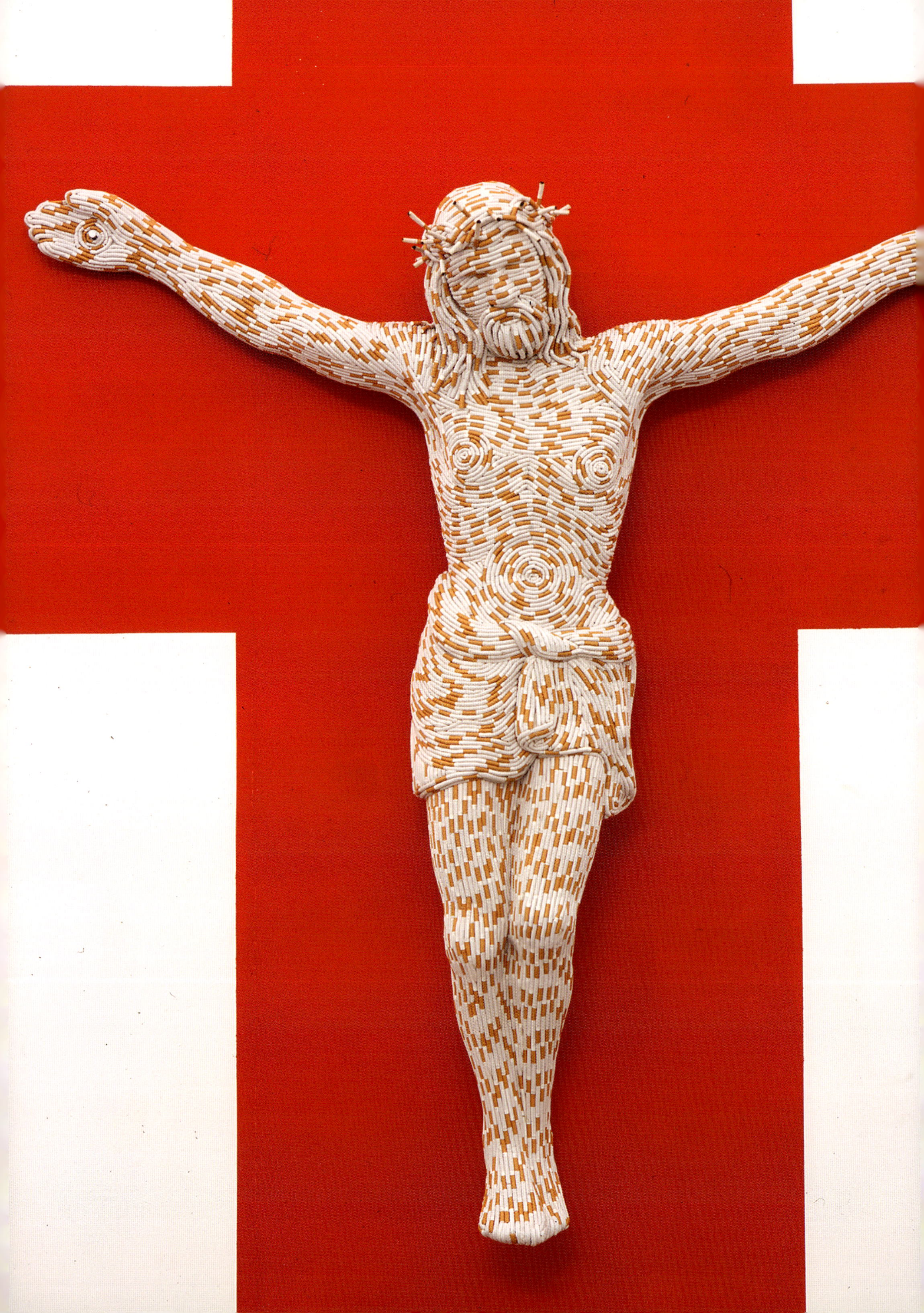

Sarah Lucas, *Christ You Know It Ain't Easy* (detail), 2003, Marlboro cigarettes and mixed media, lifesize, © the artist, courtesy of Sadie Coles HQ, London

This life-sized sculpture of the crucifixion of Christ, made entirely from Marlboro Light cigarettes, was exhibited in 2004 at the Tate Britain in a show called *In-A-Gadda-Da-Vida* (from the corrupt pronunciation of 'In the Garden of Eden'). The show's curator, Gregor Muir, believes the work to be a statement about the power of consumerism today – conspicuous consumption, not religion, is now the opiate of the people.

THE POWER OF OFFENSIVE IMAGES

Introduction

Once upon a time in Denmark, a children's book author named Kåre Bluitgen wanted to make a book about the life of the Prophet Muhammad. Bluitgen complained he couldn't find anyone to make illustrations for it, because artists believed depictions of the Prophet were blasphemous in Islam and they feared being attacked by religious extremists. Perhaps their apprehension was heightened by the murder of rebel filmmaker Theo Van Gogh in the liberal streets of Amsterdam after he made the film *Submission* in 2004. The ten-minute film criticised the treatment of women in Islamic society and many Dutch Muslims considered it to be blasphemous. The Islamist militant Mohammed Bouyeri took *sharia* law into his own hands as he shot the filmmaker several times, then pinned a radical, apocalyptic manifesto to his dead body with a knife, carved with apocalyptic passages from the Quran.

With Van Gogh's murder fresh in the European consciousness, the politically conservative Danish newspaper, *Jyllands-Posten*, ostensibly wished to show courage in the face of terror and help Bluitgen make his book on the Prophet Muhammad. The paper commissioned a number of cartoonists/caricaturists (not 'illustrators') to draw images of Muhammad as the artists saw him. A dozen of these were posted in the paper on 30 September 2005. Most were silly, hardly salient – a couple were so poor in quality and execution that the paper should have been downright embarrassed in retrospect for even printing them – while several of the images were nasty, aggressive, and violent depictions, such as Muhammad with a bomb for a turban and another of Muhammad clutching a sword and bearing an angry expression. What he was angry about was not indicated within the cartoon. Regardless, not much happened after the initial printing, save the protests of a few Muslim groups in Denmark. Soon after, on 17 October 2005, the independent Egyptian paper *Al Fagr* reprinted several of the images during the Muslim holy month of Ramadan, including the sword-wielding Muhammad image on the newspaper cover. Again, not much was said.

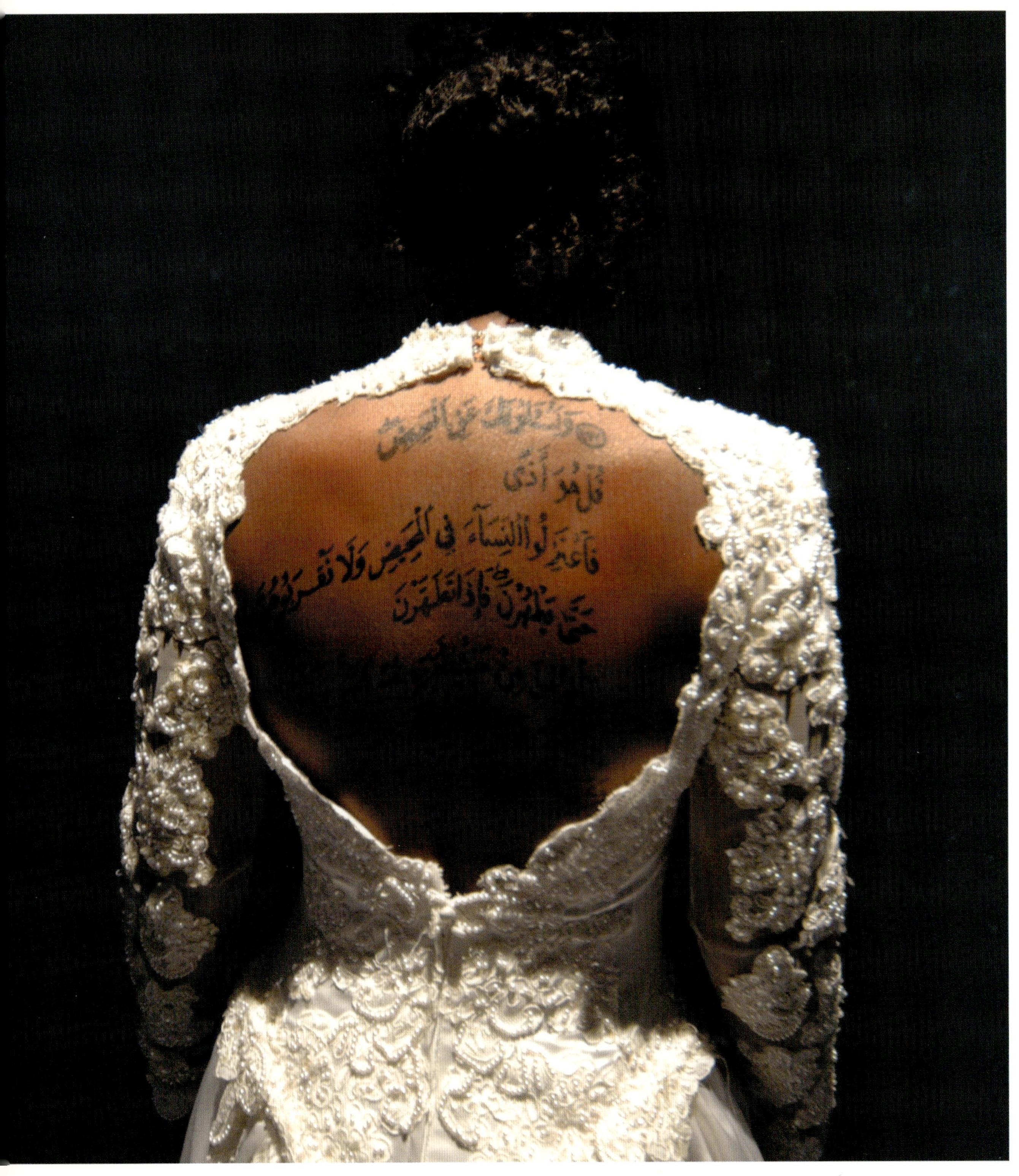
ويسألونك عن المحيض
قل هو أذى
فاعتزلوا النساء في المحيض ولا تقربوهن
حتى يطهرن فإذا تطهرن

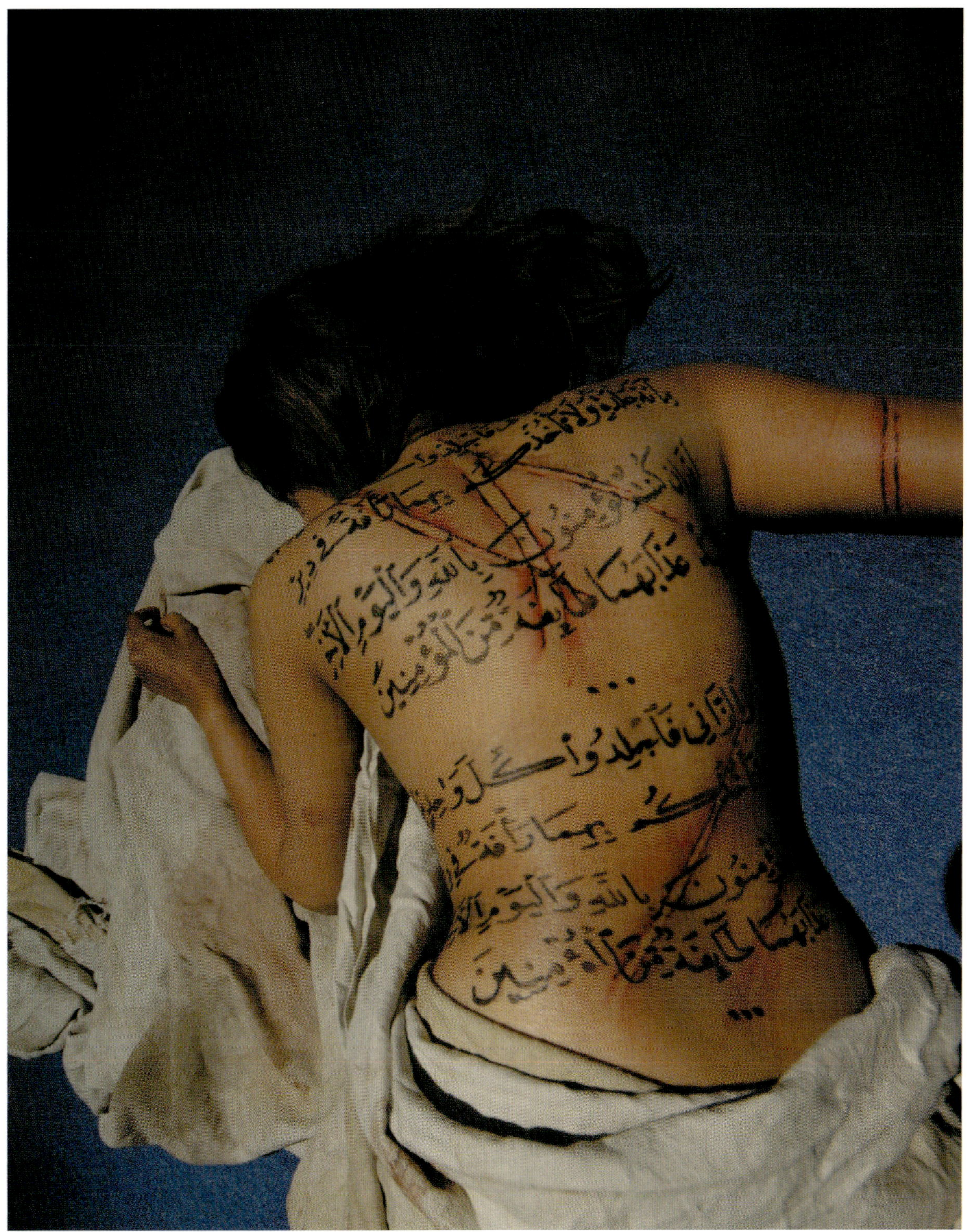

Theo Van Gogh, *Submission*, 2004, film stills, courtesy of Thomas Kist

The ten-minute English-language film takes its title from a direct translation of the word 'Islam'. The film was perceived as insulting by many Muslims due to its controversial portrayal of women within Muslim families. The film, shown on the Dutch public broadcasting network VPRO in August 2004, depicted domestic violence and inter-familial rape. These images show slashed female bodies used as vellum for verses from the Quran.

However, protests across the world, many becoming violent and even fatal, began in early February 2006 after several papers across Europe – apparently with nothing better to do than recycle four-month old stories – reprinted the images. Now the cartoons made the news, and people took notice. Pockets of Muslim groups around the world – almost entirely in war-struck, disaster-struck, poverty-struck areas – reacted against a European media, and 'the West' in general, that seemed intent on provocation – a provocation boosted by brisk sales at newsstands. Muslim leaders called for economic embargoes, flags (especially Danish) were burned, sticks and stones were thrown, fires started, people killed. If some Muslims were offended by negative portrayals of what they found sacred (namely, Muhammad), many Western journalists, bloggers, and barroom pundits responded by showing what the modern West holds sacred (namely, free expression).

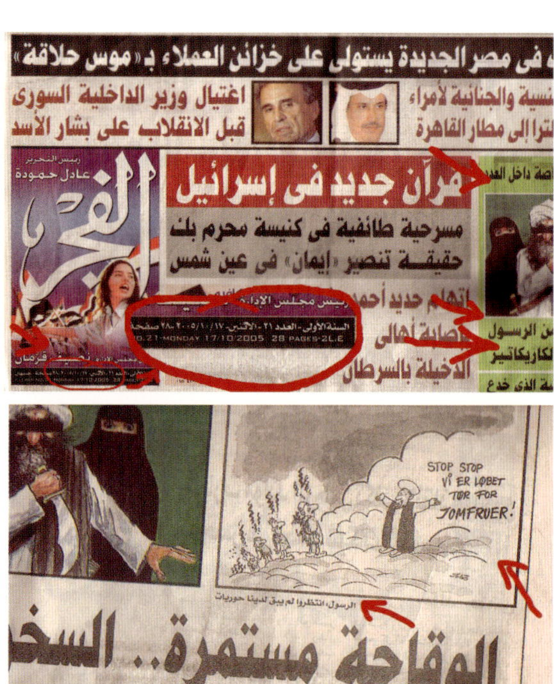

اغتيال وزير الداخلية السورى
قبل الانقلاب على بشار الأسد
الفجر
مسرحية طائفية فى كنيسة محرم بك
حقيقة تنصير «إيمان» فى عين شمس
الوقاحة مستمرة..

Shots from www.sandmonkey.org, reproducing pages of 17 October 2005 edition of *El Fagr*, courtesy of Alex Adam aka Sandmonkey

These now infamous Danish cartoons were published by the Egyptian newspaper, *El Fagr*, during the holy month of Ramadan. A subsequent UN report focused on the need to combat 'Islamophobia', suggesting that "beliefs should not be humiliated under the veil of freedom of expression". Sandmonkey, the Cairo-based blogger, was one of many to disseminate the images across the internet, in solidarity with the illustrators, *Jyllands-Posten* and the right to freedom of expression.

To understand the place and function of blasphemy, it is necessary to take stock of the power of images, and the ways they 'call out' to people.

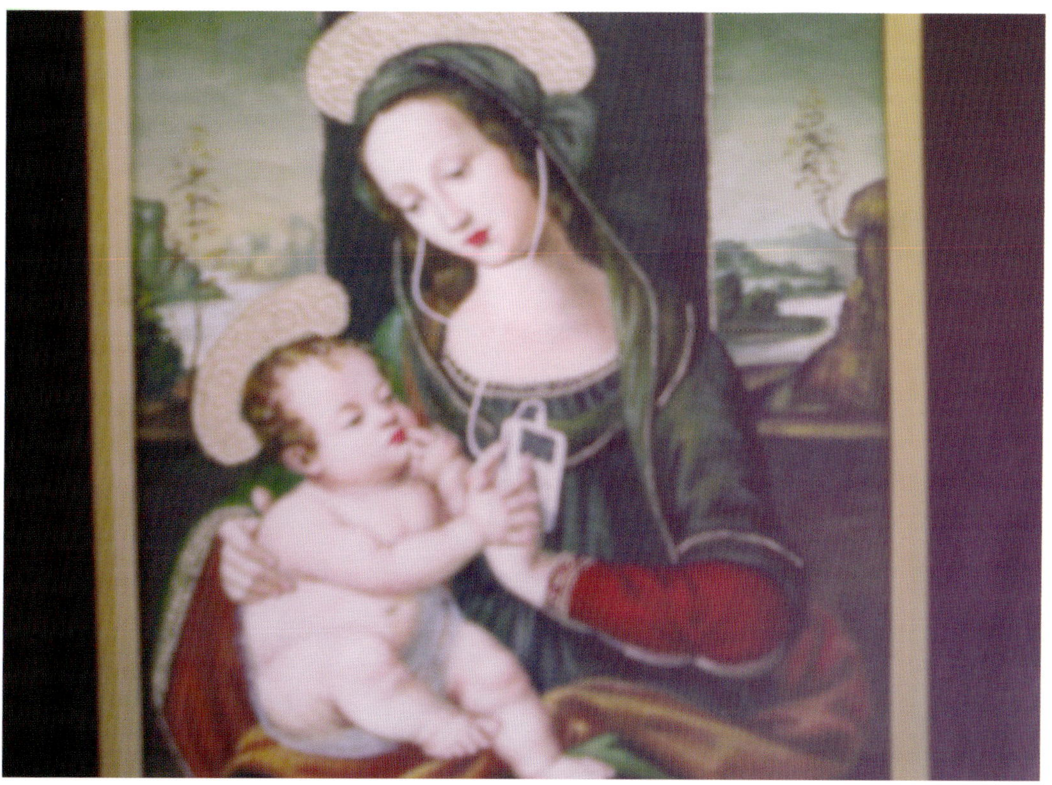

Robin Banks aka Banksy, *Silent Night*, 2004, oils, courtesy of the artist

Banksy, the Bristol-based 'anarch-artist', agreed for his work to be included only if the Danish Muhammad cartoons featured as well. This piece, in the same vein as Lucas's work, playfully invokes capitalism and materialism as the new religion.

While the issues raised through the so-called Danish cartoon controversy touch on a number of facets of human life – economic, political, social, religious – the flint-stone that sparked the upheavals was a handful of images. Even if side-stepping the socio-political issues, *The New York Times* art critic Michael Kimmelman pointed out the power of images in the midst of the riots: "To many people, pictures will always, mysteriously, embody the things they depict. Among the issues to be hashed out in this affair, there's a lesson to be gleaned about art: Even a dumb cartoon may not be so dumb if it calls out to someone."[1] Artists' intentions are one thing, formal evaluation of images another, and the reception of images – in spite of how 'dumb' they may be – still another. To understand the place and function of blasphemy, it is necessary to take stock of the power of images, and the ways they 'call out' to people.

Kimmelman's editorial draws on the work of art historian, David Freedberg, who sums up this imagistic 'calling out' in his significant study, *The Power of Images*:

> People are sexually aroused by pictures and sculptures; they break pictures and sculptures; they mutilate them, kiss them, cry before them, and go on journeys to them; they are calmed by them, stirred by them, and incited to revolt. They give thanks by means of them, expect to be elevated by them, and are moved to the highest levels of empathy and fear. They have always responded in these ways; they still do. They do so in societies we call primitive and in modern societies; in East and West, in Africa, America, Asia, and Europe.[2]

Marcus Harvey, *Myra*, 1995, acrylic on canvas, 396 x 320 cm, courtesy of White Cube/Jay Jopling

Based on a mug shot of one of the Moors Murderers, Myra Hindley, and created from the stencilled handprints of young children, the work angered many who saw it as exploiting the suffering of the victims and their families. At the *Sensation* show in September 1997, the painting was defaced on two separate occasions, using Indian ink and eggs. A glass case and two security guards were employed to protect the work. Surprisingly, when exhibited in New York, this image did not spark public protest. Instead, Chris Ofili's portrait of the Virgin Mary was attacked by a Christian brandishing white paint.

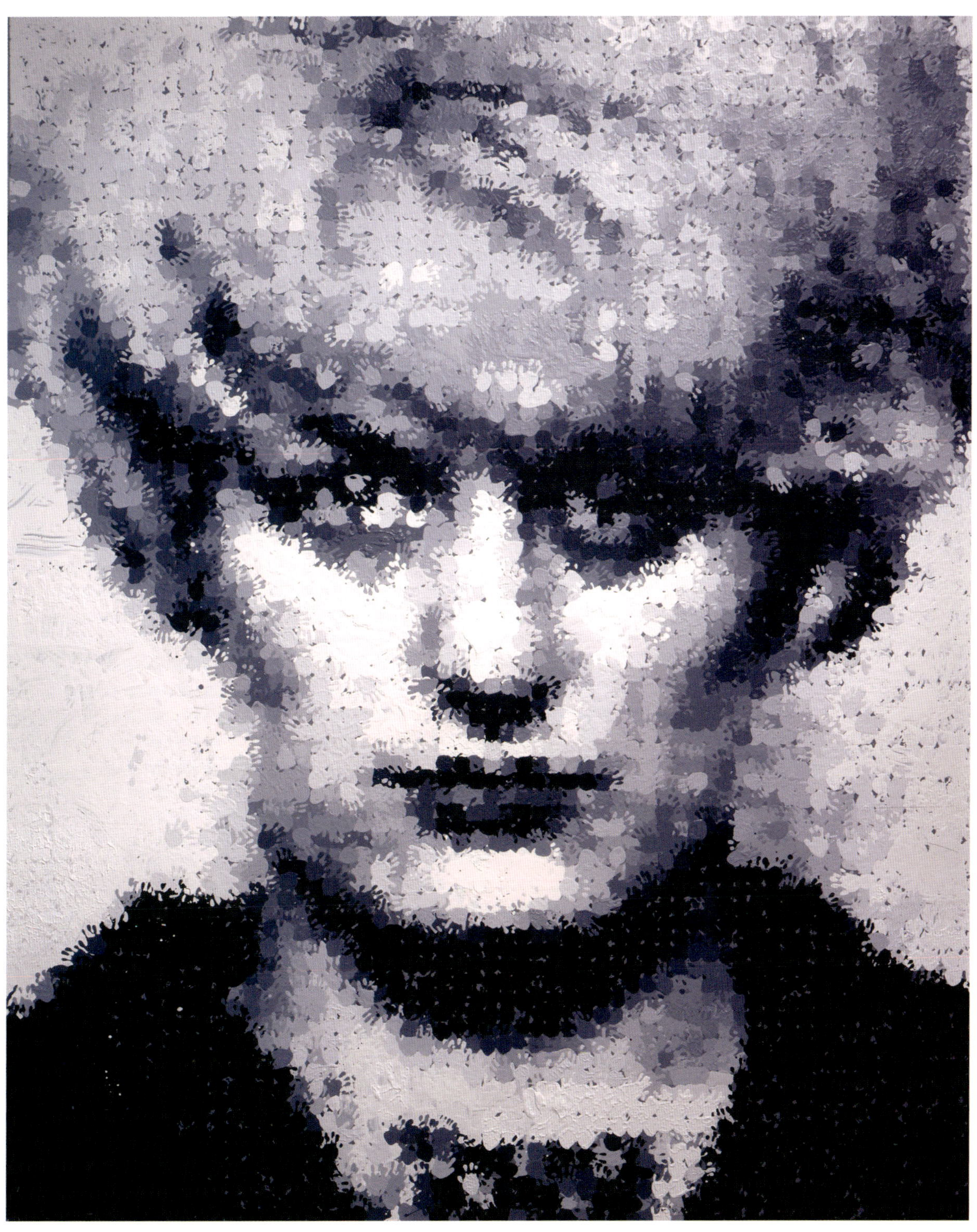

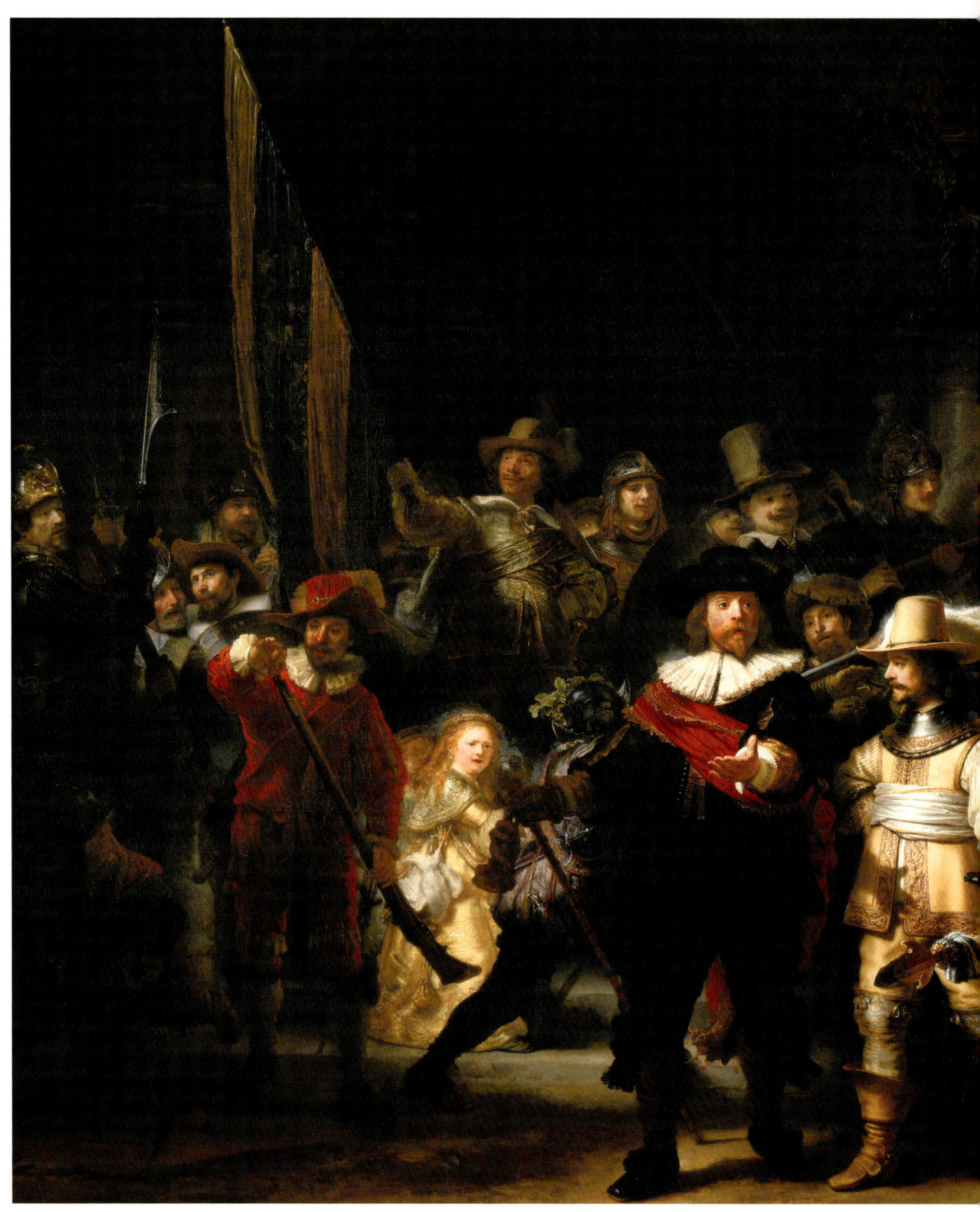

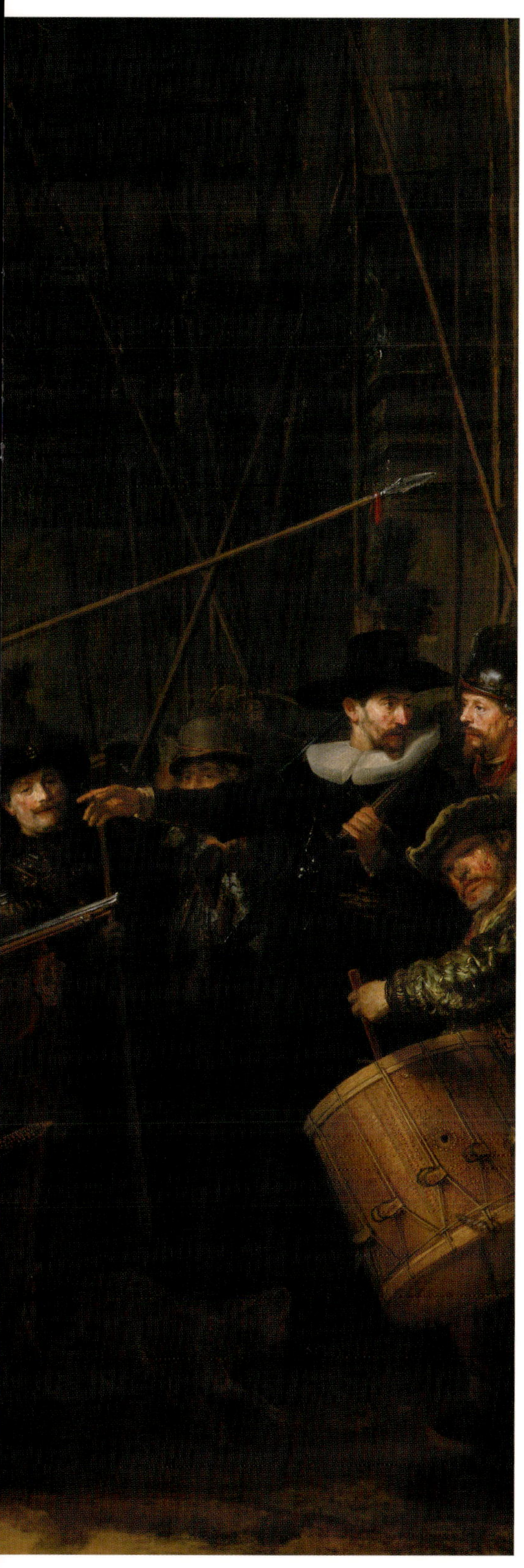

The power of images would seem to emerge through some quasi-alchemical process: fine ink lines drawn on paper, curves here, straight line there, and Bam! There is a depiction that will really provoke someone. Or maybe: a little pigment, a little oil, a surface to work on, and there's a representation, slightly skewed from the 'real world', that induces tears, that rouses people from their dogmatic slumber and makes them journey hundreds of miles to bask in the presence of the image. That the Frank Gehry-designed Guggenheim Museum in Bilbao, Spain, has helped revitalise this post-industrial city tells us much about the ways pilgrimage (in the modern guise of 'tourism') continues to rely on the material realities of images and their attractive power. Images gain seemingly immaterial energy, or aura, from raw materials, causing physical responses on the part of viewers. And while there is much to say about the crying, kissing, and journeying that surround images, in this book I am looking at the indictment of blasphemy, and so we must delve into related responses to images such as censorship, iconoclasm, and sometimes just downright destruction.

Rembrandt van Rijn, *The Night Watch* (The Militia Company of Captain Frans Banning Cocq), 1642, oil on canvas, 371 x 445 cm, courtesy of Rijksmuseum, Amsterdam

This painting has been savaged three times over the past hundred years at Amsterdam's Rijksmuseum, most severely in 1975, when it was slashed by Wilhelmus de Rijk with a bread knife stolen from his hotel. During this latter act of vandalism, the attack focused on the figure of Captain Frans Banning Cocq, whom de Rijk perceived as being the personification of evil. Throughout the attack, he claimed, "I have been sent by the Lord. I have been forced to do this by forces out of this Earth." The Rijksmuseum would only authorise this unscathed version of the painting to be reproduced in this book.

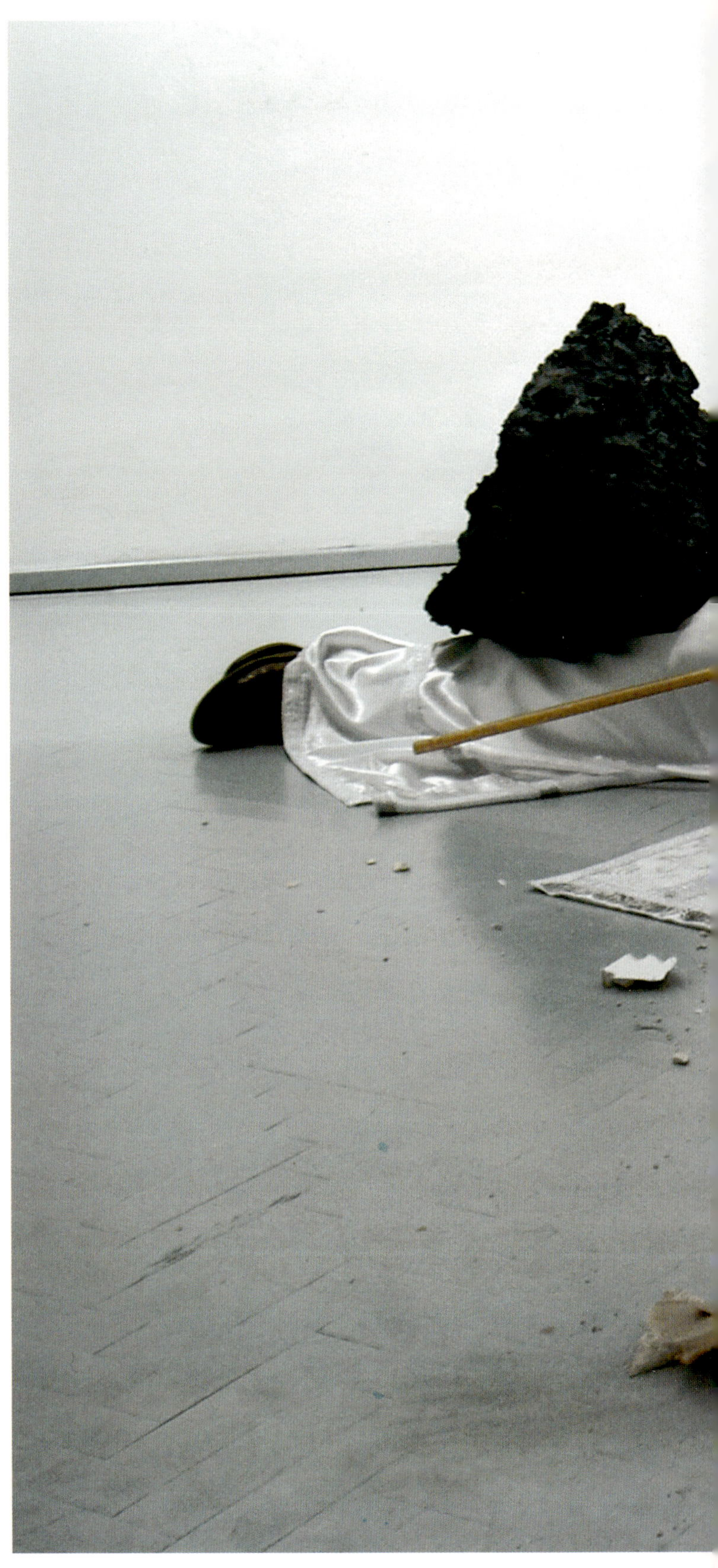

Ciprian Muresan, *The End of the Five Year Plan*, 2004, sculpture (wax, textile, plaster), human size, photography Carmen Gociu, courtesy of Protokoll and the artist

The Romanian artist exhibited this piece in his 2004 solo show at Studio Protokoll, in Cluj, Romania. The work obviously references Cattelan's earlier *La Nona Ora*, but this time combines the downfall of the Orthodox Christian church with the failure of Soviet Communism. With both these forms of authority having lost their influence, Russia and much of Eastern Europe has opened the door to Capitalism as a replacement.

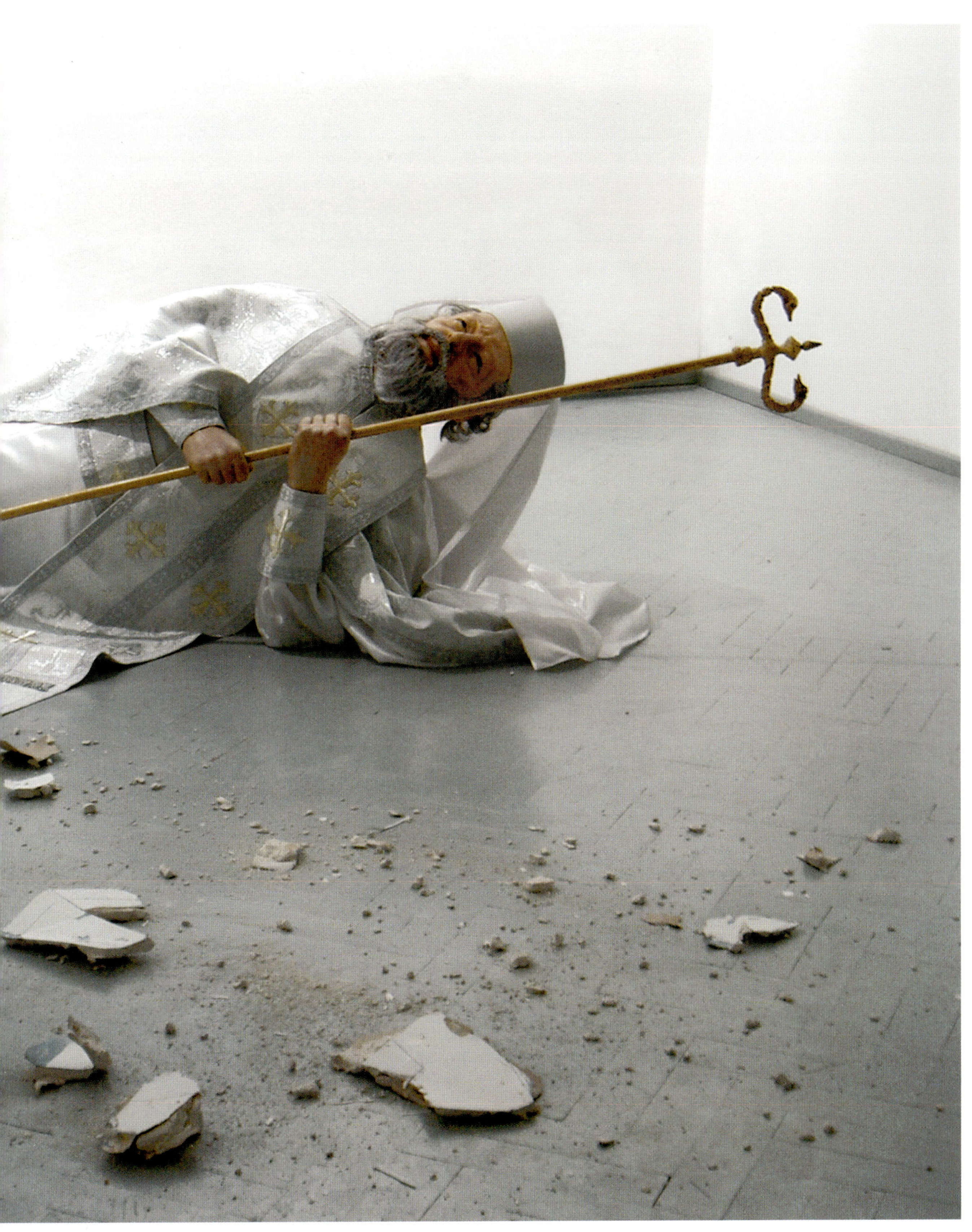

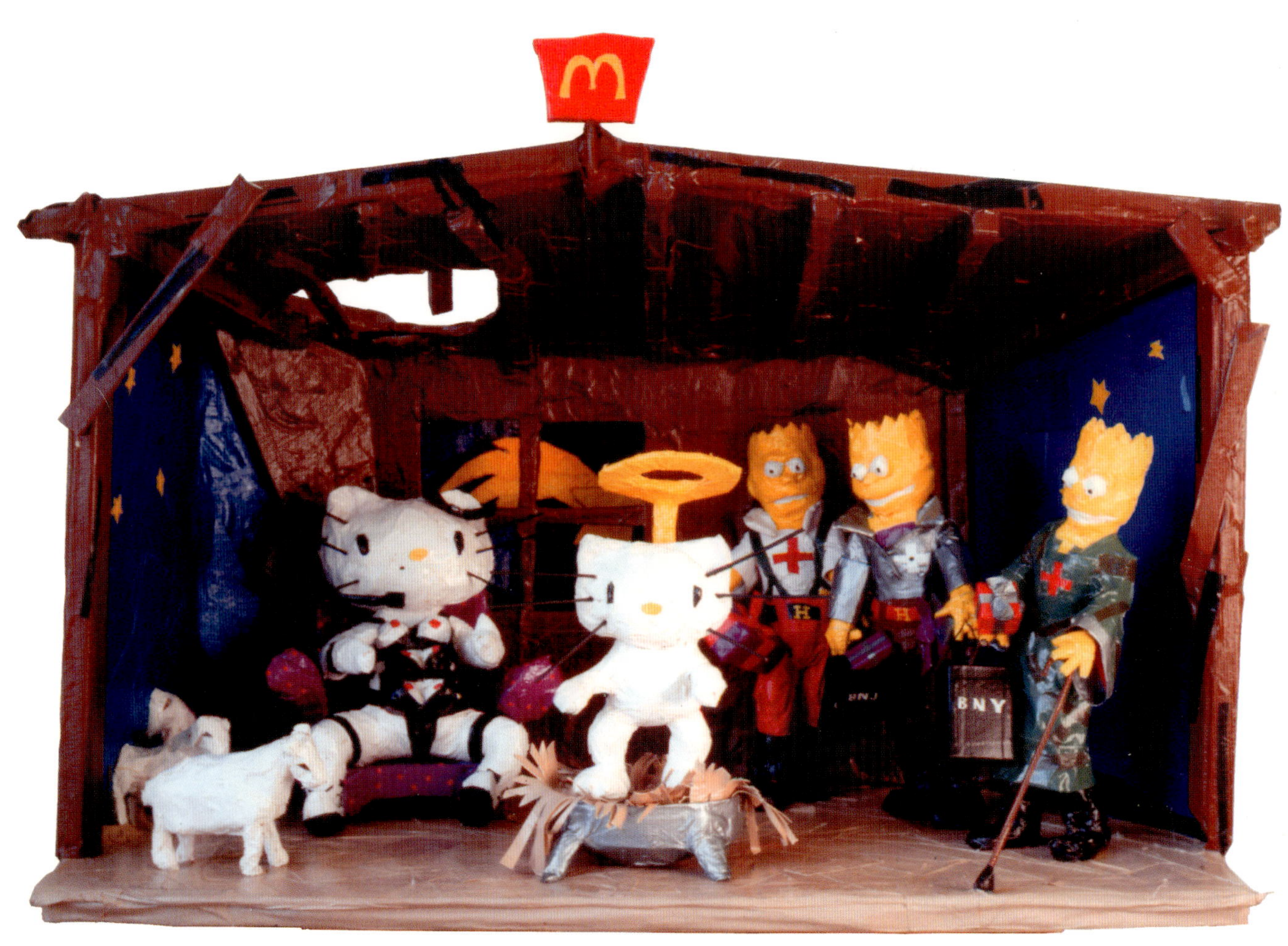
BNY

The cartoons, and the responses to them by rioters, journalists, politicians, and religious leaders, implicitly lay out many of the issues taken up in the following pages. Blasphemy is a contested, fluid, and dynamic category of meaning. Such taboo arts serve as powerful components in the making and shaping of society since they reveal a general public's lusts, longings, fears, and repulsions. Leonard Levy, who has spilled more scholarly ink than anyone on the subject of blasphemy in recent times, states "Blasphemy is a litmus test of the standards a society feels it must enforce to preserve its unity, its peace, its morality, and above all its salvation."[3] Blasphemy, and the *accusation* of blasphemy, is a culturally symbolic marker that helps define societies and religious traditions, as well as provide identities for people in terms of gender, race, class, and sexuality. Some seemingly blasphemous images are ignored or overlooked by the masses, while religious and political authorities exploit other seemingly tame images. Oftentimes, those with the most authority, politically and/or religiously, win the battle. But not always.

This book provides a general overview of blasphemy in the visual arts, including painting, calligraphy, illuminated manuscripts, photography, advertisement, graphic design, and film. Through these various media juxtapositions between local artistic practices and hierarchical authority systems in Muslim, Jewish, and Christian histories are explored. In the end I query the status of blasphemy in the modern age as sacred symbols shift from conventional religious subjects – whether it be God, Mohammed, Jesus, Quran, or Torah – to liberal values such as friendship, education, freedom of expression, and the democratic nation-state. This is no comprehensive study, nor does it uncover any startling new historical findings. Instead, by bringing together a wide variety of historical events, and their sometimes mythical retellings, this book attempts a synthetic view that cuts across cultures, religions, eras, languages, nations, and visual media in order to provide perspectives on issues that are vital to contemporary life: censorship; human rights; church (and mosque and synagogue) versus state; the role of the artist in society; governmental funding for art; the rise of modernity, postmodernity and the concomitant rise of fundamentalism; and the ongoing need for humans to make meaning of life through symbolic activities.

Tom Sachs, *Hello Kitty Nativity Scene*, 1994, mixed media, courtesy of the artist

This sculpture, or work of 'bricolage' as Sachs prefers to describe it, commenting on the commercialism of Christmas featured in a window display at Barney's department store. The artist became the target of the Catholic League, who said that the piece defamed Christianity. A campaign of protests, death threats and hate mail ensued, resulting in Barney's removing the piece, which was originally intended to be auctioned off for charity.

The first chapter begins with the problem of defining blasphemy. It is a slippery term that has now been used in various forms for a few millennia to apply to a variety of activities, performances, speeches, writings, and images by individuals and groups. I will chart some of these historical definitions, specifically in the theological traditions of Judaism, Christianity, and Islam. As this study is in English, and starts with the contemporary English understanding of the term, it is in the first instance necessary to figure out if languages like Hebrew, Greek, Latin, or Arabic have equivalent terms. Without getting stuck on pinning down 'correct' translations or etymologies, I instead argue for a loose definition via the terms sacred and profane, categories which themselves are ever shifting. Moving away from an essential definition of blasphemy, my aim is to highlight the multiple uses to which the accusation of blasphemy has been strategically put, to show how blasphemy emerges somewhere between the production and reception of images.

Following on from these definitions, the second chapter suggests that blasphemy is intimately, though not exclusively, tied to issues of power. There is a power of images that must be accounted for, and then there is the power of authority figures and their pronouncements on the images. Historically speaking, definitions of blasphemy centre on a *verbal* rather than a *visual* affront against the sacred; indeed, the roots of the term relate it to 'evil speech'. Major recent historical works on blasphemy have little more than a few passing comments about blasphemous images, so I offer a perspective on how images function like, and unlike, verbal utterances against the sacred. At issue here is a theological and theoretical divergence between the power of words and the power of images. The differences and overlaps between political and religious authority are critical to take into account, even as they are ultimately impossible to separate. The power of images also works in the opposite direction, as people without social power (often in terms of race, class, and gender) utilise images in transgressive ways to assert power.

The final chapter explores blasphemous images in the modern, liberal, nation-state. What happens to blasphemy in the wake of secularisation, and the separation of religion and government? Is it, as TS Eliot suggested, "a world in which blasphemy is impossible"?[4] I do not simply reiterate a 'secularisation thesis', that the modern age has shed its religious moorings; instead such progressive thinking is problematised, and the persistence of religious influence on political power structures will be shown. This chapter will look at critical artworks made in the post-Second World War United States and Soviet Union, exploring issues surrounding flag displays and political ideologies. In the contemporary world, targets of blasphemy are often shifted from the traditionally sacred – gods, prophets, and holy books – to the 'gods of modernity' such as the nation-state, education, friendship, and freedom of expression.

Oreet Ashery, *Self Portrait as Marcus Fisher I*, 2000, digital print mounted on MDF, dimensions variable, a collaboration with Manuel Vason, courtesy of the artist

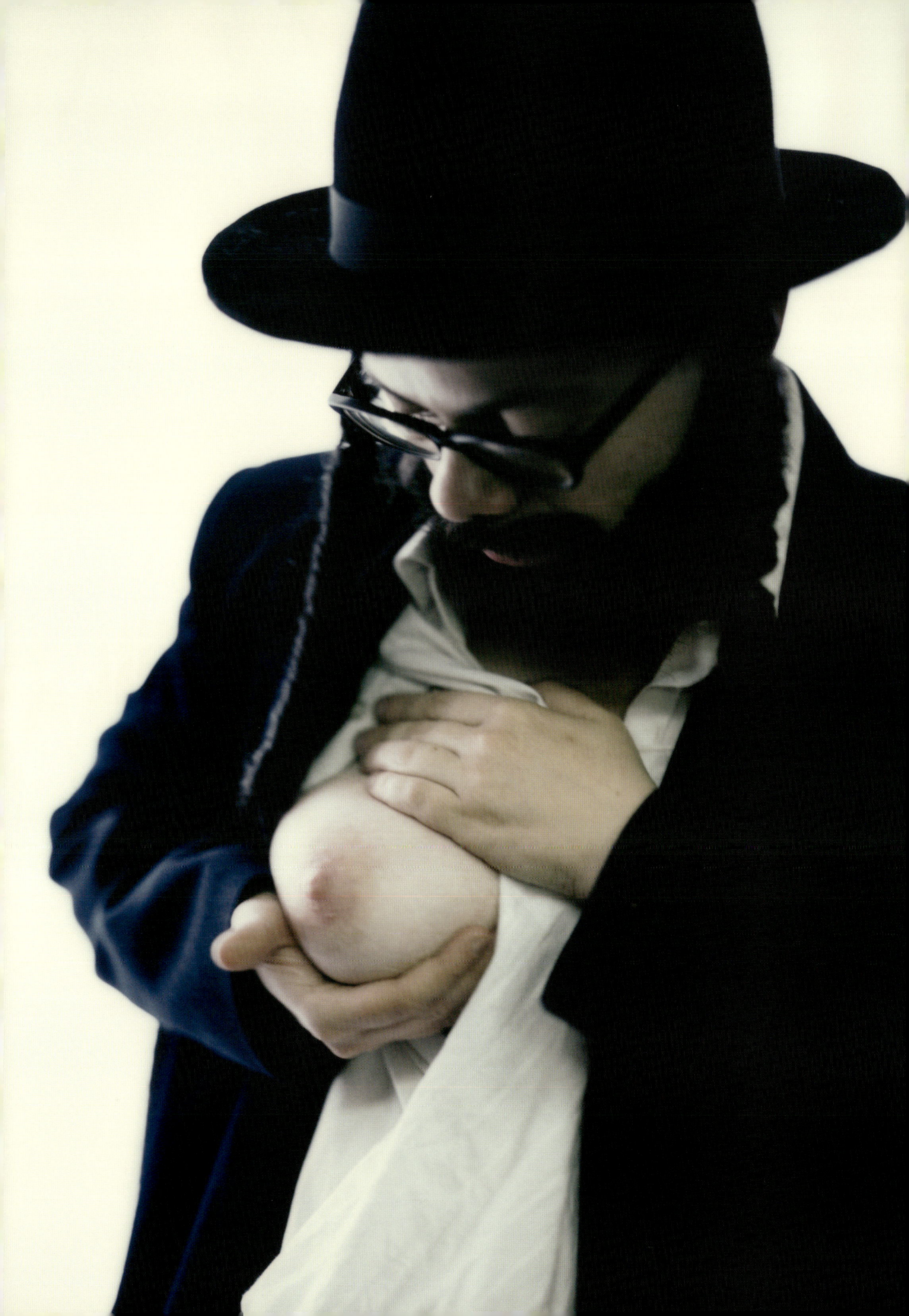

DEFINING AND DELIMITING BLASPHEMY

Chapter One

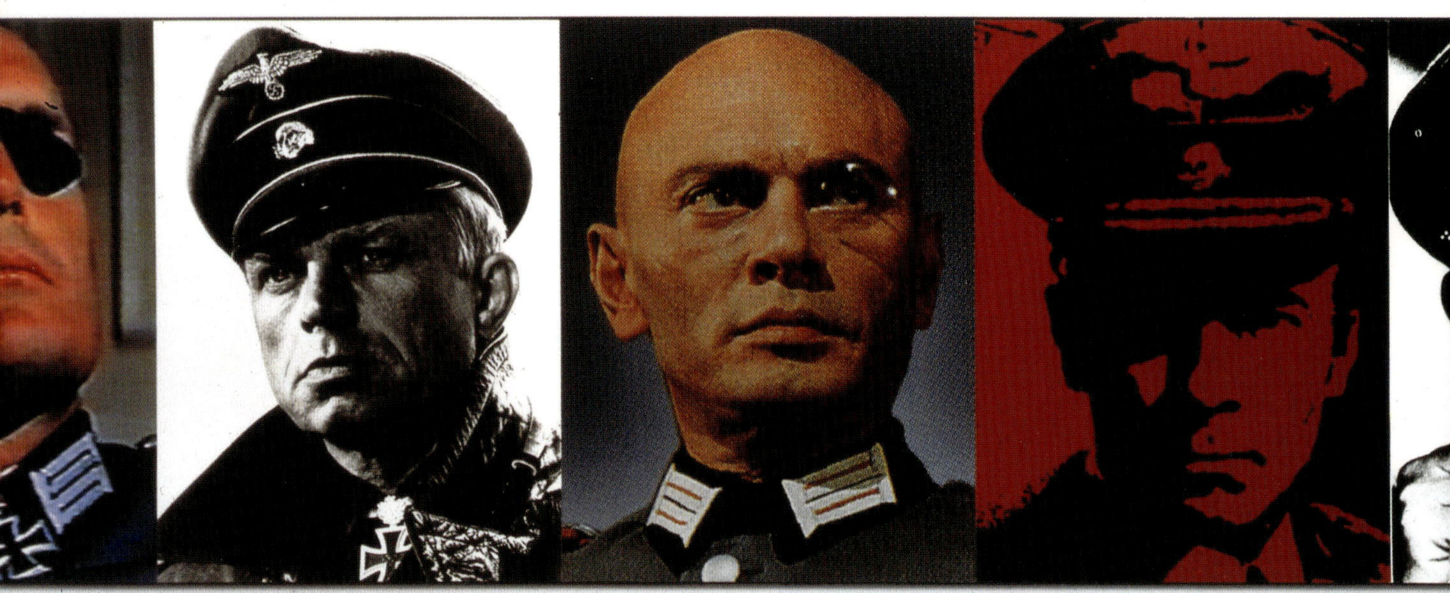

Piotr Uklanski, *The Nazis* (detail), 1998, 166 chromogenic, black and white and colour photographs laminated and mounted on board, 166 panels, each 36 x 25 cm, courtesy of Galerie Emmanuel Perrotin, Paris and Miami/ Gavin Brown Enterprise, New York

This photo-installation by the Polish-born artist was first shown at London's Photographers' Gallery, before touring other spaces, including the Jewish Museum in New York. The piece consists of 166 36 x 25 cm C-prints of film actors playing Nazi characters, and was put together from film stills without the actors' permission. When exhibited in Poland, the installation was vandalised by actor Daniel Olbrychski, who slashed four images, including that of himself playing Karl Kremer, a Nazi officer, in Claude Lelouch's *Les Uns et Les Autres*. Other actors featured in the piece include Yul Brynner, Ralph Fiennes, Dirk Bogarde, Clint Eastwood, Max von Sydow, Omar Sharif, Frank Sinatra and Jean-Paul Belmondo, the latter of whom was one of several who gave their blessing to Olbrychski's protest. The installation is Uklanski's attempt to mediate between mass Hollywood culture and sombre critical reflection, simultaneously inflating and deflating one of the twentieth century's horror stories, turning real history into cliché.

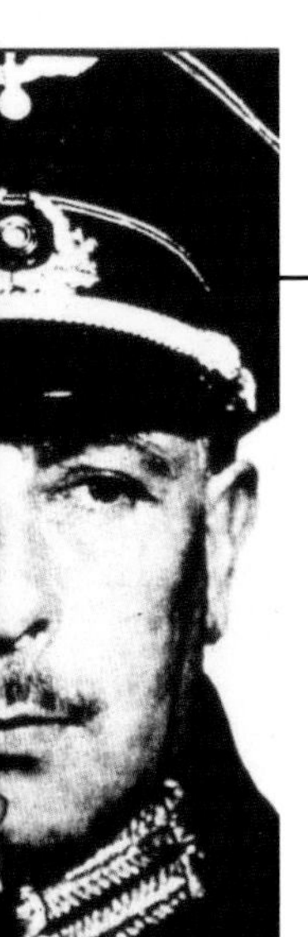

DEFINING AND DELIMITING BLASPHEMY

Chapter One

> New opinions often appear first as jokes and fancies, then as blasphemies and treason, then as questions open to discussion, and finally as established truths.
>
> GEORGE BERNARD SHAW, *Annajanska*

To a concurring opinion statement from a 1952 US Supreme Court censorship case, Justice Felix Frankfurter appended a lengthy list of definitions for the terms 'sacrilegious' and 'blasphemy', culled from dozens of English dictionaries stretching back to the seventeenth century. His point was to prove that neither term had a consistent, objective meaning that would allow legal conclusions to be drawn from them. It also showed how both terms were entangled with each other, and so simply choosing the correct term was problematic from the start. Definitions ranged from "stealing from the church" to "profaning things devoted to God", from "language tending to the dishonour of God" to "to attribute to God that which is contrary to his nature". Frankfurter's reasoned approach to the topic, outlining the utter subjectivity of charges of blasphemy and sacrilege, helped make this one of the final court cases in the United States dealing with such issues.[1]

At the heart of the case was a short film by Italian director Roberto Rossellini called *The Miracle*, for which another great Italian director, Federico Fellini, wrote the screenplay. In the film a somewhat confused and inebriated shepherdess has sex with a wandering stranger (played by Fellini himself), envisioning him to be St Joseph. And when she becomes pregnant she imagines the child must be divine as well – after all the 'real' St Joseph was the quasi-father of Jesus. The woman is mocked and scorned by her neighbours for her beliefs, and in the end she flees town and gives birth in a church on top of a mountain. The National League of Decency, a private Catholic organisation, called the film "a sacrilegious and blasphemous mockery of Christian religious truth", making sure they got both terms in – while in New York, Francis Cardinal Spellman led protests against the screening of the film.[2] Once called the "American Pope", Cardinal Spellman was stridently anti-communist, pro-McCarthy, and argued early on for US military involvement in Vietnam. His protests against Rossellini's film were successful, causing the New York film board to ban screenings of it, relying on a state law that allowed censorship boards to deny licenses to commercially screen films that were deemed "... obscene, indecent, immoral, inhuman, sacrilegious...". The Supreme Court ultimately reversed the New York State ruling, asserting the right to free speech set out in the First Amendment, effectively rewriting the laws on censorship and film which had been in place since the dawn of theatres in the United States. Literature had been protected until this point, but not film.

While the ramifications of this story are worth an entire book themselves, I want to draw attention to two aspects of it. The first concerns the difficulties with defining the term, and the remainder of this chapter sets out some of the ways the term has been utilised in religious traditions and contemporary societies. Along the way I provide some new attempts at defining blasphemy from the perspective of religious visual culture, and through the interrelated terms sacred and profane. The second lesson from the Supreme Court case regards the power of images and their ability to provoke, critique, and stir human emotion, inciting organised protests, court cases, instances of iconoclasm, and federal laws. On the flip side, certain humans have been able to control the energies of images, to speak those thousand words that a picture tells, and circumvent their function. The power of images and their relation to blasphemy and authority will be examined in the next chapter.

Defining Blasphemy

As Justice Frankfurter suggests, definitions of blasphemy (and related terms) are slippery, subjective, and susceptible to manipulation by those seeking power. The opinion statement by the US Supreme Court over *The Miracle* case argued that censorship is questionable on grounds of sacrilege or blasphemy since "the censor is set adrift upon a boundless sea amid a myriad of conflicting currents of religious views, with no charts but those provided by the most vocal and powerful orthodoxies".[3] In other words, blasphemy and sacrilege cannot be pinned down in a universal, timeless manner, but are prone to endless changes in religious meaning and through power mongering. For it is in the *accusing* itself, and in the greater environment in which the charges are made, that we find the profound power of blasphemy. It is one of those terms that has gained its lasting resonance not through semantic stability, but through its instability, its endless manipulability. Blasphemy's history is intertwined with other terms such as sacrilege and heresy, most directly, but also with the obscene, impious, idolatrous, offensive, subversive, and taboo, as well as its condemnation in the forms of iconoclasm, censorship, and excommunication, not to mention imprisonment, torture, and execution.

This does not mean definitions are impossible. Indeed, my goal here is to rethink blasphemy in light of the visual culture of a twenty-first century Western society that pretends it no longer believes in the hocus-pocus of spiritually charged images. Every society has its taboos, and the concept of blasphemy allows us to look to the forbidden symbols and activities of our past, in order to enquire about our own present list of taboos. In so doing, we come up against the structures and strictures of our current culture, enabling a certain

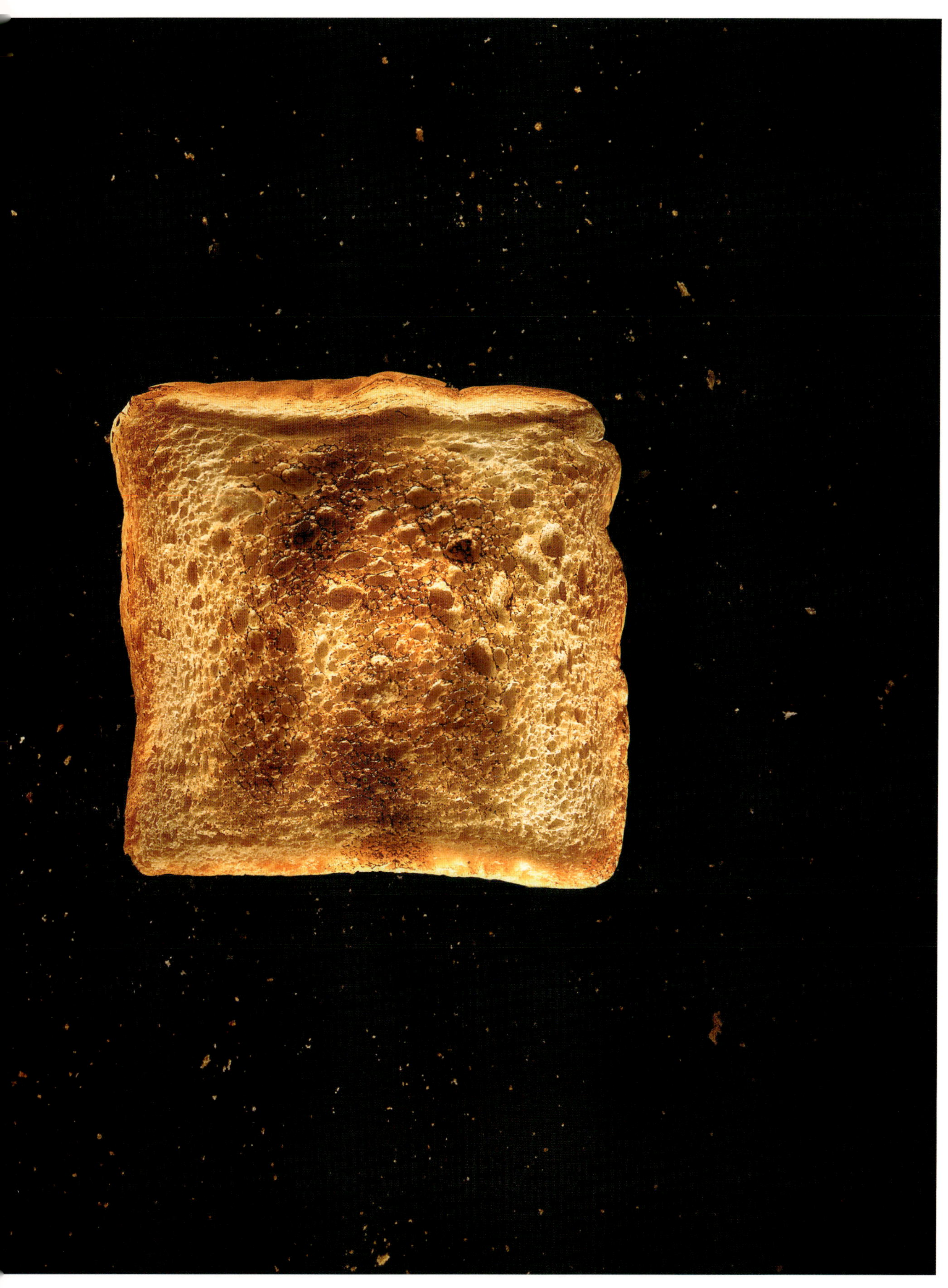

charting of the permissible and forbidden that defines contemporary life. I begin, then, with some initial attempts at definition.

The word blasphemy, in its most literal form, taken from its Greek roots, means 'evil speech'. Since that is a bit ambiguous, common definitions such as "contemptuous speech about God", "defamation of the divine" or "treason against God", have all been used, though none of these definitions exactly fit the purposes of this book.[4] The Greek root '-pheme' relates it to speech, and as this is a book about images, we have to wonder about how the term is related both to the verbal and the visual, the speaking and the showing. Also, the restriction to language about 'God' or even 'the divine' can be a bit strained, since what will be seen in the following is that books, persons, ideas, ideologies, and nations, can also seemingly be blasphemed against.

A number of contemporary dictionaries and encyclopedias suggest a more neutral definition relating to 'profane speech'. While the vagaries abide, this is getting closer to my interests herein. In reference to religion, language about the profane can be useful, especially since it is set in contrast to the term sacred (or as it is sometimes called, 'holy'). Contrary to popular parlance, the profane is not inherently negative. It is only the everyday, the ordinary. The simplest way to

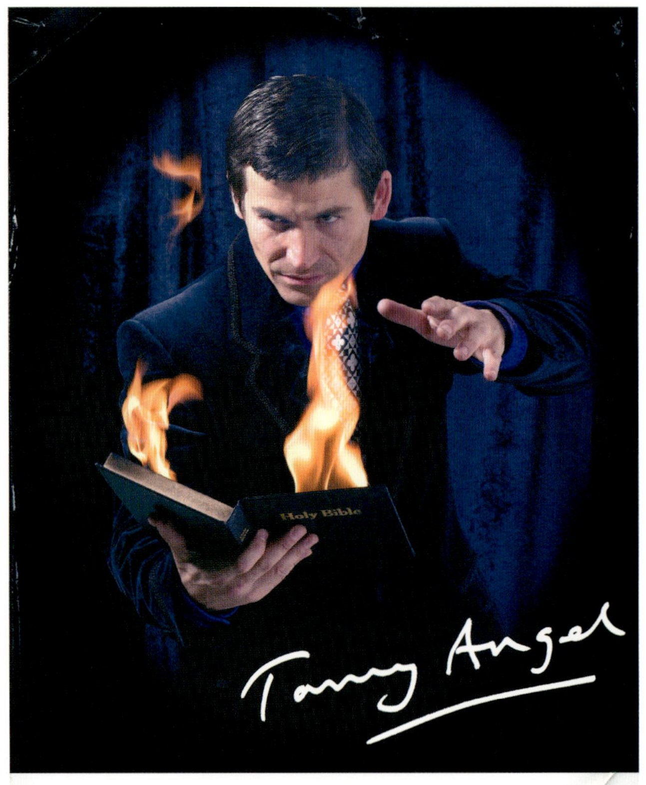

PREVIOUS PAGE: **Chip Simons**, *Jesus Toast*, 2005, original shot on 6x6 camera colour reversal film, scanned on imacon scanner, output as digital C-print, print size 36 x 28 cm, frame size 61 x 51 cm, courtesy of the artist

To make your own 'Personal Jesus Toast', visit Eric Gillin's site, *The Black Table at www.blacktable.com/gillin041202.htm*

ABOVE: **Jonathan Allen**, *Tommy Angel*, 2006, performance/photographs, courtesy of David Risley Gallery

Allen's fictitious 'gospel magician' persona blends glitzy Vegas showmanship with Christian fundamentalism.

Allah Bless America

Jesus is My Co-Pilot

Christian Democrat... and proud of it !!

GOD BLESS AMERICA

GOD ROCKS

My God is alive - sorry about yours

HONK IF YOU LOVE JESUS

Jesus Loves Truck Drivers

American Car Bumper Stickers

think of the sacred and profane is to note the difference between the Sabbath day (whether Saturday or Sunday is not an issue here) and the other days of the week. The Sabbath is sacred, the other six days are profane. The sacred Sabbath reminds people of how the world could and should be, the profane keeps us rooted in how it is, the here and now. Also important is the fact that in all Judaism, there is a specific division between the two: sunset on Friday. There is literally a temporal border, like the need to wash one's hands or take off one's shoes before entering a mosque or temple. And through these divisions we realise how the sacred and the profane need each other for their very definitions. The sacred provides meaning and orientation for the profane; the profane sustains the sacred.

In relation to blasphemy, what must be accounted for is the all-important border *between* these poles. In its most literal definition, the sacred is that which is 'set apart' from the profane. The sacred refers to beings (human and otherwise), places, objects, and times which are elevated, and are charged by divine and/or human forces with power beyond that of the commonplace. The sacred has the power to bless, to cure, to make meaning and provide orientation in life, just as it has the power to kill, destroy, and generally make life miserable. Consider most encounters with sacred beings found in the Jewish, Christian, and Muslim scriptures: the initial meeting always results in the profane human being afraid in the face of the sacred being (Abram's vision of the God who wishes to bless him, Mary during the angel Gabriel's annunciation, God's revelations to Muhammad in the cave on Mount Hira). Within such a sacred history, the smug contemporary bumper sticker on cars exclaiming, "God is my co-pilot" is as blasphemous as any crucifix submerged in urine because it does not respect the difference between the sacred and profane.

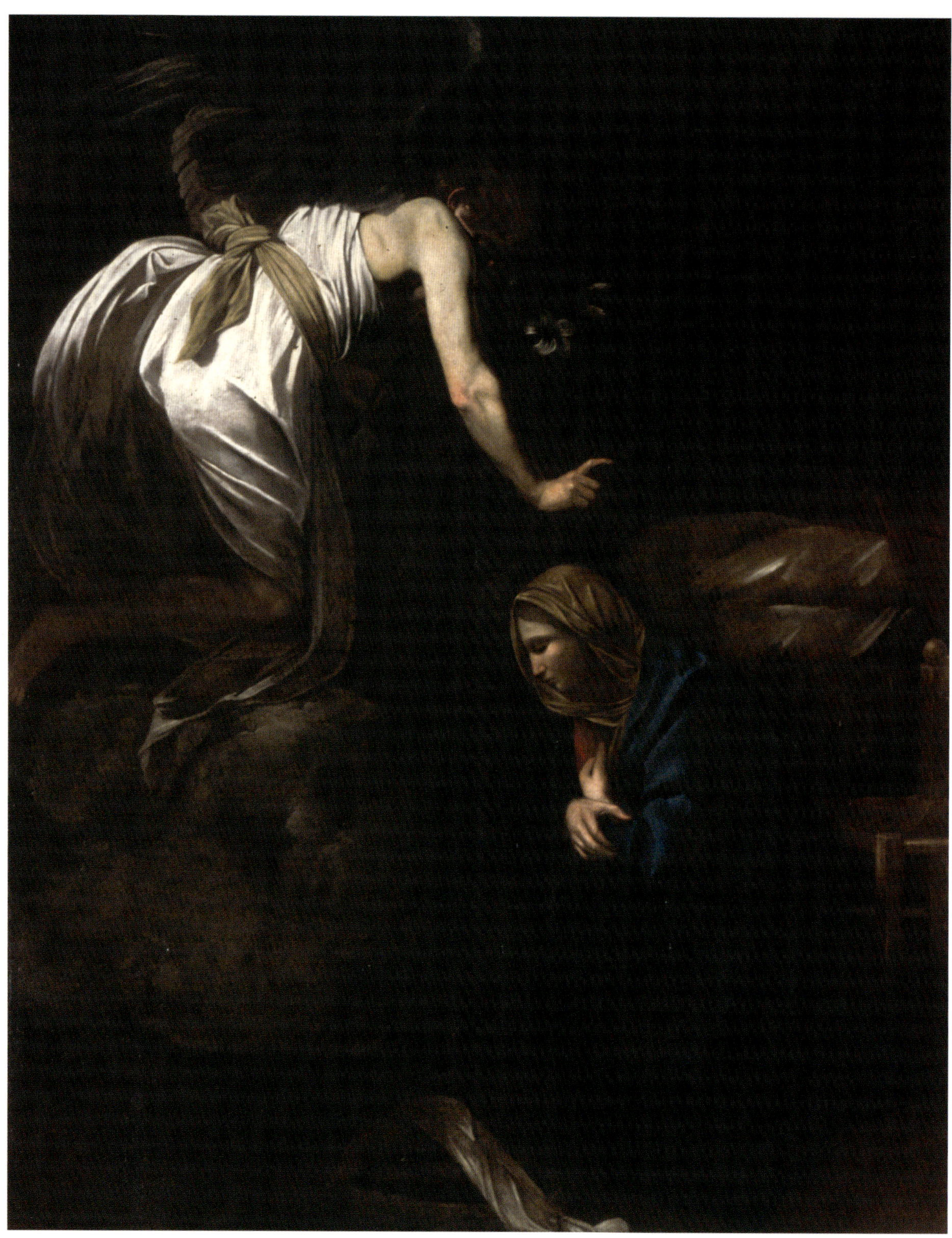

Michelangelo Merisi da Caravaggio,
Annonciation (The Annunciation), 1608–1609, oil on canvas,
285 x 205 cm, photography Claude Philippot,
courtesy of Musée des Beaux-Arts, Nancy

One of Christianity's most meaningful encounters between the human and the divine.

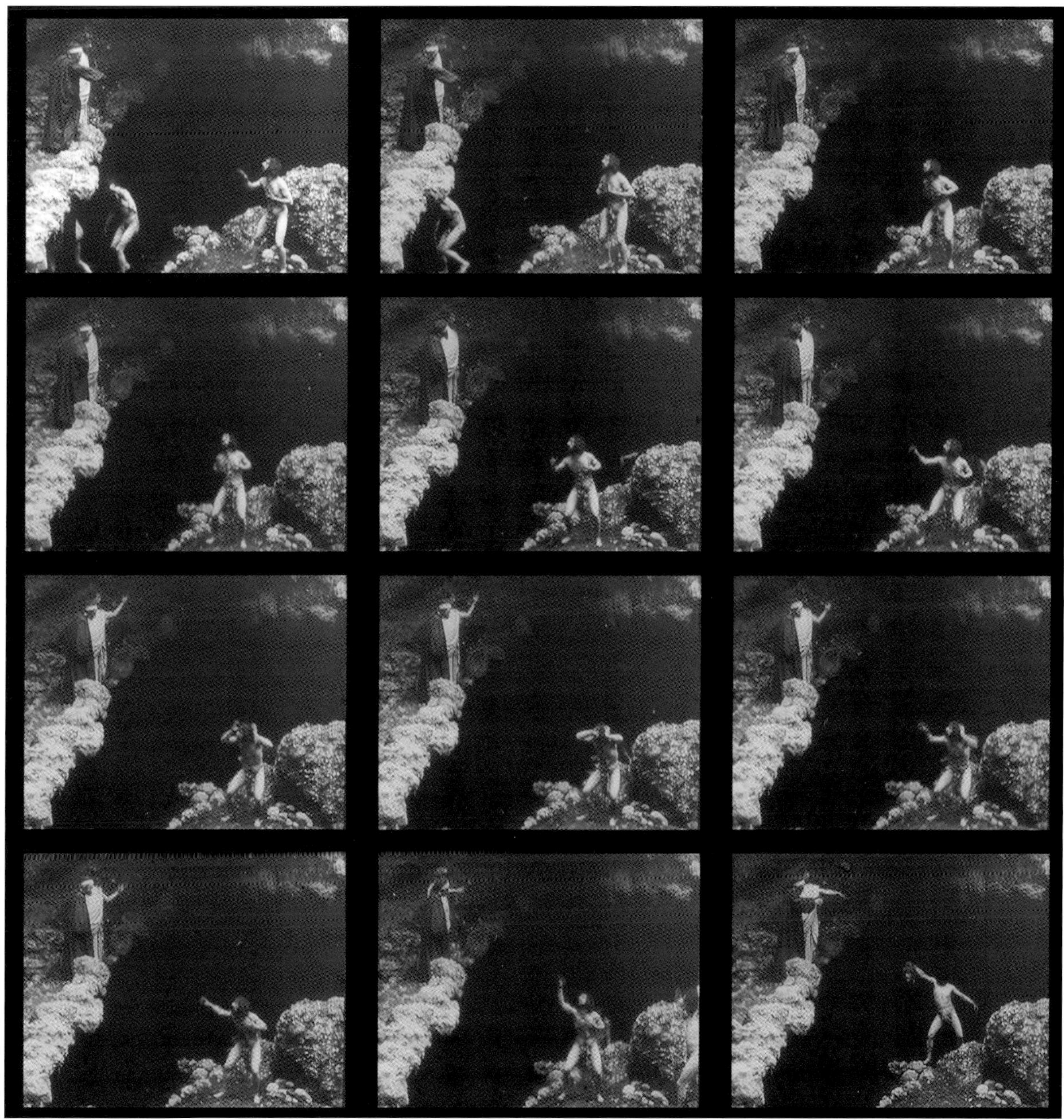

Giuseppe di Liguoro, *L'Inferno* [stills], 1911, film, courtesy of and produced by Tim Pearce for Eye 4 Films (available on DVD from www.linferno.com)

This sequence from di Liguoro's silent film, based on Dante's *Inferno* and inspired by the art of Gustave Doré, shows God's revelation to the Prophet Muhammad, who is portrayed in an unflattering and mocking way.

Blasphemy is fundamentally about transgression, about crossing the lines between the sacred and the profane in seemingly improper ways.

Because of the power of the sacred, there are rules and rituals that must be followed in the correct manner in order for the profane to come into contact with it. There is a dividing line between the two, but there are always ritualistic passages that allow those lines to be crossed – taking off shoes, washing hands, lighting candles – or that transform the one into the other. There are passages between the sacred and the profane such as 'consecration' ceremonies (ordaining priests, blessing new spaces, etc.) and even 'deconsecration' ceremonies (old buildings, images, or persons no longer serve their functions and are ritualistically brought back into the profane realm). Social, political, theological, economic, and historical authorities keep these categories in place, tell when and how they may be crossed, and thus establish and maintain order.

Tony Garifalakis, *Nothing's Song* (installation view), 2006, mixed media, dimensions variable, above: uncensored version, below: censored version, courtesy of the artist

As part of the *Silenzi Project* in Venice alongside five other artists, Garifalakis was initially told that the studio space for the work was to be six deconsecrated churches. Shortly before the project began, the artists were informed that the sites were, in fact, working, consecrated churches. Garifalakis ran into trouble when a priest, whose church of San Lio he was working in, objected to what he saw as a celebration of death and Satanism, rather than an intended comment on contemporary consumer culture, via the use of traditional Christian imagery. *Silenzi*'s Italian curator decided to pull Garifalakis out of the exhibition entirely, and it was only when threatened by the Australian curator with the removal of the work of all three of the Australian artists taking part, that he was allowed to participate. He was, however, forced to censor his piece, which he did by turning all the 'offensive' work to face the wall. Garifalakis also insisted that a statement was placed on the wall, saying that his work had been censored.

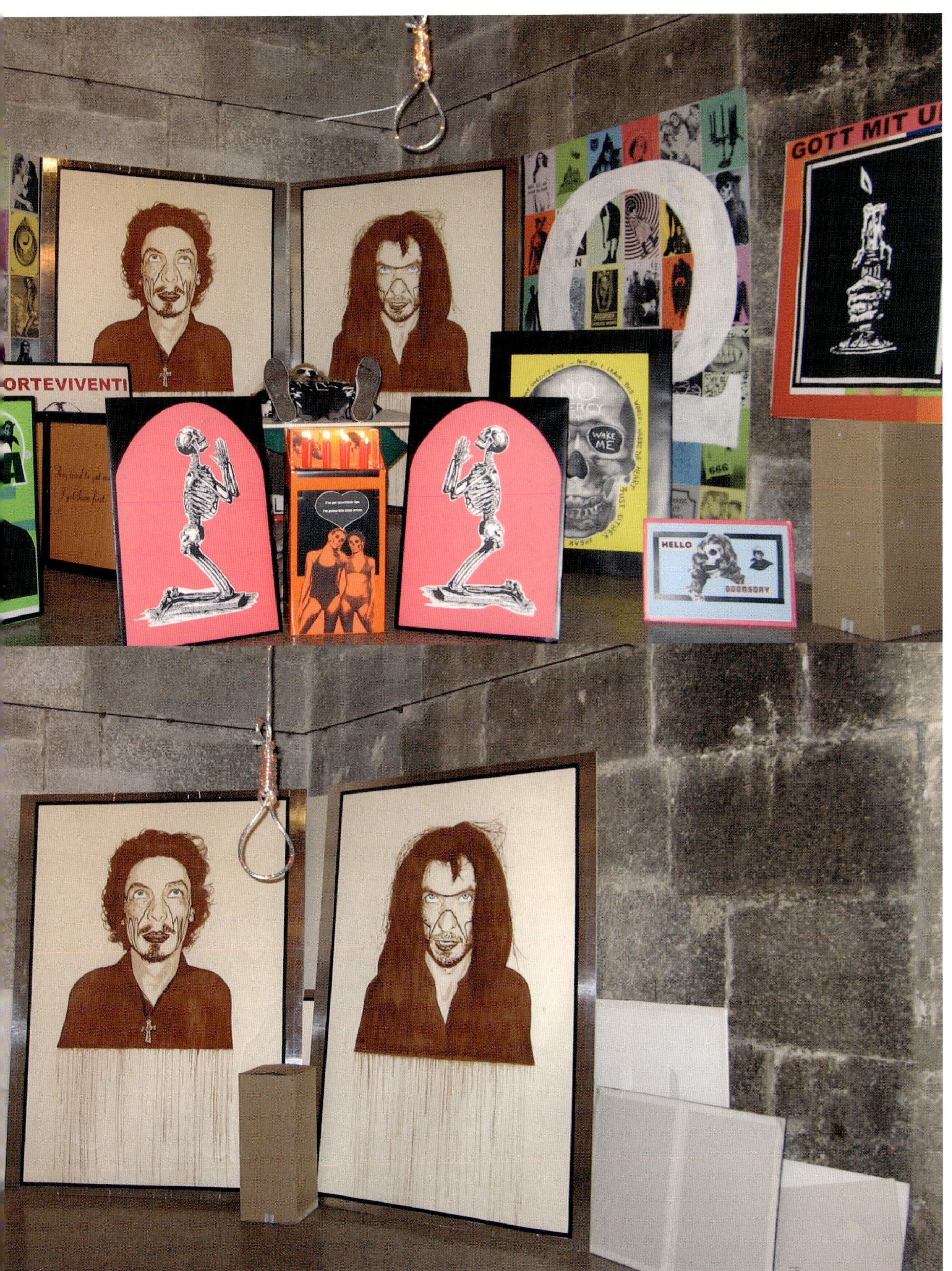
GOTT MIT U
ORTEVIVENTI
WAKE ME
666
HELLO
DOOMSDAY

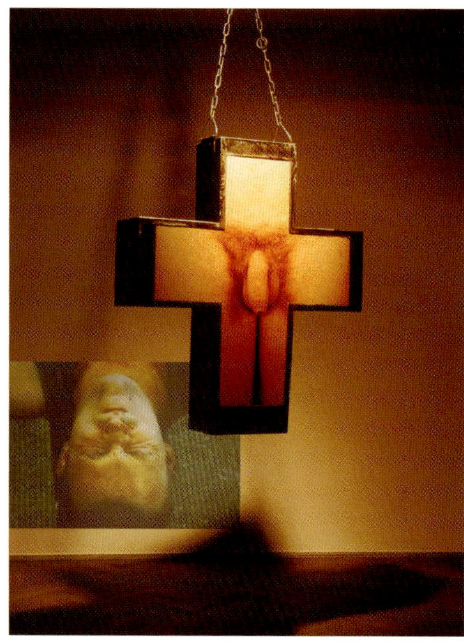

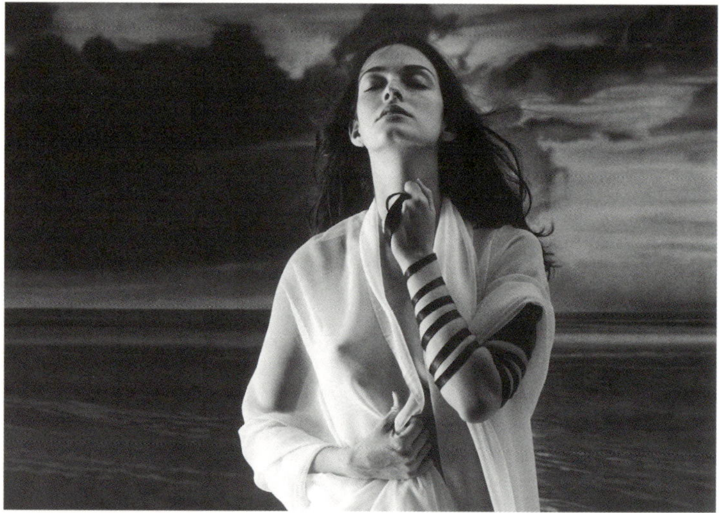

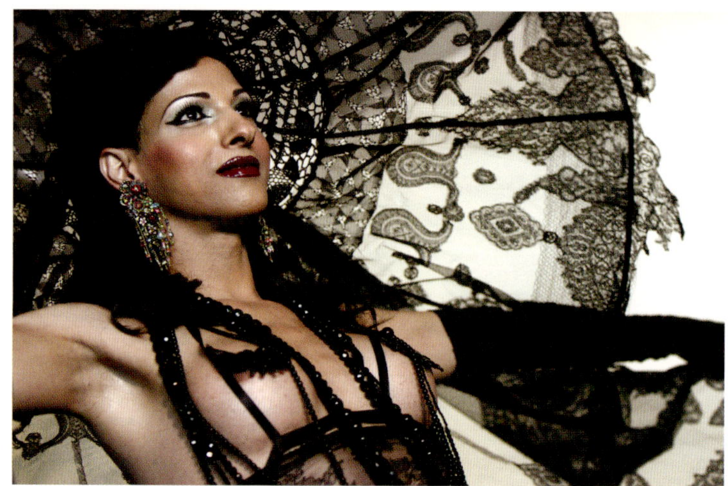

ABOVE (CLOCKWISE FROM TOP LEFT): **Dorota Nieznalska**, *Pasja* (Passion), 2002, multimedia installation with video, courtesy of the artist

The Wyspa Progress Foundation, with which Nieznalska is connected, is conducting a campaign to overturn her conviction. If you would like to sign an open letter in support of this campaign, please contact: wyspa_mode@wp.pl.

Leonard Nimoy, *The Shekhina Project*, 2002, photographic series, courtesy of R Michelson Galleries (www.RMichelson.com)

Based on the kabbalistic myth of the Shekhina, the estranged female counterpart to God, Leonard Nimoy's provocative series of photographs explores the sexual subtext of this story of loss and desire.

Dana International, promotional image courtesy EMPICS

Born Yaron Cohenin Tel Aviv, Israel on 2 February 1972, the Israeli transsexual popsinger's notoriety stems from her winning entry at the 1998 Eurovision Song Contest. She drew controversy from many Israelis who thought it was shameless for a transsexual to represent their country.

OPPOSITE: **Katarzyna Kozyra**, *Blood Ties*, 1995, colour photographs, courtesy of Zacheta National Gallery of Art and the artist

The bottom two panels were displayed as a billboard on the streets of Poland and were censored for their depiction of nudes with religious symbols and the pairing of Christian with Islamic imagery.

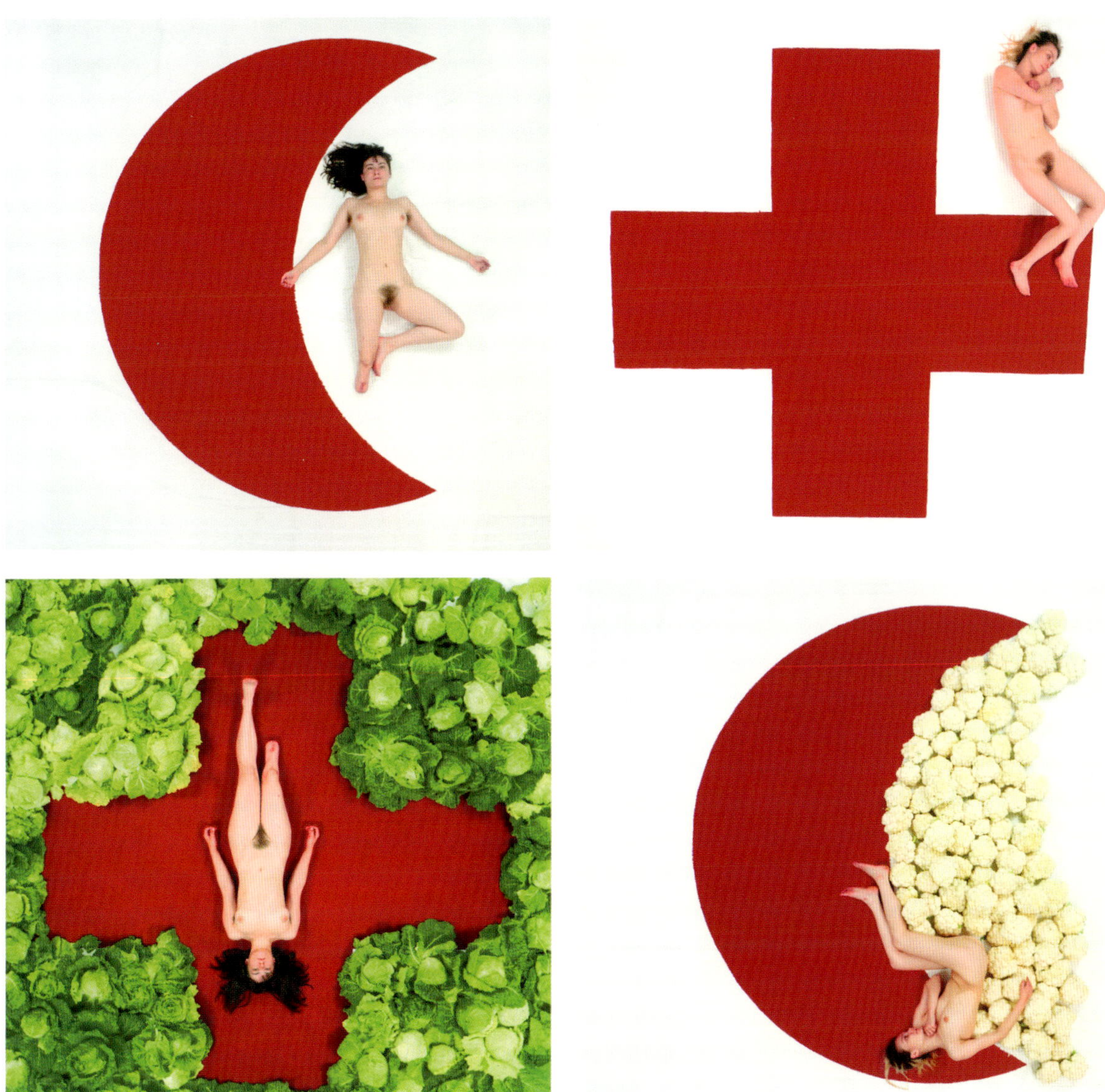

With the sacred-profane partition in place, I suggest that blasphemy is fundamentally about transgression, about crossing the lines between the sacred and the profane in seemingly improper ways. Blasphemy does not play by established rules, does not respect the traditions of socially acceptable ways of ritualising, and may even poke fun at well-respected symbols and myths. An image of male genitalia displayed on a screen in the shape of a Greek cross garners the Polish artist Dorota Nieznalska a criminal charge with a sentence of community service and payback of court costs. Maqbool Fida Husain, a Muslim artist, painted an abstract nude image of 'Mother India', and has been subject to right-wing Hindu groups leveling legal charges and death threats against him. Dana International, the transsexual singer who won the 1998 Eurovision Song Contest, performed a traditional Sabbath song in Jerusalem's Old City, with her performance being met with accusations of blasphemy by an Orthodox rabbi. A naked woman is photographed across sacred symbols of crosses and crescents, as in Katarzyna Kozyra's 1999 Blood Ties, causing outrage, censorship, and charges of blasphemy, again, in Poland. A near naked woman wears tefillin in a dramatic photo by Leonard Nimoy, stirring Orthodox Jews to accuse him of sacrilege.

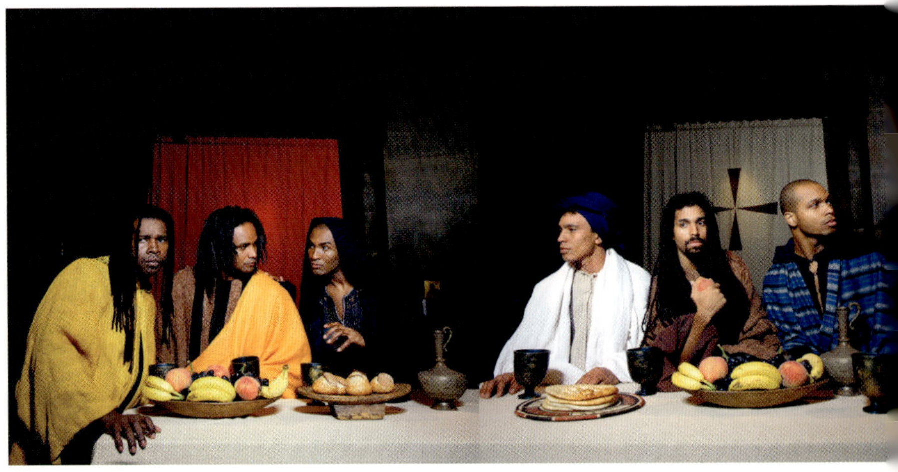

Another naked woman, this time black and accompanied by an all-black cast (save a white Judas), stands in the role of Jesus in a restaging of Leonardo's famous tableaux in Renée Cox's *Yo Mama's Last Supper*, upsetting Catholic leaders and city mayors. And in case anyone thinks such issues are resigned to the modern age, the history of Michelangelo's Sistine Chapel fresco is a prime example of how many in the Vatican considered the nude figures to be problematic, eventually causing many of the 'privates' to be covered over (by Michelangelo's apprentice Daniele da Volterra). Each of these cases helps point toward the ways in which blasphemous images have to do with an impure mixing. There is nothing in itself immoral or evil about urine, dung, or nudity – they are simply elements of natural, profane life as humans – but when these are mixed with the potency of sacred symbols, then tongues begin wagging.

No work of art is blasphemous in and of itself; it must be deemed so from within religious and/or political power structures.

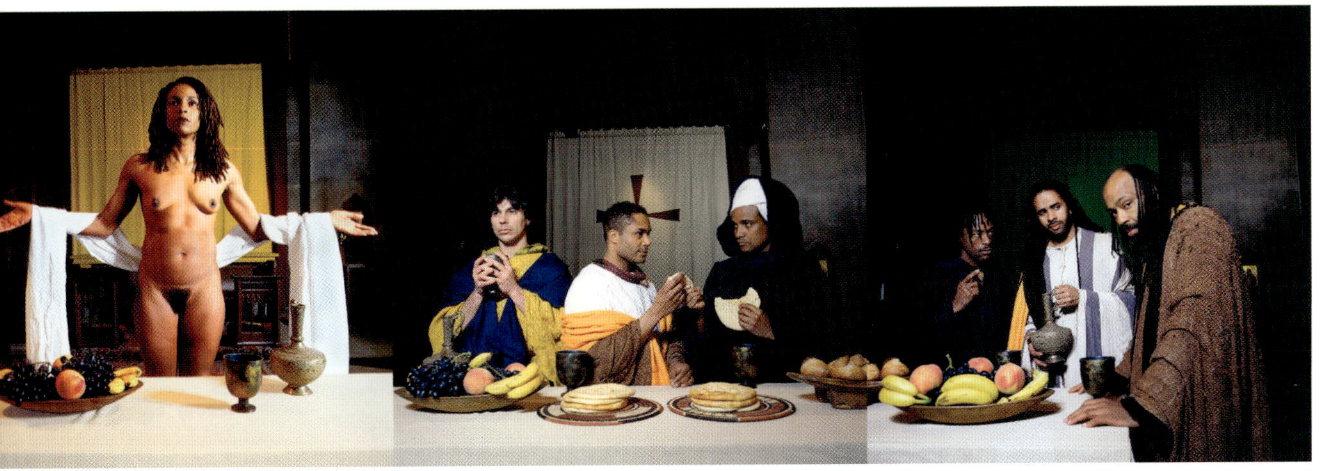

Renée Cox, *Yo Mama's Last Supper*, 1996, Cibachrome print, courtesy of the Robert Miller Gallery and the artist

New York Mayor Rudy Giuliani, who also spoke out against the work of Chris Ofili, condemned this piece as "Anti-Catholic". *Yo Mama's Last Supper* depicts the artist, an African-American woman, taking the place of Christ in Leonardo's version of the Last Supper, flanked on either side by African-American Disciples. It is unclear whether the piece was attacked for its use of nudity in a religious context or because of her envisioning Jesus as a black woman. Cox, who was raised Catholic, sees her practice as more personal than polemical, speaking of her own intimate experience of religion.

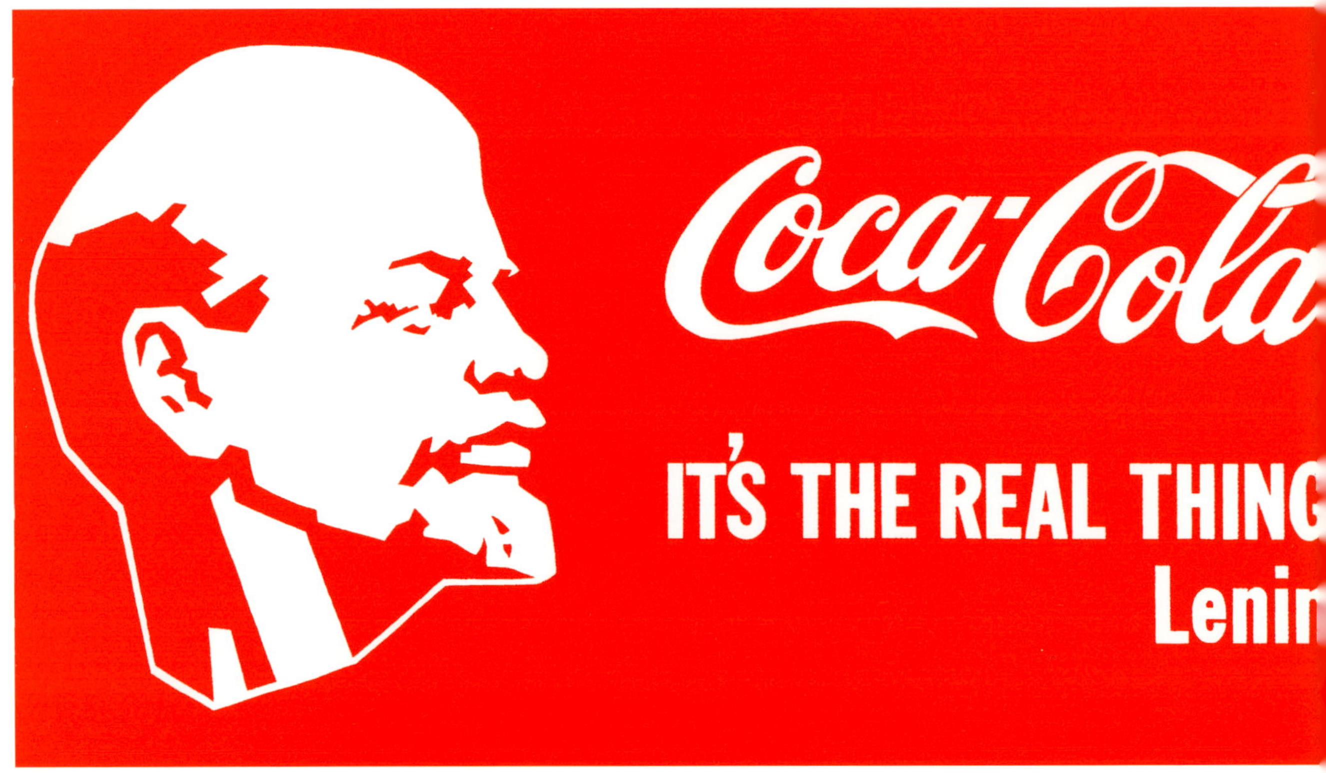

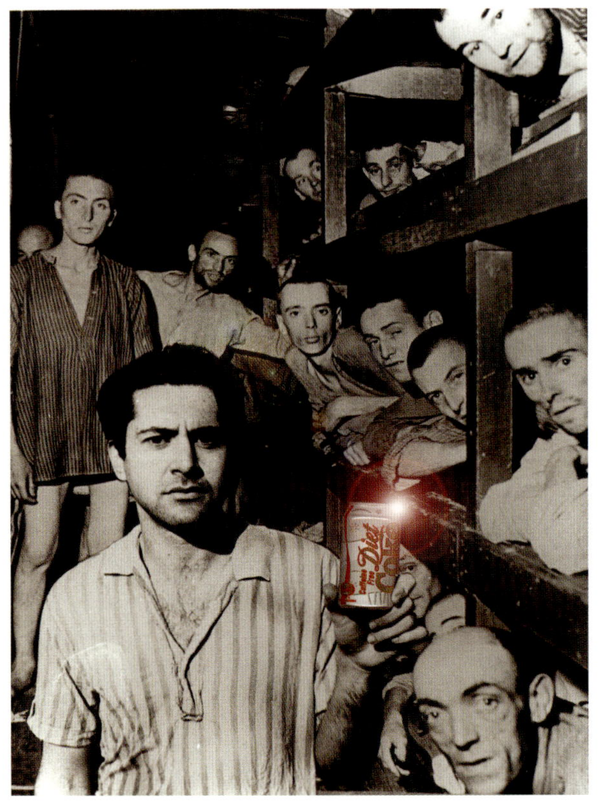

ABOVE: **Alexander Kosolapov**, *Lenin Coca Cola,* 2000, silkscreen on paper, 100 x 70 cm, and *This Is My Blood*, 2000, silkscreen on paper, 100 x 70 cm, courtesy of the artist

Alexander Kosolapov's striking images have solicited outrage and even vandalism in his native Russia. Members of the Russian Orthodox Church, an increasingly prominent political force in Russia, literally defaced the image of Jesus in *This is My Blood.* Born in Russia but living in America, Alexander's work draws parallels between Soviet propaganda, advertising, and the religious icons of the past. By juxtaposing religion with advertising, he not only mixes the sacred and the sacrilegious but also equates the tactics of religious half-truths with that of persuasive corporate visual rhetoric.

RIGHT: **Alan Schechner,** *Self Portrait at Buchenwald: It's the Real Thing,* 1991–1993, digitally manipulated print, courtesy of the artist

Schechner is telling us to look harder, to search beyond the apparently 'real' surface of our political and media representations and to question whether images are real or not? The work places the holocaust in historical and politics and asks us to consider the society in which the holocaust happened. Allessandro Imperato. (See Schechner's website: www.dottycommies.com for further details.)

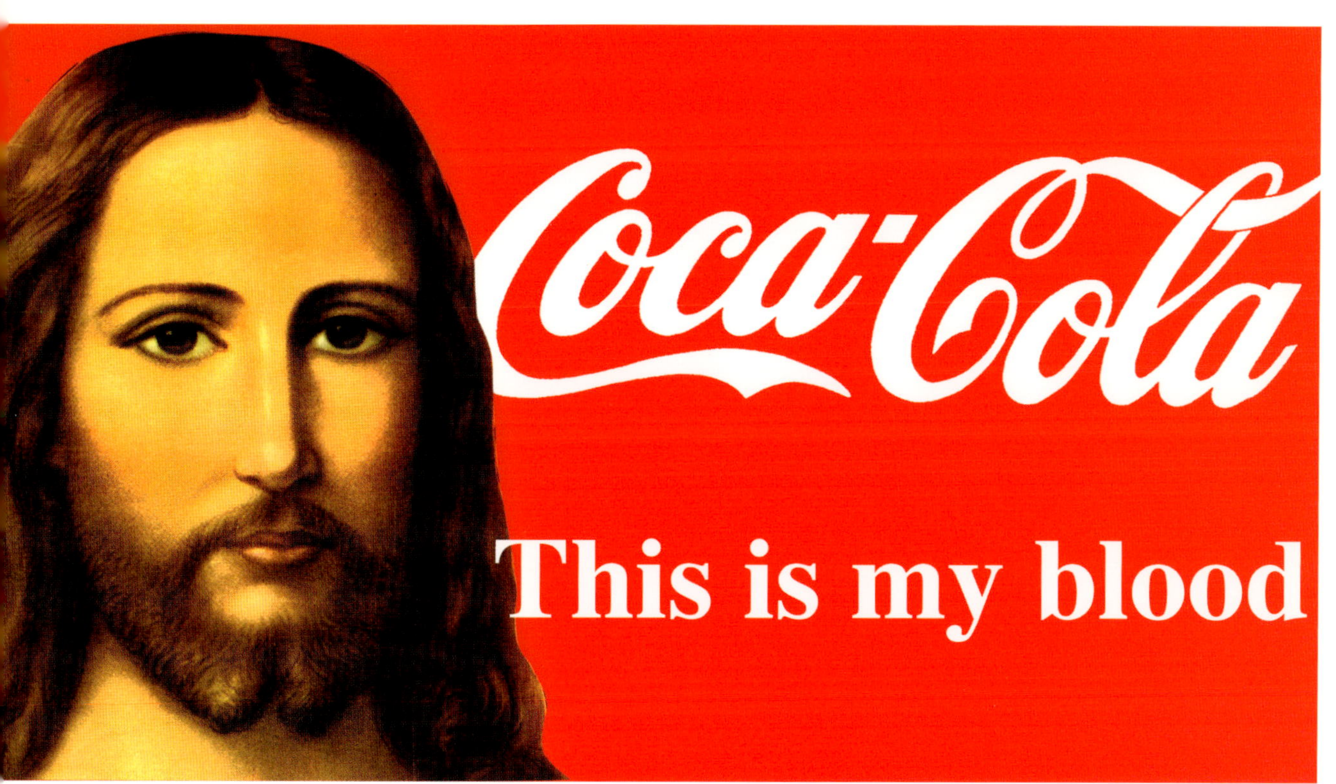

There are no specific formal qualities that blasphemous images share, though sexuality/nudity and bodily fluids seem to register in a great many of them. Collectively they point toward a society's dis-ease with the human body itself, that most intimate and yet most foreign of entities. We will see such 'impure' mixings again and again. Meanwhile, one *leitmotif* throughout contemporary contentious imagery deals with the ubiquitous logos of consumer capitalism. One of the most universal, and therefore profane, dimensions of life in the twenty-first century is consumerism and the mass marketing that drives it. Artists have responded with critique and satire as they reappropriate the images of mass consumption. The Russian artist Alexander Kosolapov has worked such themes into several pieces, and been roundly condemned for his improper mixings. In *This is My Blood*, Kosolapov mixes the Coca-Cola logo with an iconic image of Jesus Christ, while in several other pieces he mixes iconic images of Lenin with McDonald's imagery. In another vein, Alan Schechner has retouched Holocaust images by digitally inserting consumer products into well known photos from Buchenwald and elsewhere. While these were not considered blasphemous from a religious authoritative position, one can see again an improper mixing of what some people consider sacred and profane, only here it is a consumer product that appears to have the power to desecrate.

The offences taken by certain people in each of these instances all have to do with their own conceptions as to what is sacred and what is profane. I hastily note that in each of the instances noted here, *some* religious authorities found the artworks blasphemous or offensive, while others did not. There are ways to show how urine, dung, and nudity are *not* the negative elements some believe them to be, but in particular contexts the 'mixture' seems too transgressive for certain authority figures.[5] For now, I am concerned to provide some background for why people have believed and continue to believe certain images to be blasphemous.

Let me set up a brief contrast between three images to show the ambiguity as to what might be considered blasphemous in particular times and places; when the mixings between sacred and profane are acceptable and when they are not. Chris Ofili's now well-known *Holy Virgin Mary* – with its pornographic cut-outs surrounding the Virgin, and the elephant dung fashioned at her breast – was originally composed in 1996, and bought by Charles Saatchi, a wealthy British businessman, soon after. In 1997, Saatchi set up an exhibition called *Sensation* from his own collection, held at the Royal Academy of Art in London. Not much of anything was said about Ofili's work, since the news media was busy with controversy surrounding Marcus Harvey's disturbing portrait of the serial killer Myra Hindley. When *Sensation* opened at the Brooklyn Museum in New York in the autumn of 1999, however, Mayor Rudolf Giuliani decided that Ofili's piece was sacrilegious and began a quasi-religious/morality campaign to eliminate funding for the museum. Giuliani lost all political and economic attempts to censor the image, but the controversy had multiple effects, including the prompting of Australia's National Gallery of Art to cancel their planned exhibiting of *Sensation*.

In a somewhat similar image to Ofili's, from a fifteenth century Book of Hours (a personal, Christian devotional reader very popular in medieval Europe) from France, we find an illustration of Pentecost – the Holy Spirit descends on the followers of Jesus as described in the second chapter of Acts. It is a beautiful pious image, located in a beautiful

Illustration of Pentecost from The Book of Hours, Rouen, France, c. 1470–1480, illuminated manuscript (parchment), 20 x 13 cm, courtesy of the Newberry Library, Chicago

The image depicts the Christian festival of Whitsunday, held on the seventh Sunday after Easter, which celebrates the descent of the Holy Spirit on the disciples of Jesus after his Ascension.

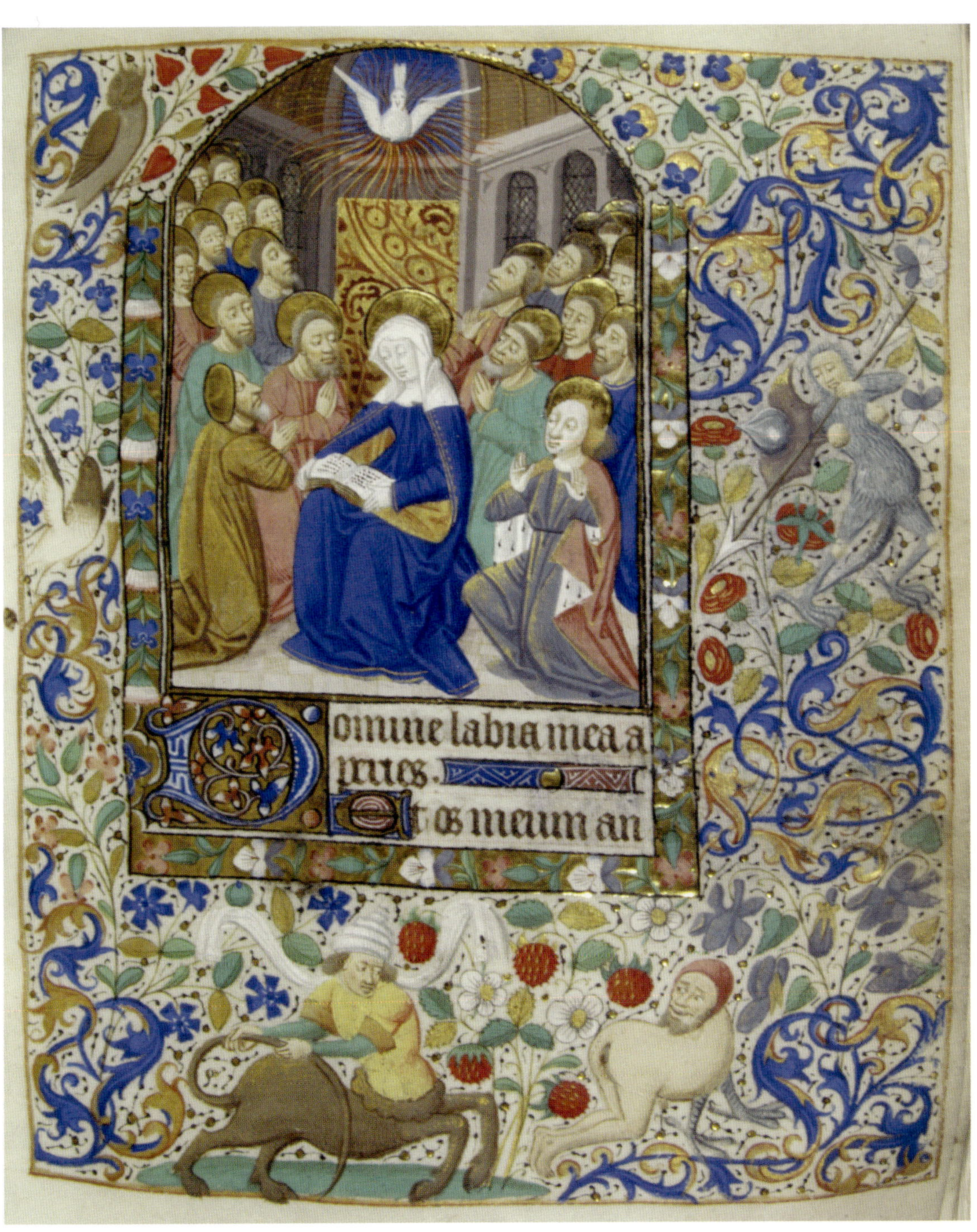
Domine labia mea a
peries.
Et os meum an

pious book. Nonetheless, in the lower frame of the image are two beast-men, frolicking in some anal-sexual adventure. As with Ofili's image, the religious personages that are the focus of the image are accompanied by a certain aberrant sexuality. The manuscript contains no evidence of censoring of these images, and while it is impossible to tell how many people have seen the image in the past half-millenium, none of those who did seemed to be compelled to act against it.

Compare these, finally, with a relatively crude drawing found in a grammar book. The grammar book would have been used by Latin students and contained writings by Ovid. The images have little to do with the text they accompany and are merely meaningless marginalia. Most of the images throughout the book developed out of wordplays and depict people engaged in various activities, a few of them with scatological references and anal sexuality. We see in the image here that such marginalia wasn't deemed appropriate by everyone and heavy censorship occurred. As opposed to the somewhat sacred status of the Book of Hours, however, this was just a profane grammar book. But what was depicted was obviously not pleasing and someone felt the need for censorship.[6]

All of the previous indicates that a blasphemous image is not a category of *being* in itself, but it is an entity that proffers a confusion between the sacred and profane, challenging the accepted norms. No work of art is blasphemous in and of itself; it must be deemed so from within religious and/or political power structures, whether small or large scale, and there are many examples in which an image has appeared without comment in one setting only to explode with controversy in another. In short, a blasphemous image needs both an artist and an accuser. The context for accusation includes everything from religious dogmatic assertions to media coverage to political posturing made by authorities seeking to appear as defenders of social decorum and morality. Throughout *Blasphemy: Art That Offends*, the visual culture of the blasphemous image is emphasised, pointing toward the fact that images do not exist in isolation from cultural norms and values.

MS 99, **Regulae Grammaticae**, c. 1450, illuminated manuscript, courtesy of the University of Chicago Library

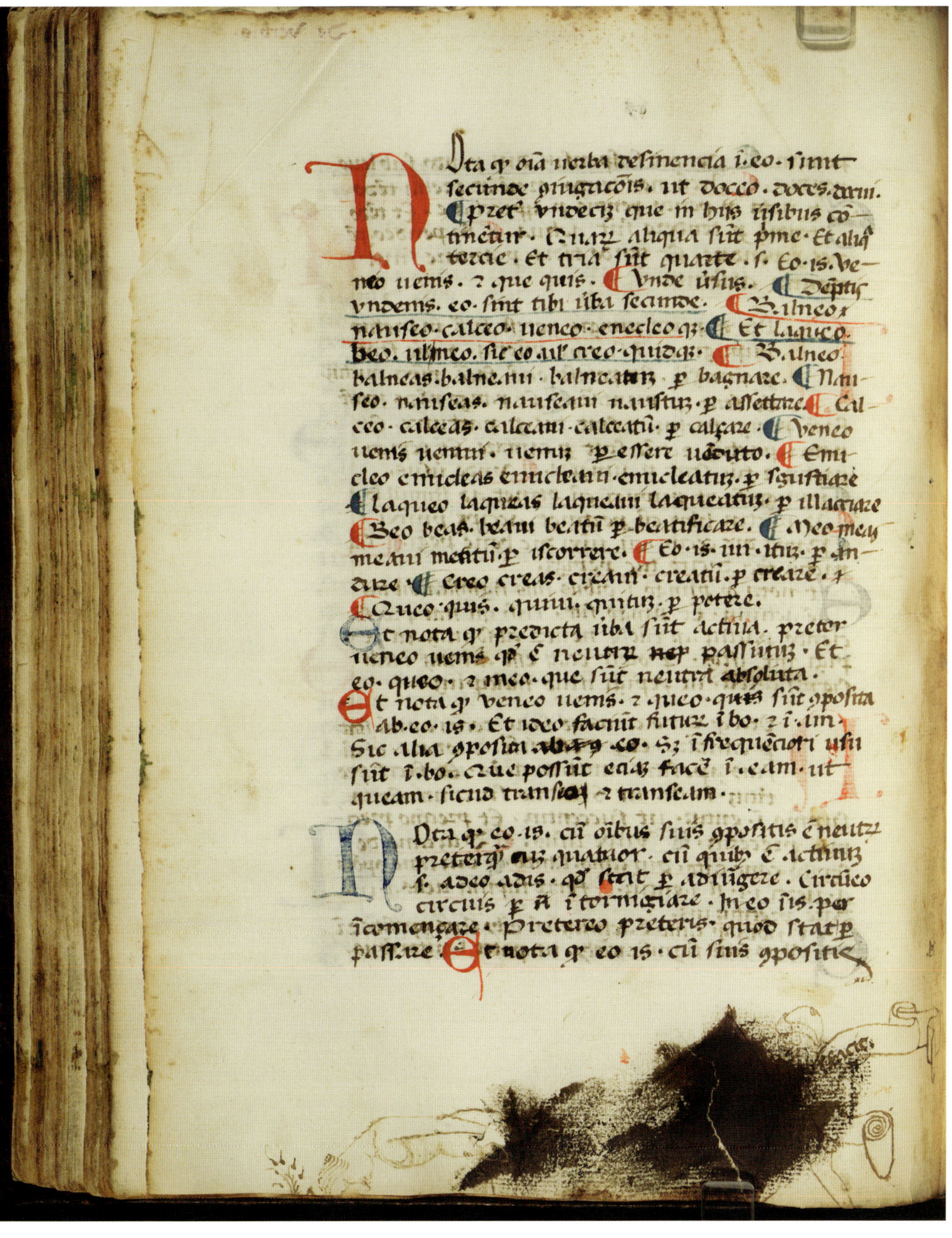
Nota quod omnia uerba desinencia in eo sunt
secunde coniugacionis. ut doceo. doces. docui.
Preter undecim que in his uersibus con-
tinentur. Quarum aliqua sunt prime. Et alique
tercie. Et tria sunt quarte. scilicet Eo. is. Veneo uenis. et queo quis. Unde uersus. Depticis
undenis. eo. sunt tibi uerba secunde. Balneo et
nauseo. calceo. ueneo. enucleo que. Et laqueo.
beo. ultimo. sic eo aut creo quidem. Balneo
balneas. balneaui. balneatum. pro bagnare. Nauseo. nauseas. nauseaui nauseatum. pro assettare. Calceo. calceas. calceaui. calceatum. pro calzare. Veneo
uenis uenium. uenitum pro essere uenduto. Enucleo enucleas enucleaui. enucleatum. pro sguisciare
laqueo laqueas laqueaui laqueatum. pro illaciare
Beo beas. beaui beatum pro beatificare. Meo meas
meaui meatum pro scorrere. Eo. is. iui. itum. pro an-
dare. Creo creas. creaui. creatum. pro creare. et
Queo quis. quiui. quitum. pro potere.
Et nota quod predicta uerba sunt actiua. preter
ueneo uenis quod est neutrum ~~nec~~ passiuum. Et
eo. queo. et meo. que sunt neutra absoluta.
Et nota quod ueneo uenis. et queo. quis sunt composita
ab eo. is. Et ideo faciunt futurum in bo. et in am.
Sic alia composita ~~ab eo~~ eo. Sed in frequenciori usu
sunt in bo. Que possunt eciam facere in eam. ut
queam. sicud transeo et transeam.
Nota quod eo. is. cum omnibus suis compositis est neutrum
preterquam cum quatuor. cum quibus est actiuum
scilicet adeo adis. quod stat pro adiungere. Circueo
circuis pro id est intorniçiare. Ineo inis. per
incomençare. Preterreo preteris. quod stat pro
passare. Et nota quod eo is. cum suis compositis

Some Historical Dimensions of Blasphemy in Judaism, Christianity, and Islam

To provide historical background to the concept of blasphemy, I will briefly sketch some of the Western religious histories and uses of the term. Since the word itself stems from the Greek, it is never clear whether it can be easily translated into other languages, and thus whether the concept exists in the same way in Judaism, Islam, and Christianity. The three religions have always been, and continue to be, intimately linked. Contemporary aphorisms about our current 'global community' and religious pluralism have some truth, but tend to disregard the many times and places in which these three religious traditions (and others) have coexisted in the past millennia.

Judaism

Ancient Hebrew, the language of some of the oldest sacred texts in the world – what Jews often call the Tanakh, and Christians the Old Testament – does not have one consistent term that might be translated as blasphemy. The authoritative, Greek, third century BCE translation of the Hebrew Bible, known as the Septuagint, used the Greek *blasphemia* to translate a number of Hebrew words (including *naqab*, *qalal*, *gadaf*, and *ne'atsah*) focused on cursing, reviling, despising, and/or insulting God (Numbers 15.30; 2 Kings 19.6, 22; Isaiah 52.5; Ezekiel 35.12, Daniel 3.29, Nehemiah 9). Meanwhile, there is a long tradition in Judaism of arguing or bargaining with God, beginning with Abraham's pleas that God not destroy Sodom and Gomorrah (Genesis 18.16-33) and extending through modern Hasidism and particularly in post-Holocaust theology. Such conversation and argumentation with God has a long and pious tradition in Judaism, though many Christians and Muslims might find this a bit too close to blasphemy.[7]

Ancient Jewish laws on blasphemy oftentimes went further than a direct insulting of God, and some of the more common crimes of blasphemy are variations on the third commandment: "You shall not take the name of the Lord your God in vain" (Exodus 20.7). What becomes critical to note is the shift from the more direct cursing of God to the linguistically charged cursing of God's *name*. The name cursing seems to have the larger history, continuing into the present day. Throughout Jewish history the name of God itself is holy, sacred, and must not be uttered by mere mortal, profane people. Here too, one can see the semi-permeable boundaries between the sacred and profane as established by ritual, for at one point in history a tradition emerged in which the name of God was uttered one time a year (at Yom Kippur), in one specific place (the Holy of Holies at the centre of the Temple), by one specific person (the chief priest). Otherwise, God's true name has been kept from the masses, while many substitute names have arisen for the sake of everyday, profane, life.

The notorious and hilarious 1979 film, *Monty Python's Life of Brian*, was decried as blasphemous around the world and banned from numerous European countries for years. The film pushes at the boundaries of what is sacred and profane, since the eponymous 'everyman' Brian is born at the same time as Jesus Christ in a manger down the street. But as Brian's mother clearly tells a crowd of Brian followers: "He's not the Messiah, he's a very naughty boy!" One scene in the film ironically deals with some of the ambiguities and extremities to which blasphemy might be considered in the ancient Israelite tradition. An old man is accused of blasphemy for speaking the name 'Jehovah', and a crowd has gathered to stone him (including women, dressed as men, in order to be allowed to the stoning –

thereby playing with the gender differences that often accompany the splits between the sacred and profane, a subject taken up further in the next chapter). A priestly figure appears and reads off the charges, during which time the priest must, of course, mention that the man's offence was speaking the name of Jehovah. The crowd immediately begins to throw stones *at the priest* since he too had just spoken the name 'Jehovah'. Here is a film accused of blasphemy, even as it actually revisits some of the very history of blasphemy.

The Pythons didn't just make this up either. The Hebrew scriptures imply the problems with accusing someone of cursing God's name, since doing so without actually repeating the curse is impossible. And later on, the prominent twelfth century theologian, poet, and astrologer from the Iberian peninsula, Rabbi Avraham ibn Ezra, made a related comment which might have pleased the Monty Python team. Known for his meticulous works on Hebrew grammar and commentaries on the Torah, ibn Ezra notes how the Exodus 20 command against using God's name is widespread, and yet anyone accused of it will swear by God's name that they are not doing so!

One final, initial point about the Jewish charge of blasphemy. In a string of other commandments following the so-called Ten Commandments, Exodus 22.27 explains that "You must not revile God", and quickly amends this divine-oriented command with the earthly, "nor curse a chief of your own people". Blasphemy constantly oscillates between divine law and earthly governance, and the status of the sacred wavers between the heavenly and the earthly.

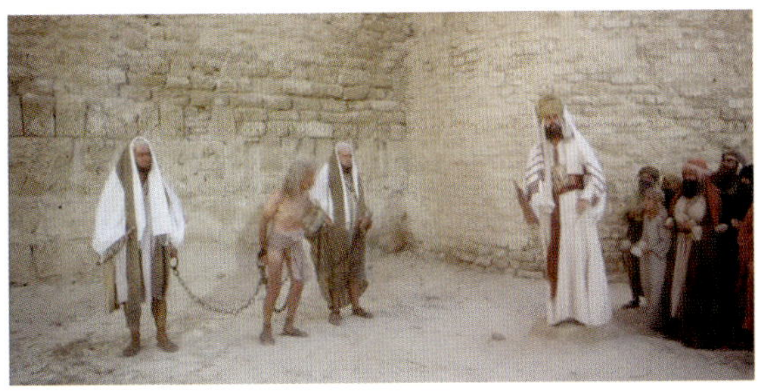

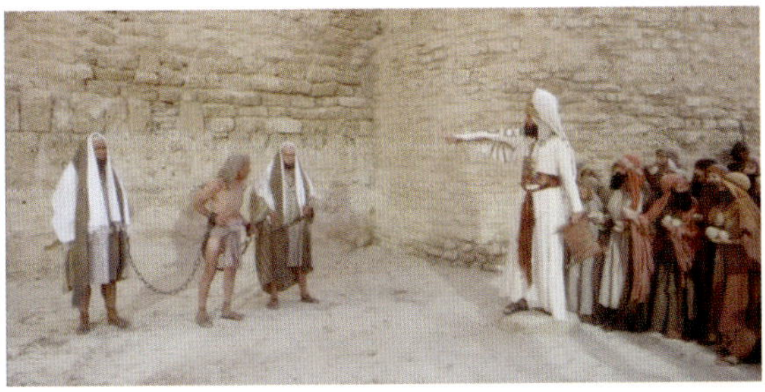

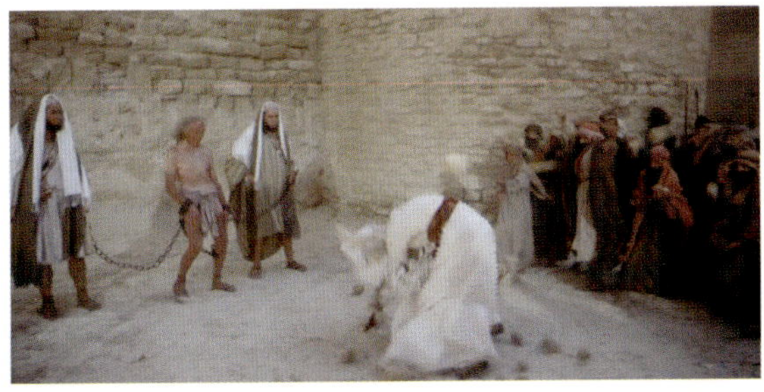

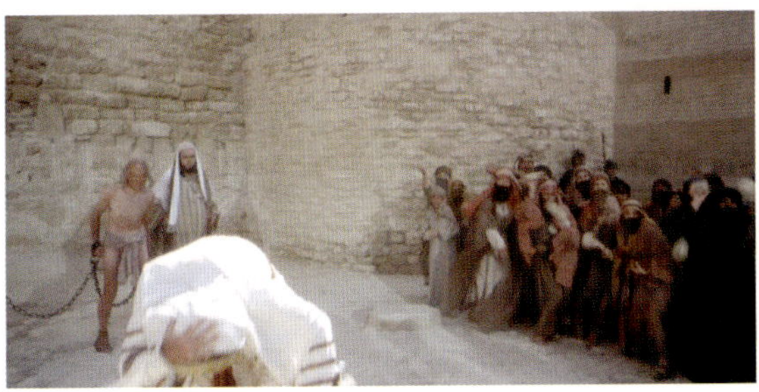

Terry Jones, *Monty Python's Life of Brian* [screen shots], 1979, film, courtesy of Python (Monty) Pictures Limited

Monty Python's Life Of Brian is a comedy written by and starring the cast of Monty Python. The film documents the life of Brian Cohen, a man born on the same night as Jesus. Seen by many as a critique of excessive religious fervor, the film is also perceived by many as a religious satire of organised religion. In the past, the film has been described as a racket involving hypocrisy and zealotry, and has harshly been called a sacreligious film deserving censorship.

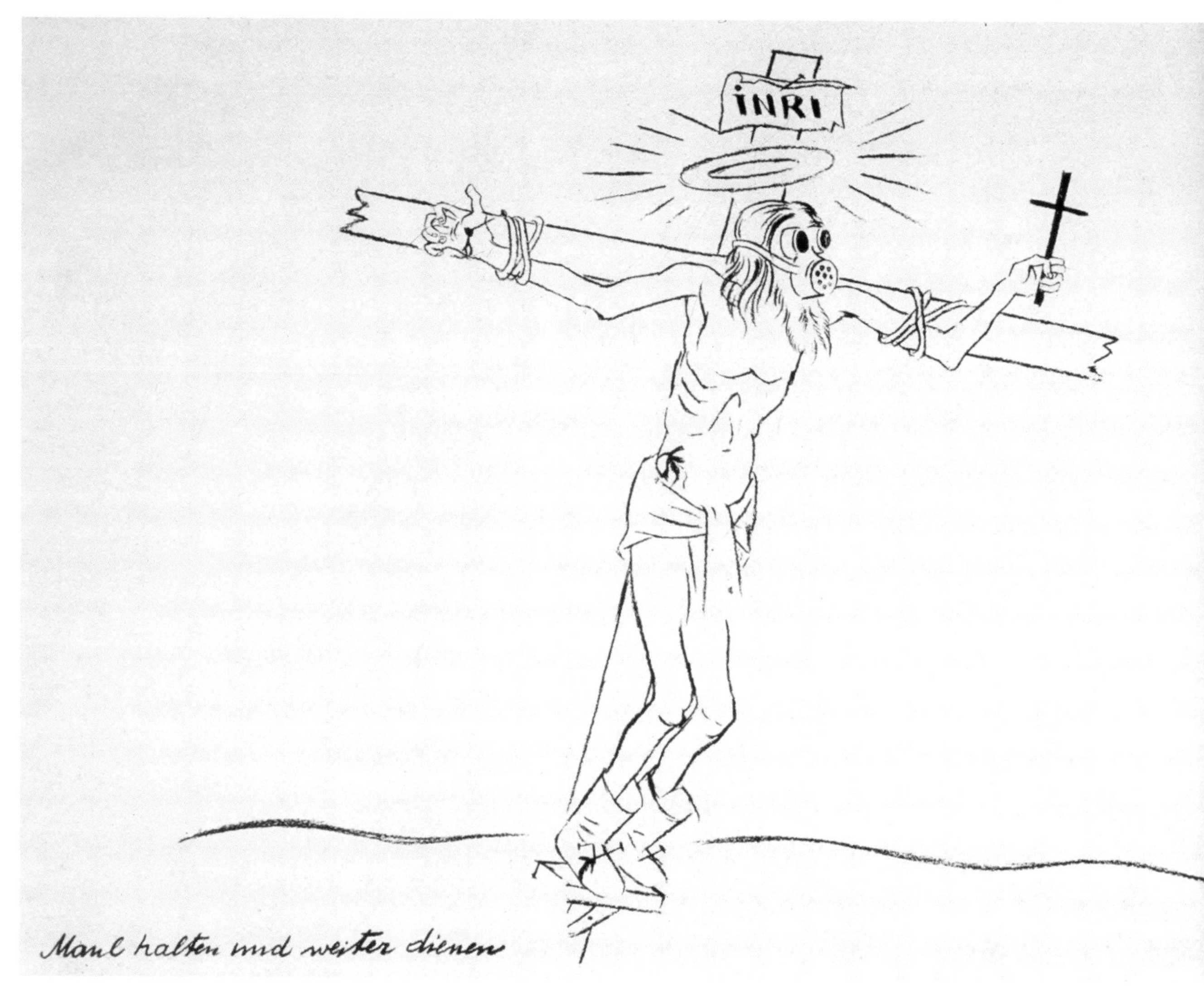

George Grosz, *Christ in a Gas Mask*, 1923, ink on paper,
Photo archive Ralph Jentsch, Rome, © DACS, London 2006

In the same year that Grosz created *Ecce Homo*, 1923, the German authorities confiscated the artist's prints, fining him for "offending public morals". By 1928, Grosz was arrested and put on trial for blasphemy. The court decided to have one of his many 'offending' prints – *Christ in a Gas Mask* – destroyed.

Christianity

Christianity picked up much of its 'theo-logic' (that is, its rules, regulations, and belief statements relating specifically to God) from Judaism, even as it improvised in order to emerge as a religion distinct from its Jewish and, eventually, Roman, roots. Indeed, if looking through an encyclopedia, library, or the Internet, one of the first places the researcher is pointed is to the trial of Jesus, implied by the Gospels as being a blasphemy trial against Jesus. In the Christian retelling, this trial is turned on its head and becomes a rhetorical indictment against the blasphemous Sanhedrin who refused to acknowledge the Messianic nature of Jesus. To clarify, in some of the Gospel accounts (Mark and Matthew most explicitly) Jesus is accused of blasphemy. In the retelling of the trial, as canonised in the Christian New Testament, those who accused Jesus are the real blasphemers since within the narrative structure they did not recognise the divinity of the Christ.

But then in another historical turn, Jesus Christ certainly must hold the title as 'the Most Blasphemed Against Holy Figure', especially in the modern West. Images of Jesus that have been accused of blasphemy in the last hundred years have included great political statements by George Grosz, which led to the artist's indictment of blasphemy in Germany in the 1920s; and Kamera Skura and Kunst-Fu's joint Czech-Slovak entry in the 2003 Venice Biennale called *Superstar*, which consists of a cruciform statue of Jesus Christ moved from the cross to the gymnasium. Gerhard Haderer's little comic book *The Life of Jesus* – borrowing a popular title from the nineteenth century quest for the historical Jesus – sold hundreds of thousands of copies throughout Europe but also landed the artist a six-month prison sentence by the Orthodox-inspired Greek government (though later repealed); and Gilbert and George's recent exhibition in London, *Sonofagod Pictures: Was Jesus Heterosexual?* prompted Conservative Minister Ann Widdecombe to label the pictures "blasphemous in the extreme, as [Gilbert and George] will find out when finally they stand before the Son of God".[8] Perhaps Jesus is an easy target since Christianity, to put it bluntly, is the religion that made blasphemy popular. Because of its global prominence, its ability to infiltrate many of the world's cultures, Christian attitudes toward blasphemy have had a long-lasting influence on other religious traditions, as well as the political and legal structures of contemporary nations.

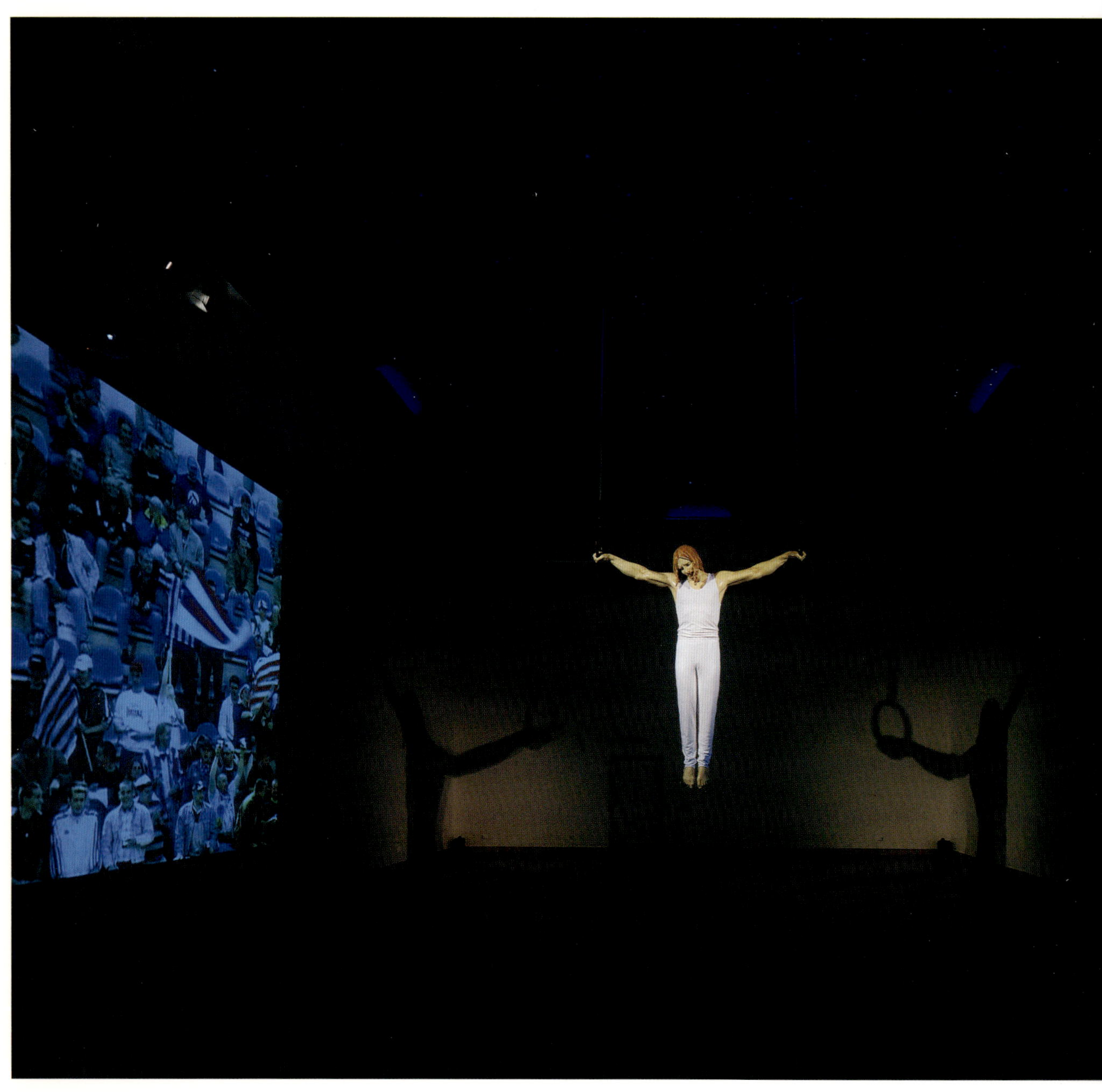

Kamera Skura and Kunst Fu, *Superstar*, 2003, multimedia installation with video, courtesy of the artists

Here the two artists have collaborted to create an intriguing, lyrical and subversive visual satement. The installation has been described as a world in which sports stars and physical prowess are worshipped. The object of adoration here being a Christ figure kitted out in a gym suit.

Historically, early Christianity set about the intellectual task of getting their story straight. The paradoxical understanding that Jesus is both divine and human at the same time made it very difficult to put the theology into words (just what part of Jesus was human and what part divine?), and the task of a few centuries' worth of theological councils was to articulate a more stable definition of the Incarnation. After that was settled, the bishops and scholars turned to the task of defining the Trinity, another paradoxical formulation that attempted to reconcile monotheism with a three-parted deity. As many councils met and formulated what became Christian orthodoxy, they simultaneously rejected those who did not adhere to their statements, and the term blasphemy was hurled from one group to another, and back again. In other words, it has been primarily theological positions that have been considered blasphemous in Christianity: one had to have the correct theological understanding of Jesus Christ and the Trinity. So important was having the right view, that the sixth century Emperor Justinian declared that if blasphemy is not punished God will become angry, and famine, earthquake, and pestilence will follow. So he made it a capital offence. Such a decree, it must be noted in passing, followed the first great outbreak of the bubonic plague across Europe in 540.

Once the early theological doctrines were established, and alongside Christianity's rise as the official religion of the Holy Roman Empire, the term 'heresy' became the more prominent legal accusation, while blasphemy was simply used as an invective. Compared to the first 500 years of Christianity, accusations of blasphemy are seldom found in the next 1,000 years of the Church's legal language and doctrine, and when used, the two terms were commonly interchanged. The sixteenth century crystallisation of the Protestant Reformation, particularly around the figures of Martin Luther and John Calvin, was key to the revival of the term blasphemy. The Roman Catholics had legal control over the crime of heresy and decided who should be accused, why they should be accused, and what their punishment would be. They made this accusation against, amongst others, Luther, Calvin, and their followers. Thus, the Reformers had to come up with their own attack, and Luther particularly used blasphemy as the term to throw back at the Catholics, as well as the Arianists, Anabaptists, Jews, and Muslims – or simply anyone who disagreed with Luther himself. As Leonard Levy states, "It became part of the Protestant currency", and during the Catholic-Protestant wars (of words as well as swords) many people were burned at the stake for blasphemy and heresy.[9] It was not until the eighteenth century that execution was phased out as the punishment for blasphemy across Europe and North America. Laws against blasphemy remain on the books in many Western nations, even though court cases rarely transpire today.

Because the Reformers' revival of blasphemy occurred at the cusp of modernity, broadly speaking, the language was often incorporated into the charters and constitutions of new nation-states. From the seventeenth into the twentieth century, charges of blasphemy crossed from the religious to the political, even as there is never a clear distinction between the two. As I will discuss in the final chapter, modern European political philosophies began to include more and more subjects that could be blasphemed against. No longer is blasphemy limited to what religious institutions see as blasphemous – deities, texts, prophets, and doctrines – but blasphemy and its accusations are integrated into a new dimension of sacred entities: freedom of expression, education, friendship, and most prominently, the nation-state.

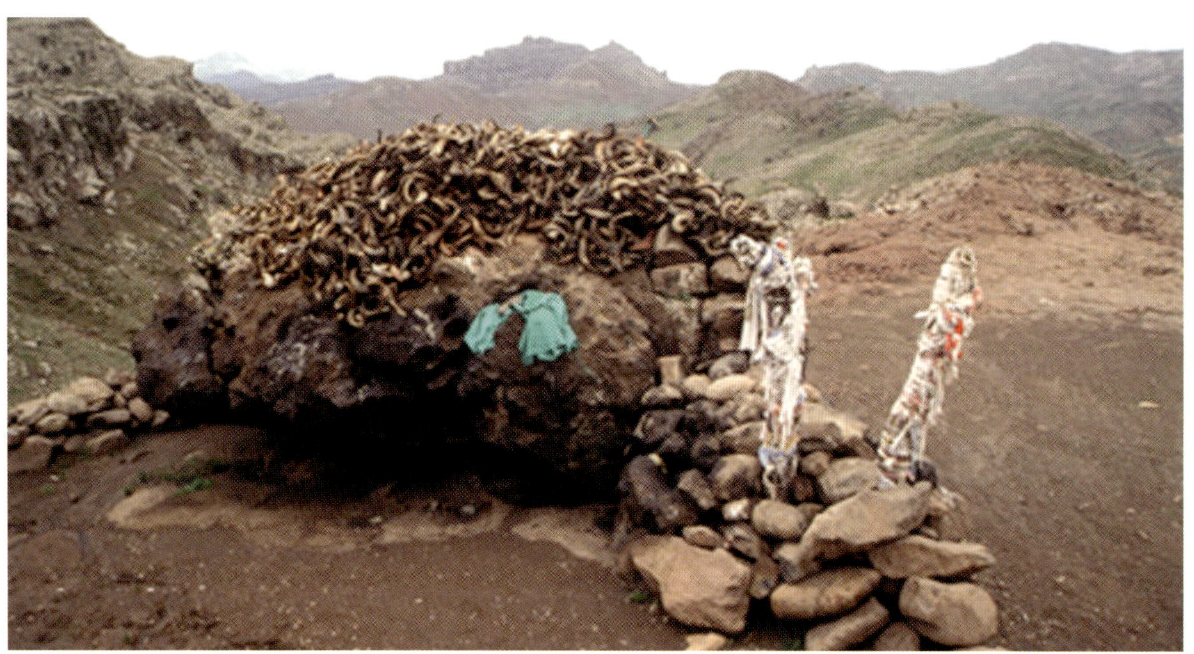

Islam

There is no direct translation of blasphemy in Arabic, and hence in Islam. However, as with Hebrew and English, Arabic has a number of interrelated terms that intersect with similar issues and theological concerns. Many scholars suggest that blasphemy can be understood through the Arabic term *kufr*, which might be translated as 'disbelief' (or 'ingratitude', of not attributing to God what should be) and is referred to extensively throughout the Quran. Its opposite is *iman*, or 'faith'. Literally, *kufr* means 'to cover up', and suggests a hiding or rejection of God's divine revelation (Quran 3.16). There is also the term for 'apostasy', *riddah*, which runs parallel. Otherwise, there is a strong relation to *shirk*, one of the gravest sins in Islam, which means "to put something before the true God". Since Islam emphasises *tawhid*, or "the absolute unity and singularity of God", nothing should challenge this: not idols, other gods, or false thoughts about the true God. *Tawhid* is among the most stringent expressions of monotheism in all the world religions, and thus *shirk* must also be taken into account in an understanding of what blasphemy might mean in Islam. As with Christianity, theological positions might be called blasphemous, and thus there is overlap with notions of heresy.[10]

Martin Gray, *The Shrine of Duzgunbaba*, courtesy of the photographer/Sacred Sites (www.sacredsites.com)
It is said that this was the sacred place of the Hittite god of storm, Teshub, even before the arrival of Islam. The mount is so named after a thirteenth century Sufi saint who took refuge within a cave at its summit. The shrine denotes a place known for its healing powers.

While there is a strong God-centred impulse in Islam similar to Judaism, much of the history of blasphemy has had Muhammad and/or the Quranic revelation as the target of blasphemous activity. The Quran indicates several instances in which Muhammad's Arab contemporaries disparaged and insulted him and the revelation (Quran 111; 9.65-66). And in the expansive tradition of Islamic law, the angels, other prophets (including Abraham and Moses), as well as religious scholarship itself (since it is an extension of the divine revelation) can all be blasphemed against. Some legal traditions include improper ritualistic activities such as wearing the clothes that a Jew or Zoroastrian might wear, or participating in religious rites outside the Islamic tradition. Metaphysically speaking, the great medieval Islamic philosophers such as al-Ghazali (d. 1111) and Ibn Sina, also known as Avicenna, (d. 1037) discussed the issues of blasphemy and infidelity from Aristotelean perspectives, particularly arguing the gravity of rejecting doctrines surrounding the omnipotence and omniscience of God. Blasphemy occurs in thought, word, and deed.

The Islamic mystical traditions of Sufism, the inner seeking after God, have quite often come under criticism and been accused of heresy from other Muslims, especially in the modern age with conservative movements such as the predominantly Saudi Wahhabi. As part of their spiritual path, Sufis often utilise the arts of dance, music, and poetry to enable this divine connection, as well as the ritual repetition of God's name (*dhikr*), and at times a veneration of Muslim saints. Because Sufis tend to understand God as permeating all being, and is thus 'inside' oneself as much as external to the self, they have been accused of speaking heretically by claiming and revealing the deity within. Al-Hallaj is one of the more famous martyrs, executed on ambiguous heresy charges in 922 CE for claiming his own divinity, speaking "I am the Truth" in the midst of a ritual chant.[11]

Likewise, the Baha'i tradition, founded in nineteenth century Iran, has close links with mainstream Islam, and has been perpetually persecuted by many mainstream Muslim groups, and especially by the Wahhabi. Many Muslim countries see Baha'i as a heretical sect of Islam, rather than its own separate religion. The founder of the movement, Baha'u'llah, was himself exiled and imprisoned for most of his life, as he taught a universalistic approach to religion, and that divine revelation is continuous (for a majority of Muslims, Muhammad was the last of the prophets and thus the revelation of the Quran was the final word).

And as with Judaism and Christianity, it is never clear where the religious ends and the political begins. Theocracy is a common understanding in Islamic tradition, for if God really is the Creator and continues to sustain the world, then there can be no separation of religion and politics. The split between religion and government is one of the 'sacred cows' of the modern West, under the influence of liberal thought, and is not shared across the world and often not in Islamic countries.

The Limits of Defining Blasphemy

Perhaps I have made my task too difficult. Rather than simplifying the term and offering a definition, I have instead added more and more terms to it. Like Justice Frankfurter, I find that researching definitions, hoping to find a clear definition of blasphemy, has instead taken me down a great rabbit hole in which concepts condense or expand, turn perceptions upside down, and generally confuse. To understand blasphemy, we have to struggle with translation, with differences in languages, cultures, theological and political outlooks across thousands of years, and there is no perfect translation. Blasphemy, to adopt an astronomical metaphor from the German cultural critic Walter Benjamin, is a 'constellation'.[12] It is a symbolic reference point made up of multiple, interconnecting points (stars). It is, furthermore, a symbol that provides orientation. Just as ancient mariners navigated by the stars, constellations tell us where we are; astrologically speaking they also tell us *who* we are. The various stars that make up the constellation called blasphemy include 'idolatry', 'heresy', 'sacrilege', 'obscenity', 'infidelity', 'immorality', and others that I have highlighted previously. What is absolutely vital to realise, and in relation to the sacred and the profane, is that a constellation is a group of stars amongst many other stars. Constellations are, above all, symbols, which means that they are material objects invested with particular meaning by their observers. The defining and delimiting of some stars from others is dependent on an audience, on communities of people who agree that this star belongs here, and that over there. Some stars just don't belong in some groups. And it is, in part, the agreement, the 'social contract', that makes such constellations meaningful.

As a way to incorporate several of the ideas and activities that light up the blasphemous constellation, I have suggested using the language of the sacred and the profane. Blasphemy is about impure crossings from one side of the sacred-profane divide to the other; about juxtaposing the sacred and the profane in times and places where they are expected to be kept separate; of twisting the profane so that it appears sacred, or making the sacred appear profane. Like a constellation, the difference between the sacred and the profane is dependent on its perceivers. These perceivers live in real space and time, arguing and agreeing, creating laws and rituals which sediment into tradition and authority. Even so, the line between the sacred and the profane is drawn in sand and the proverbial winds of time blow, covering the lines, only so they will be redrawn. The lines, even if decided by convention, are nonetheless perhaps more difficult to move than sand by wind.

And this, I believe, is where art (another great constellation of a term), helps a society to see differently. In this book I follow George Bernard Shaw's dictum provided as the epigraph above. Frequently, established truths begin as jokes, treason, and blasphemy, but slowly – depending on the conversations a society is willing to entertain – become standardised, legalised, moralised. It takes some risk to paint, draw, write, sculpt, and speak in ways that breach the sacred-profane divide. The creator faces political and religious authorities, and artists are confronted with persecution, indifference, scorn, praise, sometimes execution, sometimes a 'slap on the hand'. My aim here is to contribute to this ongoing conversation, not so as to eliminate all difference between the sacred and the profane, for that can only end in chaos, but to suggest that oppressive lines *can* be redrawn.

Mounir Fatmi, *Les Connexions*, 2003–2004,
installation with books and cables, courtesy of La B.A.N.K., Paris

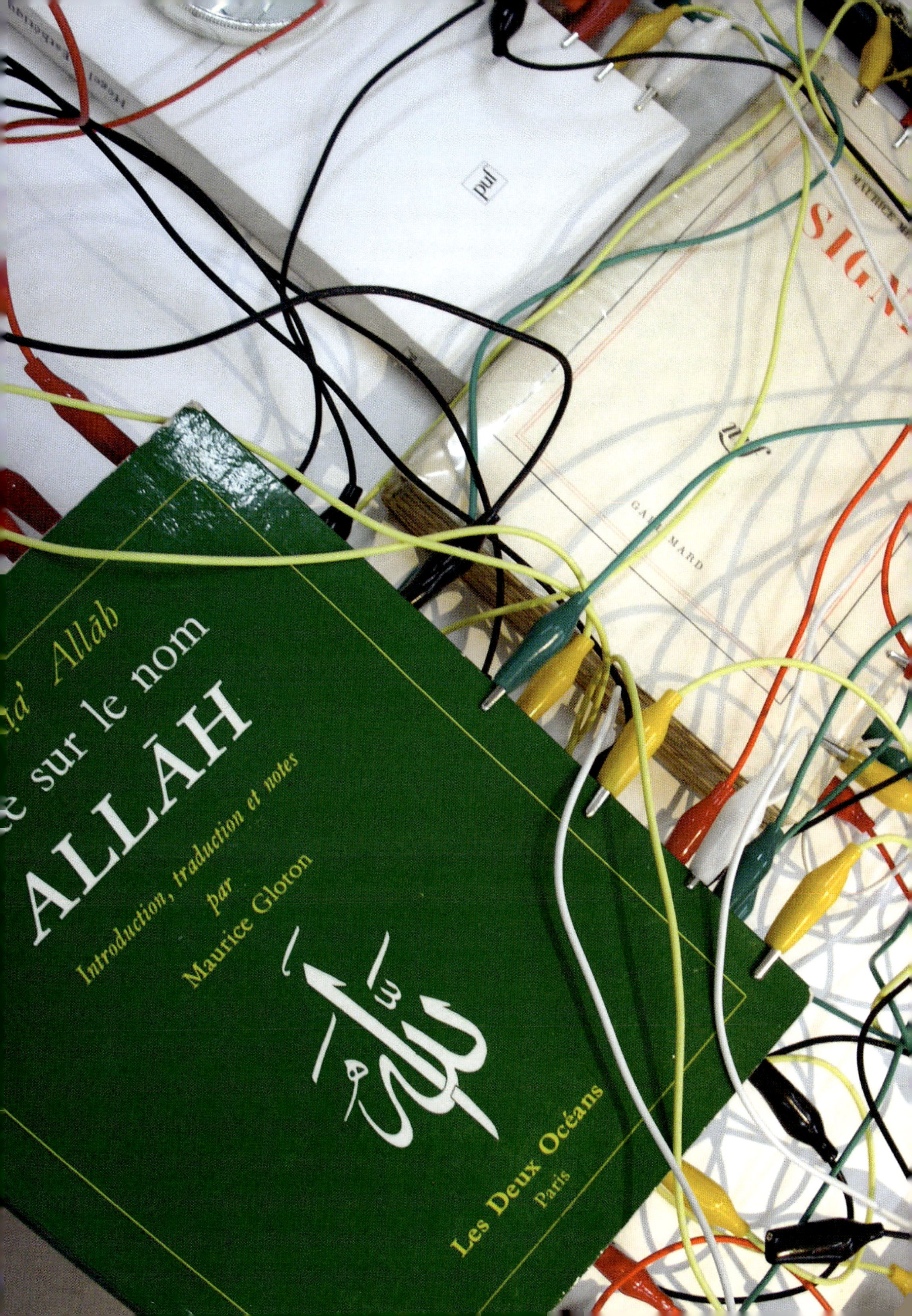

Allāh
sur le nom
ALLĀH
Introduction, traduction et notes
par
Maurice Gloton
Les Deux Océans
Paris
puf
nrf

THE POWER OF IMAGES MEETS RELIGIOUS AND POLITICAL POWER

Chapter Two

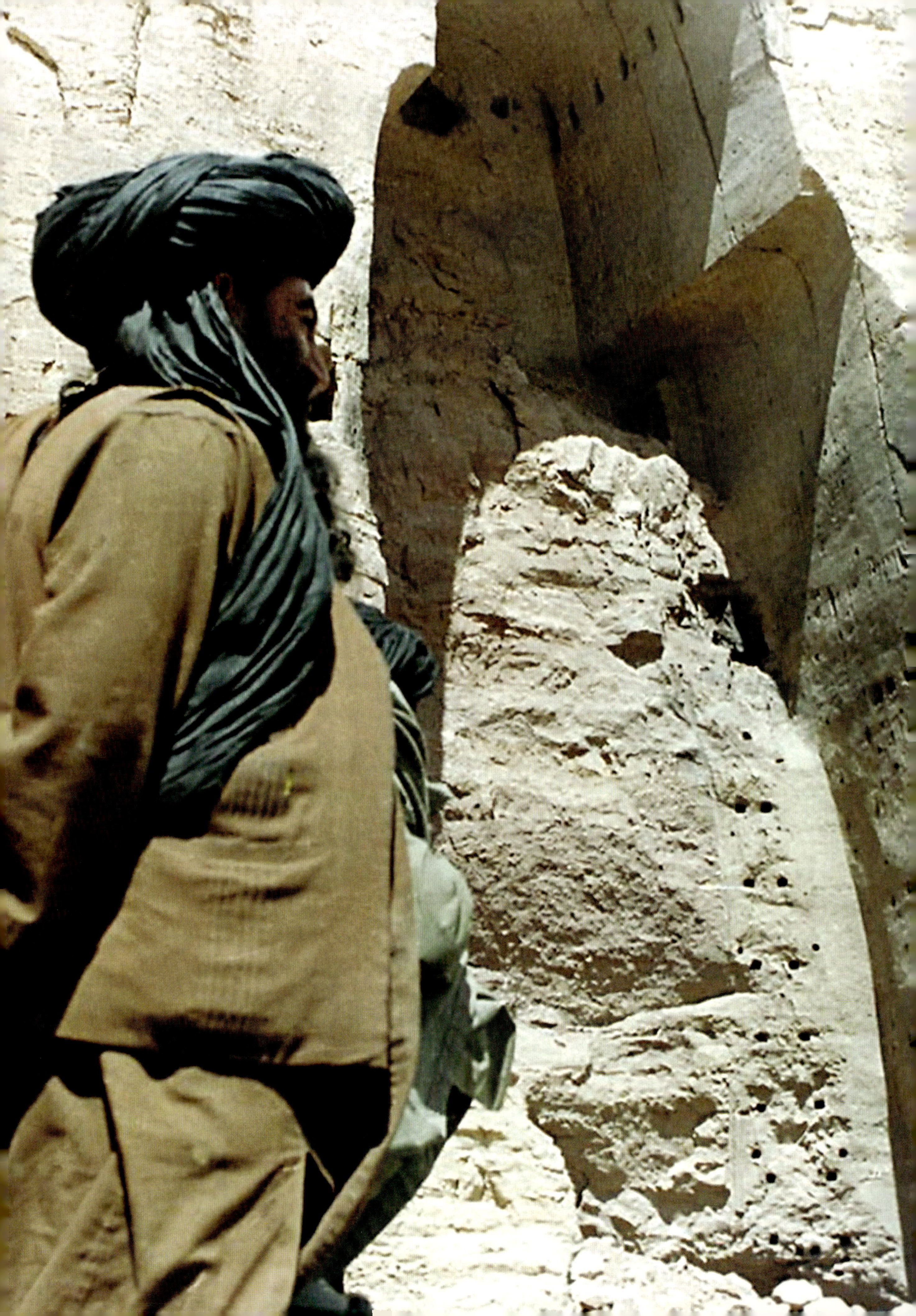

Bamiyan Buddha, Central Afghanistan,
documentary photography courtesy of EMPICS

A Taliban soldier looks up at the resulting empty space after the demolition of one of the sixth century Bamiyan Buddhas, previously carved into the cliff face.

THE POWER OF IMAGES MEETS RELIGIOUS AND POLITICAL POWER

Chapter Two

The second lesson arising from the case of Roberto Rossellini's *The Miracle*, discussed in the previous chapter, is the fact that images harbour power – sometimes secret, mysterious power, sometimes hit-you-over-the-head blatant power. Depending on the environment in which they are placed, images can set off riots, religious reformations, court cases, political posturings, and take their place among broader processes of social cohesion and social disintegration. No matter how technologically sophisticated and rationally ordered a society may be – which is to say, no matter how sceptical toward 'magical power' – there will always be images that are decried as blasphemous, sacrilegious, obscene, and/or immoral.

There is another side to this power, and that is the interpretive power held by groups and individuals who view these images, bestowing meanings upon them that bypass or exceed those intended by any artist. With regard to *The Miracle*, we find power held by Cardinal Spellman, who took the film as an opportunity to rile people and speak out against what he saw as greater immoralities in US society as a whole. His crusade may have lost in the Supreme Court, but he won many converts to his cause in the process. A picture may paint a thousand words, but there are plenty of people who can speak a thousand, even ten thousand, words about a picture and thus circumvent the artist's original intentions, to replace them with their own interpretation. Thus, bound up with the power of images is the power of the words used to interpret them. The art historian Hans Belting discusses this relationship within the history of Christianity:

> Whenever images threatened to gain undue influence within the church, theologians have sought to strip them of their power. As soon as images became more popular than the church's institutions and began to act directly in God's name, they became undesirable. It was never easy to control images with words because, like saints, they

engaged deeper levels of experience and fulfilled desires other than the ones living church authorities were able to address.... Only after the faithful had resisted all such efforts against their favorite images did theologians settle for issuing conditions and limitations governing access to them. Theologians were satisfied only when they could "explain" the images.[1]

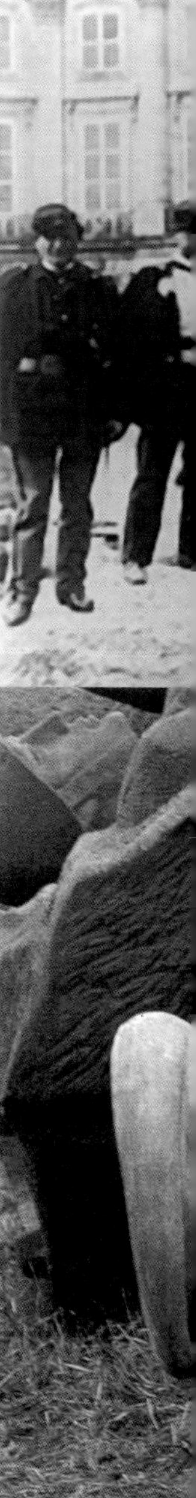

In quoting Belting here I do not intend to suggest (nor does Belting) that it is as simple as claiming church leaders use words, and the laity use images, nor that one side ultimately prevails. Rather, the power of images and the power of their interpreters are interlocked, caught in an endless dialectic. There is much to be said about the ways those with social power have tended to use verbal language for control: in a majority of religious traditions the leaders have been male, of an upper socio-economic level, and often of a particular ethnicity, and it has been this cultural elite who have been literate. Through words, political and religious authorities (or those with scant authority who want more) can transform images into scapegoats within larger cultural campaigns by decreeing them to be blasphemous. Meanwhile, images and objects, rather than written texts, have been used for widespread popular devotions, particularly among the non-literate majority.

Throughout this chapter, I present the dialectical power relations that occur betwixt and between images and their reception. While the Western monotheistic traditions of Judaism, Christianity, and Islam are each often wrongly characterised as being *aniconic* – that is, without figural representations – this chapter demonstrates the ways in which representational images have appeared throughout their histories, as well as the times authorities have worked to limit, censor, or destroy them. Images are often created *and/or* destroyed at times of religious upheaval and reform, and especially at times of new identity formation.

The key related terms at stake here are 'idolatry' and its pious, active partner 'iconoclasm'. There is also a deeper relationship between words and images that must be developed within these traditions, since words themselves, particularly when inscribed as a material, graphic marking on paper, vellum, or papyrus, become an image. Later in this chapter I outline the relation between written words and images, looking particularly at manuscripts. I then conclude by pointing to some of the ways in which blasphemous images become modes of resistance, whereby people with limited cultural power (especially in terms of gender and race) consciously enact blasphemous portrayals as a mode of subversion.

Idolatry as Blasphemy within the Abrahamic Traditions

The attack on New York's World Trade Center Towers in September 2001 was preceded a few months earlier by another highly visible destruction. In March 2001, the Taliban, the militia group that had governed Afghanistan since 1996, seeking to make themselves known to the wider world from within a deeply impoverished and ignored land, obliterated two enormous 1,500 year old statues of the Buddha carved into a cliff in Bamiyan, central Afghanistan. Apparently it took a month of artillery bombardment to eradicate them, which is not much considering the three centuries it most likely took to carve them out of the hillside. These statues were probably begun while Bamiyan was a significant Buddhist site along the Silk Road in the fifth century. Bamiyan then came under Islamic control in the ninth century CE, and for over a thousand years the statues were allowed to stand – even though at certain times various groups gathered their iconoclastic forces and hacked away at the Sage's noses and limbs. Indeed, even the notorious and reclusive Mohammed Omar (leader of the Taliban from 1996–2001, and one of the world's most wanted fugitives after the September 11 attacks) issued a practical statement about their protection in 1999, claiming that since there were no Buddhists in Afghanistan today, they couldn't actually be considered idolatrous, and the magisterial statues might even serve as a source of revenue from tourists.[2] In the end, the iconoclastic spectacle proved to be too alluring and Omar ordered their destruction. When it comes to demonstrating power, there is always a need to make statements, both verbal and visual, and what could be more spectacular than the destruction of two 55 metre high Buddhas? The story was told in news outlets around the world. This is what iconoclasm is all too often about: a visual, public event designed to portray power even, and especially, when no real power exists.

Of course, the Taliban were not the first to commit acts of iconoclasm in the struggle for power and world history is filled with parallel actions. When the Vandals (from whence the term 'vandalism') sacked Rome in 455 CE, they notoriously destroyed many of the Roman artworks in the process. The Paris Communards, in 1871, wanted to symbolise the end of the Bourbon dynasty and so toppled the Vendôme Column. And in more recent times, statues of Lenin and Stalin were removed or destroyed as the Soviet Union was dismantled. There was also the mass media spectacle of a statue of Saddam Hussein being pulled down at the start of the US led invasion of Iraq. Usually these destructive acts are carried out with plenty of photography or film equipment in the background. Such hot journalistic topics, along with the 'Danish cartoon controversy',

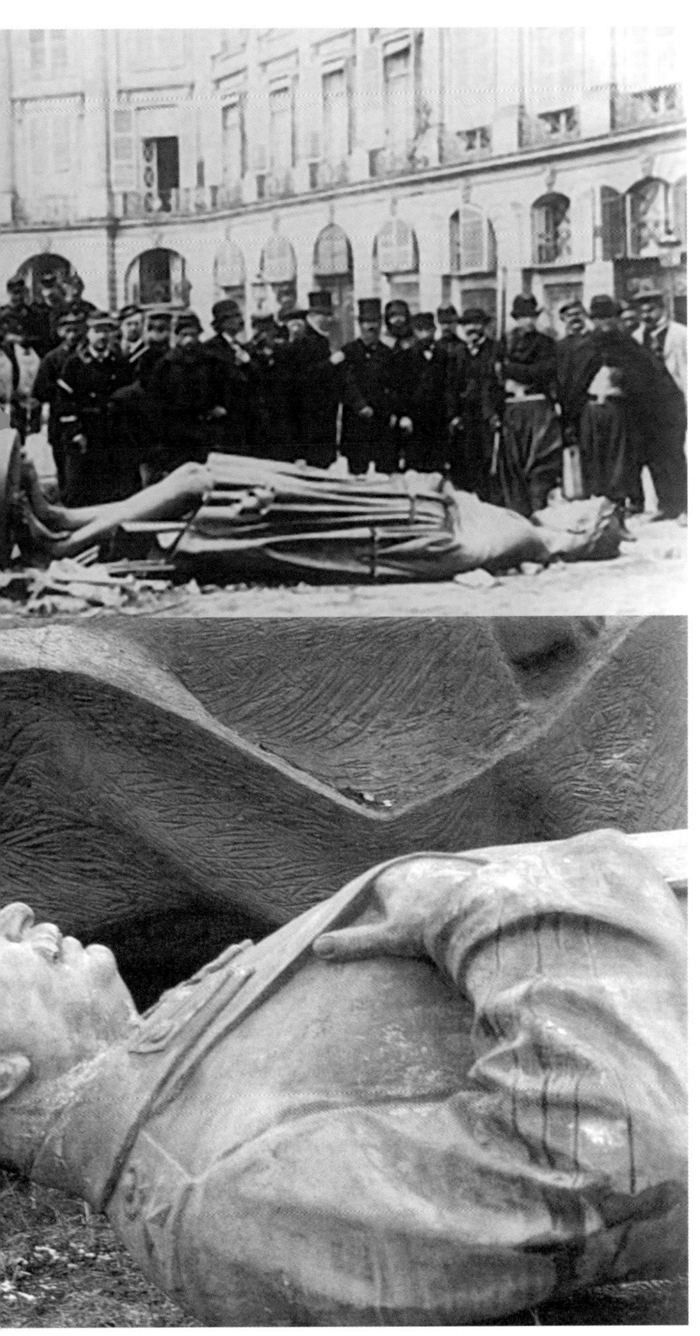

ABOVE: Communards pose with the statue from the toppled Vendôme Column, 1871.

BELOW: Fallen statue of Stalin following the break-up of the Soviet Union, photography Julian Stallabrass, 1996.

portray Islam as a religion distinctly contrary to images. News reports often make blanket statements such as "Islam forbids all figural representation". This is simply not true, nor are such easy over-generalisations true concerning the role of images in Judaism and Christianity. The lived story of the struggle over images is much more ambiguous, much more culturally and politically variant, as Mohammed Omar's actions show. Throughout history there have been many instances of Western iconoclasm, including contemporary ones, yet there are equally as many instances of the religious creation and use of images. As always, there are political, economic, and social reasons for outbreaks of iconoclasm, mixed with power struggles and the affiliated need to find scapegoats. And there are great discrepancies between the *practices* of the masses of religious people and the *ideal proscriptions* made by authority figures and authoritative texts. Looking back through religious histories, there are key points in time when reform-minded groups have made complaints and criticised the traditions of which they have been a part. For reasons of piety, economic enrichment, or in the forging of a new religious identity, reform and revivalist movements have lambasted previous ritualistic practices; chief among these practices is the use of images. Iconoclasm and charges of idolatry are often accompanied by a search for power and identity – or perhaps that should be *vice versa*. Just as the ancient Israelites' sacrifice of the scapegoat took the sins of the people and placed them on the animal, which was then sent into the wilderness, accusations of blasphemy, and the active censoring, suppressing, and destroying of images, function similarly, as they allow people to believe moral and spiritual boundaries have been rightly established and an ordered society can be maintained. It takes power to draw lines between the sacred and profane, even as images have a way of transgressing them, sneaking some improper thing across the border that some believe should not be there.

In the three Abrahamic religious traditions, God is ideally understood to be wholly transcendent of this earthly world. As such, God is beyond the possibilities of representation, making it seemingly impossible to put such concentrated, immaterial sacredness into the material, profane realm. All three traditions have, at various times, pointed back to the Second Commandment: "You shall not make for yourself a carved image, or any likeness of anything that is in heaven above, or that is in the earth beneath, or that is in the water under the earth. You shall not bow down to them or serve them" (Exodus 20.4–5). This is often considered to be the banishment of any figural, representational image-making, and not simply a prohibition against *worshipping* idols. To suggest that the divine essence of God (or the gods) could be represented in physical imagery is blasphemous in word and deed.

Abram (Abraham) Smashes the Idols, c. 1310–1320, from MS Royal 2.B.VII (Queen Mary Psalter, England), fol. 8r, illuminated manuscript, courtesy of The British Library
Abram breaks the false Gods made by his father, Thare/Terah. And below, Thare is confronted by Abram whilst he makes an idol at his work bench.

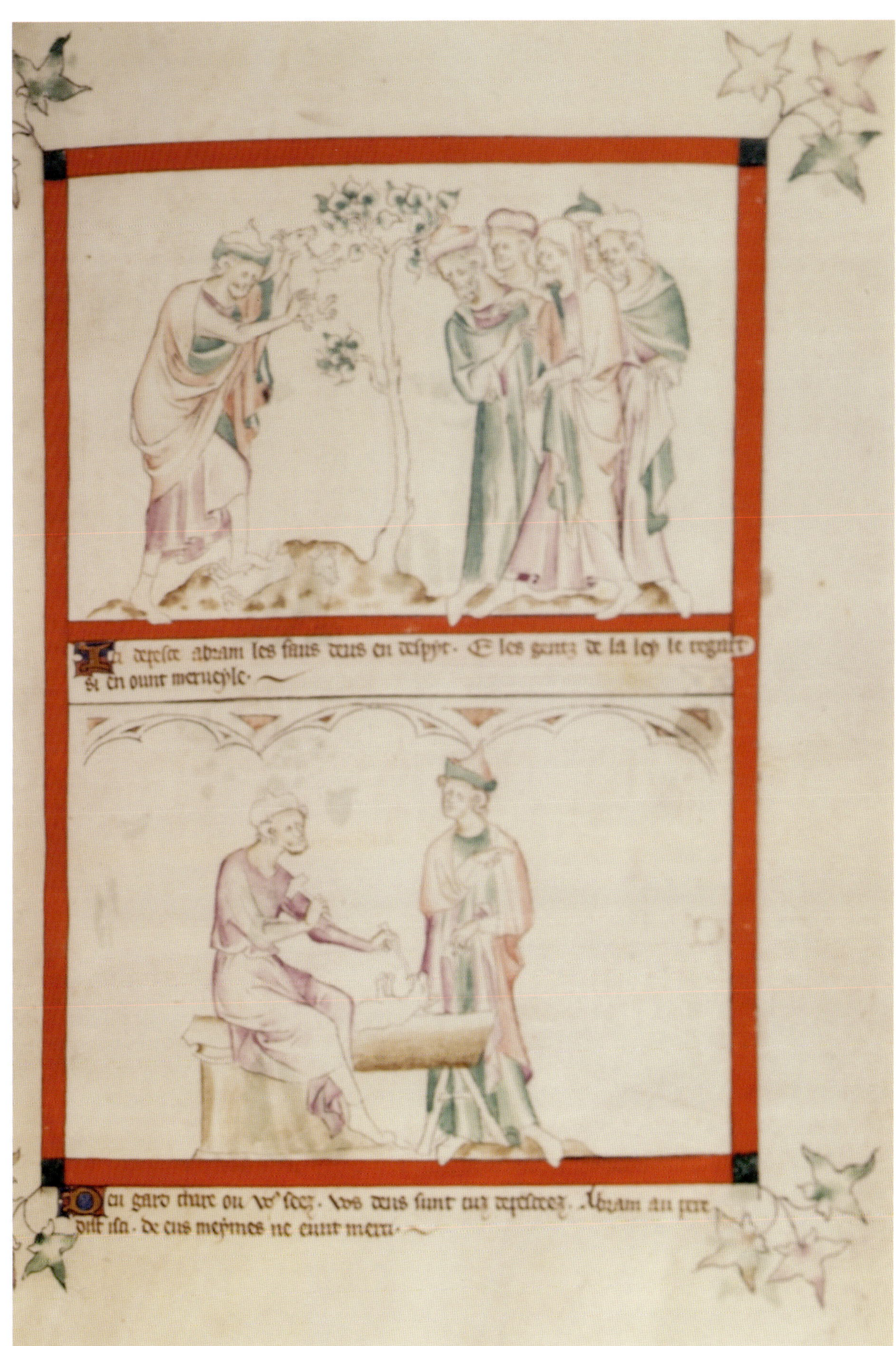

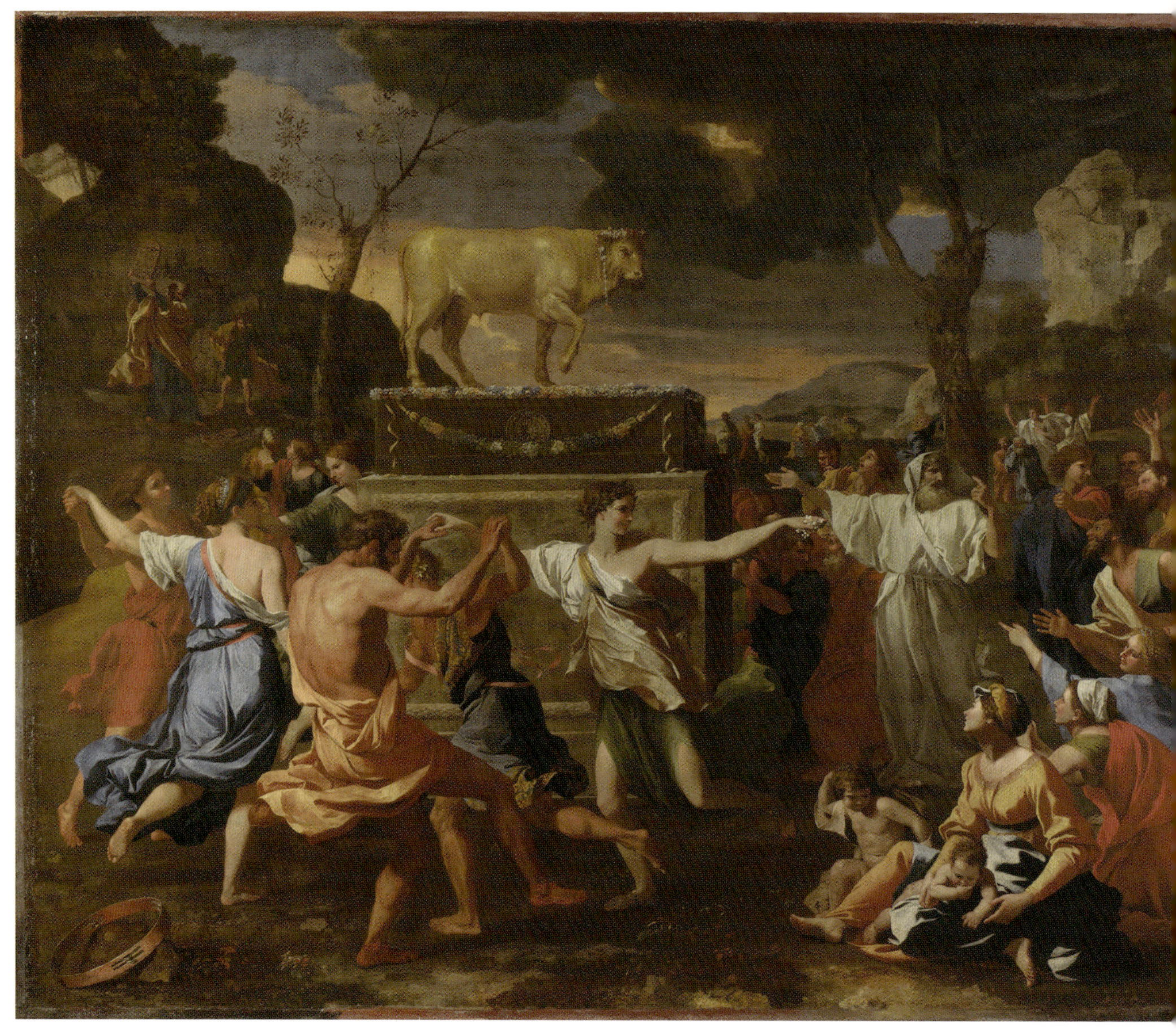

Nicolas Poussin, *The Adoration of the Golden Calf*, c. 1634, oil on canvas, laid down on board, 154 x 214 cm, courtesy of The National Gallery, London

Moses climbed Mount Sinai to receive the tablets of the Ten Commandments. During his absence the Israelites built an idol with Aaron's help and worshipped it with song and dance. On his return, Moses was so angered by this that he smashed the tablets (Exodus: 32). The National Gallery would only authorise the use of the unscathed version of this painting to be reproduced in this book.

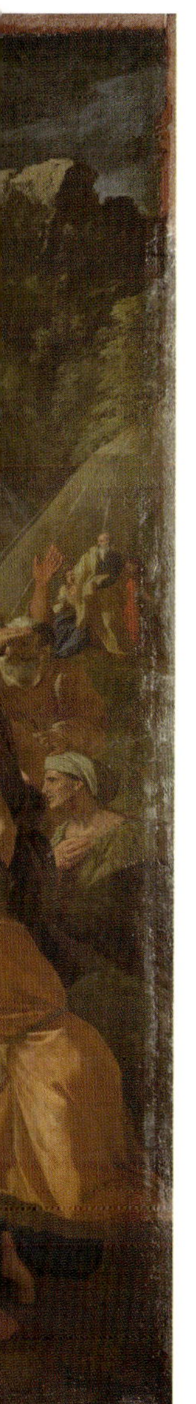

Yet, this radical divide between God and humans only works in an ideal theological way and does not hold up in practice. In spite of authoritative, theological prohibitions on images there remains a deeply *religious* – and thus, I would argue, *human* – need for intercessors, for icons and incarnations, angels and avatars, and various other passages between the heavenly and earthly, between the sacred and the profane. Sacred texts, as well as people's devotional practices, portray many sensate connections between God and human, and so traditions have developed appropriate, established ritual passages between the two. This is particularly true when it comes to images and their relation to the holy. The ancient Jewish rabbinic term for idolatry is literally 'strange worship' (*avodah zarah*), a phrasing that leaves questions: is it the deity being worshipped who is 'strange', i.e. not the true God? Or is the very *mode* of worship 'strange'? In other words, the blasphemous dilemma here is that idolatry may be about worship involving images, but it is also about conducting the proper rituals for true worship. One may worship the 'One True God', but if that is not done correctly then one is being as idolatrous and blasphemous as if one were worshipping the Golden Calf. These semi-permeable ritualistic boundaries between the sacred and profane shift from religion and religion, and even within religions there are a variety of viewpoints and customs. Theologically speaking, for Jews and Muslims, for example, the concept of the Christian Incarnation is blasphemous: God may reveal God's self to humans in speeches, whirlwinds, clouds, or pillars of fire, but never in the form of a human. Worship of Jesus Christ is, to them, certainly 'strange worship'.

And then again, throughout Christian imagery, we see the 'Old, White-Bearded Monarch' as a visible representation of God. Meanwhile, contemporary artists have, perhaps, been more true to the aniconic threads of these religions as their visions of God are often abstract, even whilst being playful, ironic, and somewhat critical. Each of the Abrahamic traditions has its own peculiar history of sacred representation, as well its own accusations of profaning images. The following is by no means a comprehensive overview, rather I mean to point toward a history of the use of images in all three traditions, and then to note particular events in which iconoclasm and accusations of idolatry have surfaced.

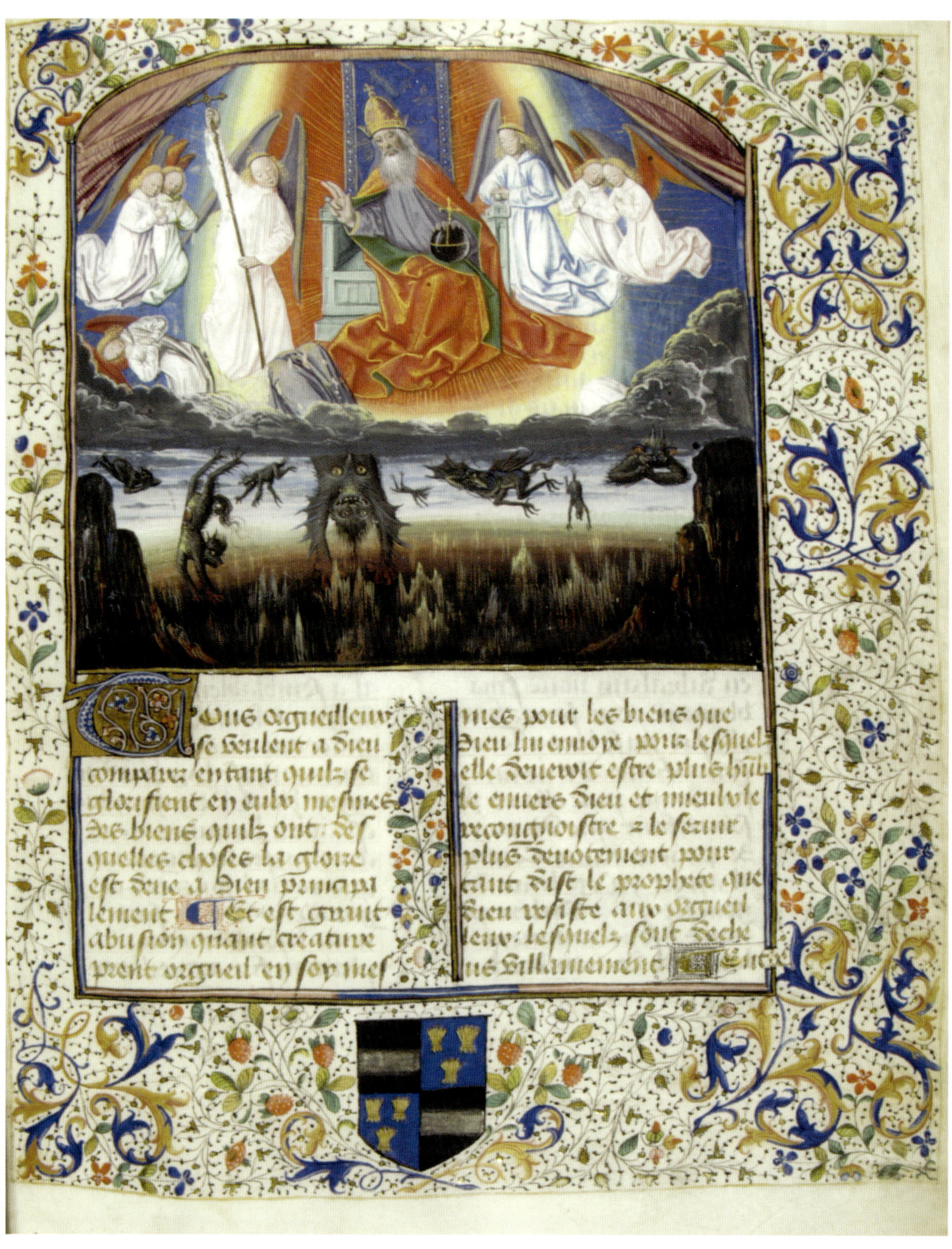

Jacques Legrand, *Illustration of God the Father Banishing Satan to Hell*, from MS55.5 (Livre de Bonnes Moeurs), Middle Ages, illuminated manuscript, courtesy of the Newberry Library, Chicago

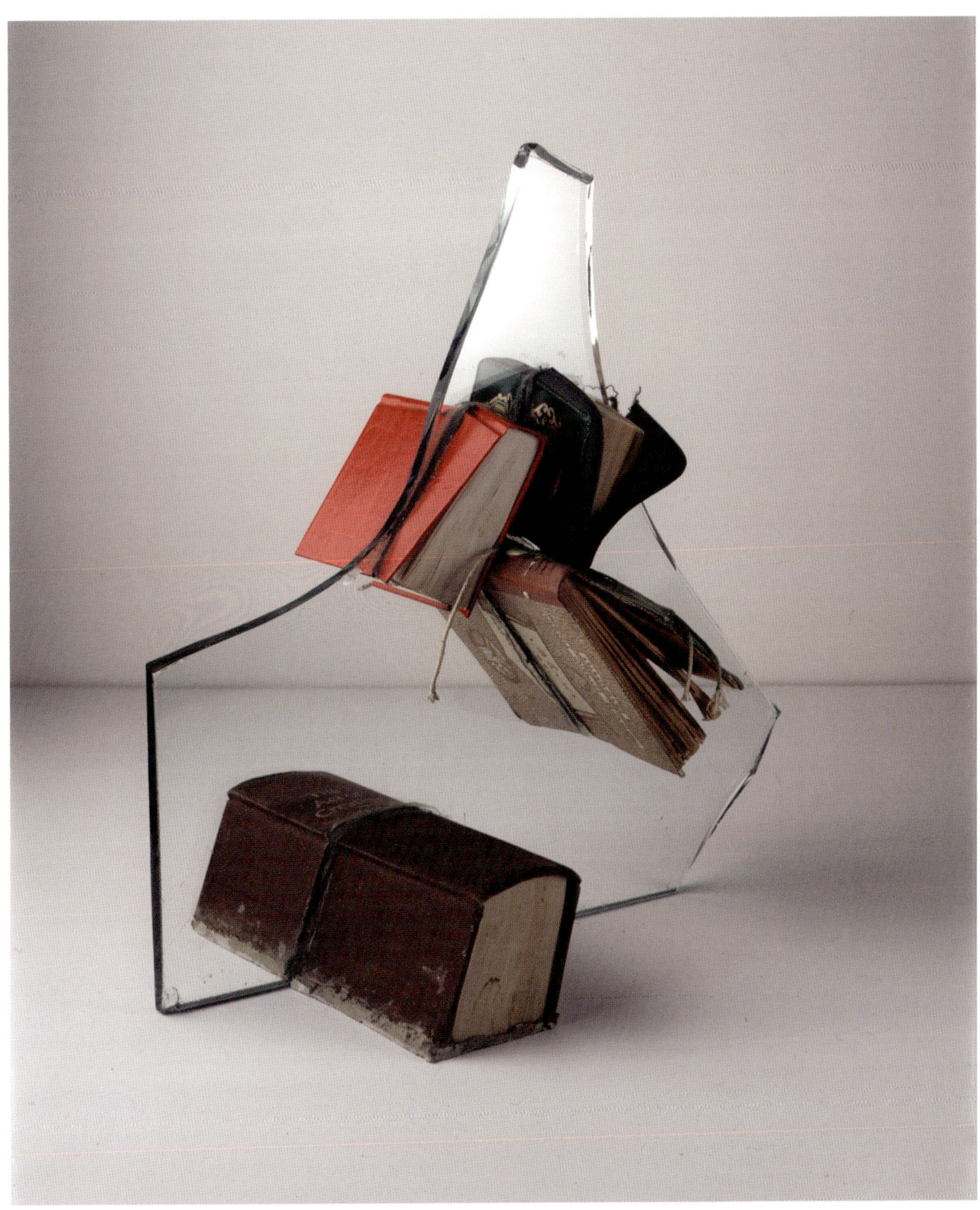

John Latham, *God is Great (#1a)*, 1990, glass, books and resin, 37 x 40 x 21 cm, photography Dave Morgan, courtesy of the Lisson Gallery and the artist

The first of Latham's *God is Great* works illustrates how the three major monotheistic religions belong to a single category of belief systems.

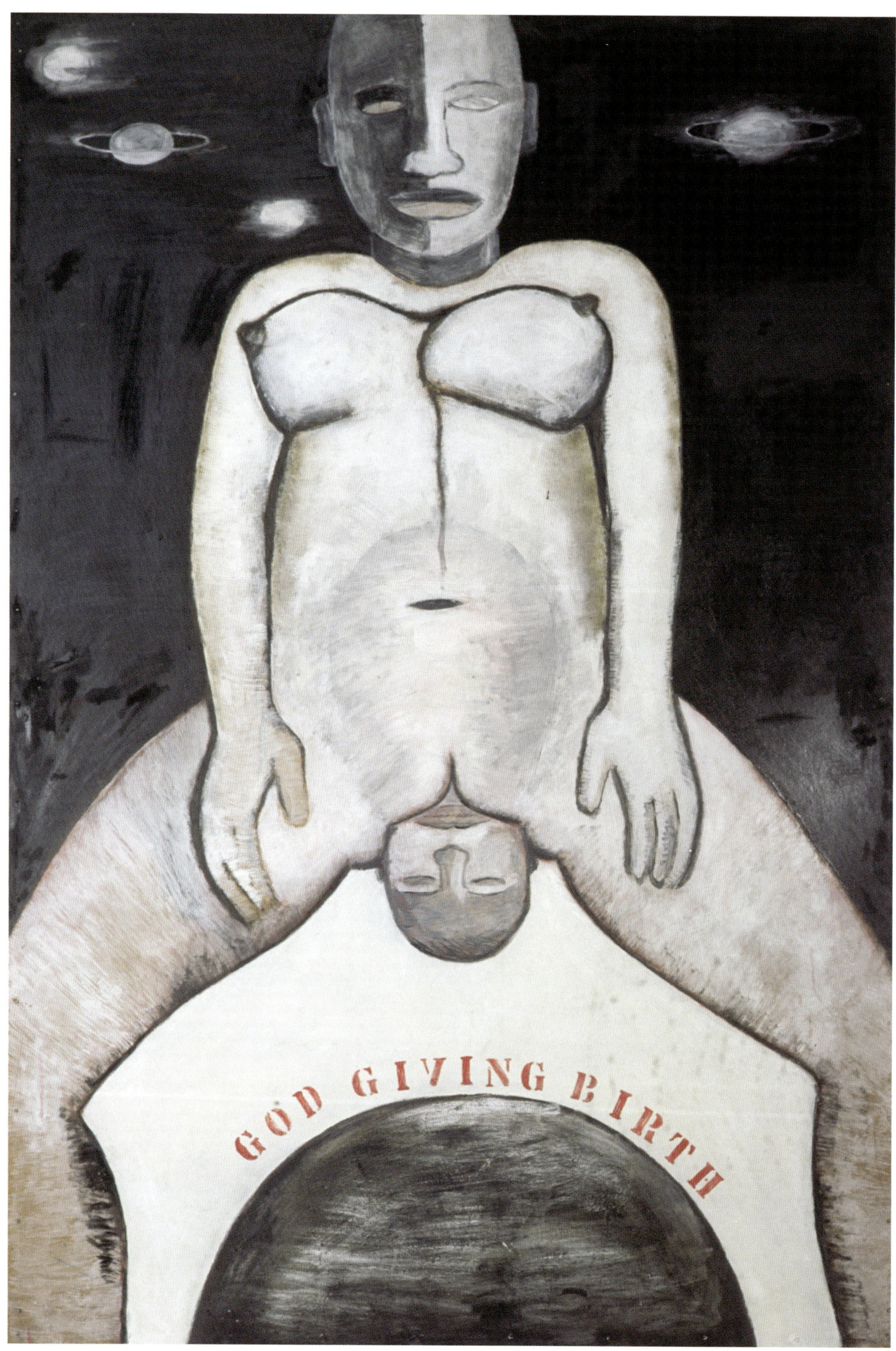
GOD GIVING BIRTH

… visions of God are often abstract, even whilst being playful, ironic, and somewhat critical.

In the Hebrew scriptures, we read of God revealing God's self to Moses, at Moses' request, in the cleft of a rock (Exodus 33.17–23). The passage goes so far as to suggest that God has a *face*, though no one can see it and live, and so God protects Moses by placing his *hand* over the opening of the cleft, only allowing Moses a glimpse of God's back. Ostensibly a story that tells of divine power, it is remarkable for its anthropomorphic verbal depiction of a God who has hands, a face, and a back. (The twelfth century Jewish philosopher Maimonides argued that such linguistic representations are just as idolatrous as the visual ones.) There are several other interesting passages in the Hebrew Bible regarding the use of images including a "household god" owned by the future King of Israel, David, and his wife Michal (I Samuel 19.11–17; for related uses of icons see Judges 18–19; Hosea 3.3–4). Even the famous story of the Golden Calf (Exodus 32) indicates how widespread image use was at the time, even if God and Moses were angered by this form of worship.

Monica Sjoo, *God Giving Birth*, 1968, 185 x 125 cm, oil painting on panel, gift of Skellefteå Kommun, courtesy of Museum Anna Nordlander

Some second-wave feminist artists rebelliously paraded the theme of birth in an attempt to lay bare and thus normalise this 'universal human experience'. Monica Sjoo exhibited *God Giving Birth*, under the recognition of many women who would describe the painting as an attempt to create a powerful symbolic image of one of the realities of femininity, women's general differentiation, and 'being' in itself. Unfortunately however, Sjoo was seen by the establishment as pushing beyond the boundaries of the acceptable. Indeed, the painting virtually lead to a prosecution under blasphemy laws.

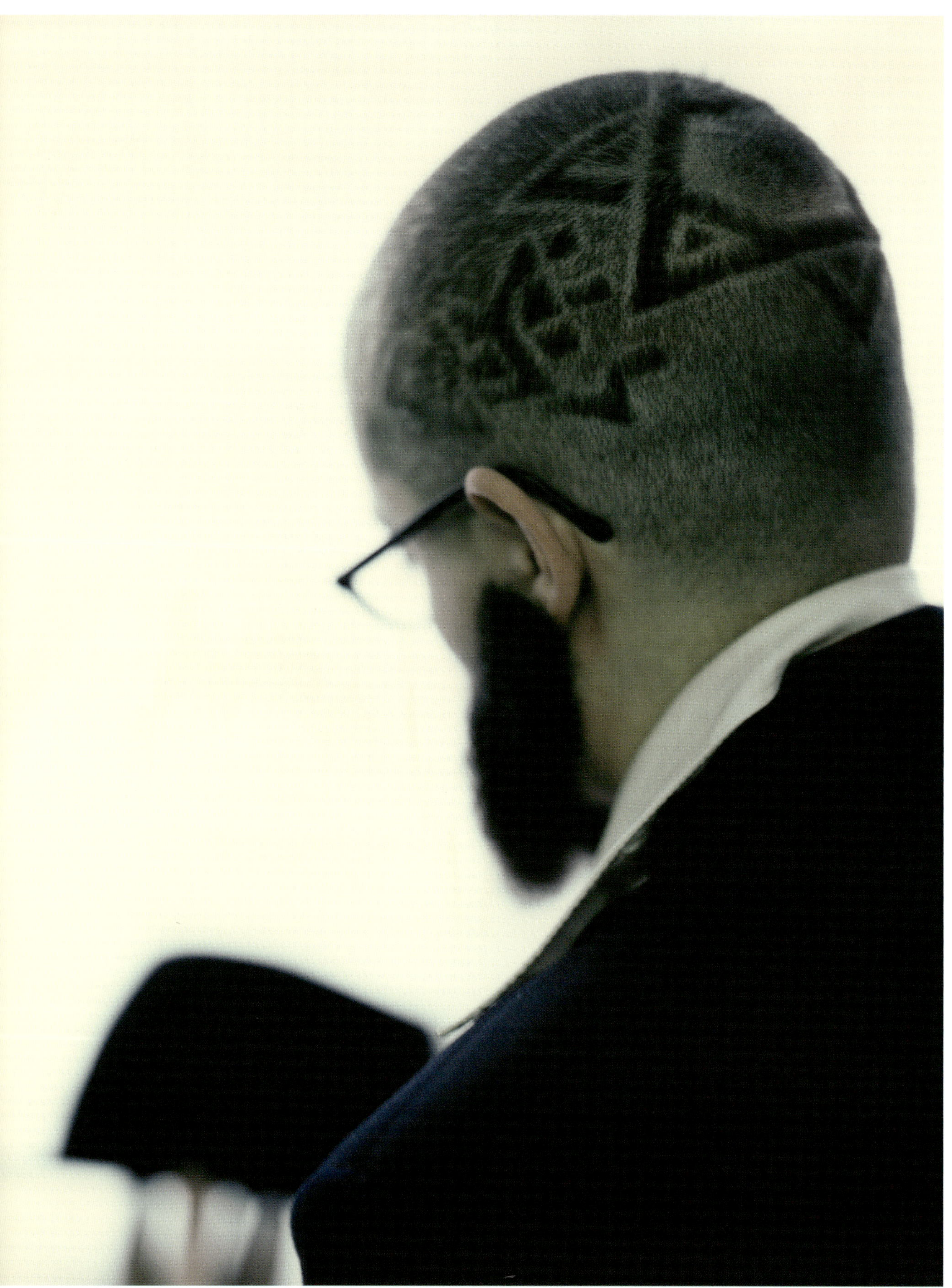

Through time, images, both symbolically abstract (such as the Star of David) and figurative (e.g. representations of biblical scenes) have continued to be used in Jewish ritual practices and everyday life. Ceremonial cups, wall hangings, mosaics, architectural relief carvings, as well as visually striking synagogue architecture, ornamentation and murals, ritual instruments, and illustrated manuscripts (among many other media) continue to evidence image-use across thousands of years of Jewish history. Particularly important are the multitude of illustrated versions of the Passover *Haggadah*. So, as many scholars have made clear over the last three decades, the idea that Jews don't have art is quite absurd. The commonly proclaimed version of an aniconic Judaism has as much grounding in modern anti-semitism as any real history of Jewish religious practices.[3]

In spite of the over-quoted Second Commandment, "thou shalt not make graven images", a number of prominent Jewish artists working in the nineteenth and twentieth centuries have created significant images. Marc Chagall's conservative Jewish upbringing was not conducive to his becoming a creator of images, and there are stories that some of his family did not approve of his profession. Nonetheless, he said, "If I were not a Jew... I wouldn't have been an artist, or I would be a different artist altogether."[4] He and many other modern Jewish artists (including Chaim Soutine, El Lissitzky, Amedeo Modigliani, Ben Shahn, RB Kitaj, and Ad Reinhardt) worked as Jews who created images – though to varying degrees of self-admitted 'Jewishness'. Chagall's work, meanwhile, was included in the *Degenerate Art* exhibition in Munich in 1937. This infamous exhibit included over 650 objects by Jewish artists, avant-gardists, and Bolsheviks. Much of the collection was eventually sold by the Nazis in Switzerland, including Chagall's *Rabbi - The Pinch of Snuff*, 1912, which was first paraded through the streets to be mocked by citizens. The following year, *Kristallnacht* occurred, and Chagall's *White Crucifixion* was created soon after. Chagall's life and career was one of exile. Originally receptive to the works of Jewish artists, the Soviet Union eventually turned against many; Chagall's murals for the Jewish theatre in Moscow, originally created in 1921, were later destroyed, and some of his paintings were removed from a 1960s exhibition in Moscow.

Oreet Ashery, *Self Portrait as Marcus Fisher II*, 2000, digital print mounted on MDF, dimensions variable, a collaboration with Manuel Vason, courtesy of the artist

The commonly proclaimed version of an aniconic Judaism has as much grounding in modern anti-semitism as any real history of Jewish religious practices.

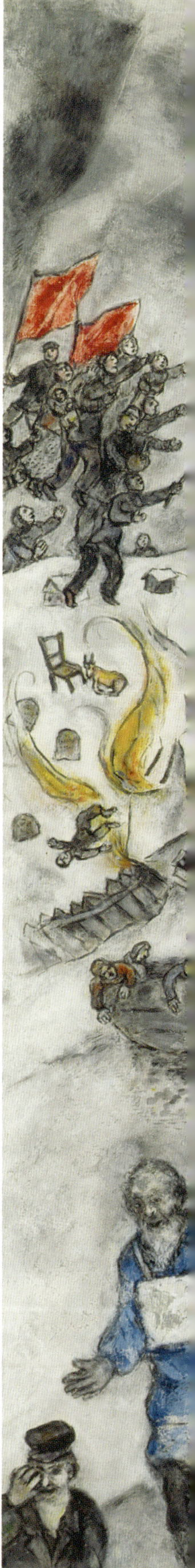

Marc Chagall, *White Crucifixion*, 1938, oil on canvas, 154 x 140 cm, gift of Alfred S Alschuler, courtesy of The Art Institute of Chicago

Chagall's juxtaposition of crucifixion and the intensity of Jewish suffering creates an interchange of religious expectation with historic reality that challenges simple assumption. He does not intend to Christianise the painting, especially in the sense of affirming any atoning resolution of the Jewish plight. Instead, in the frenzied world Chagall creates, all are caught in a vortex of destruction, binding both crucified victim and modern martyr. Chagall makes clear that the Christ figure and the Jewish penitent are one.

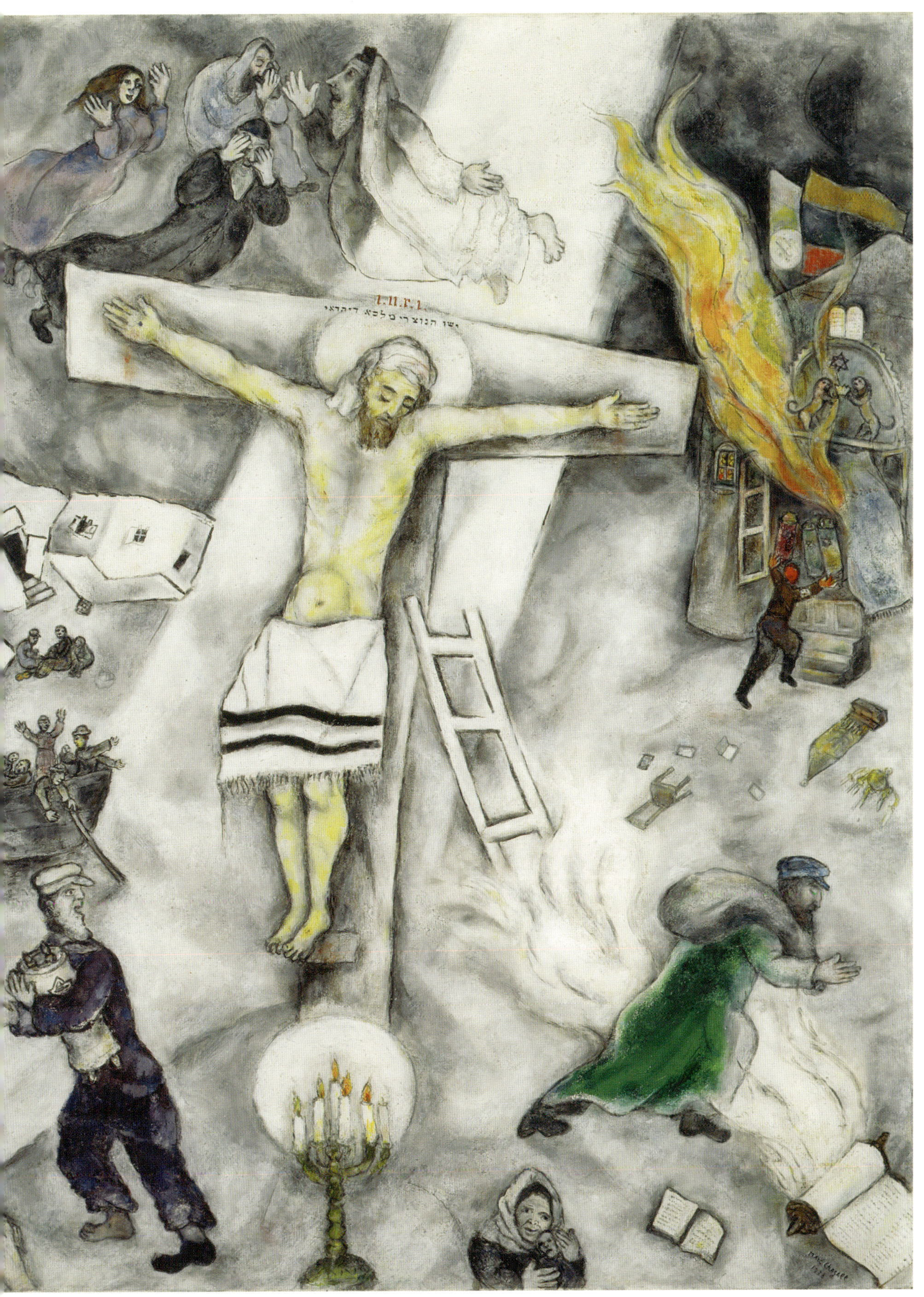
I.N.R.I.
ישו הנוצרי מלכא דיהודאי

As with several other Jewish artists in the modern age, iconic Christian images were re-appropriated and used for the artists' own purposes. Chagall's *White Crucifixion* places the crucifixion of Jesus among the European pogroms against Jews. And Mark Antokolsky's *Ecce Homo*, 1873, takes the well-known Christian image (by Rembrandt and others) and turns it into a Jewish icon. Both of these images reassert Jesus' own Jewish identity and, in a time of radical anti-semitism, serve to battle the 'Christ-killer' myth perpetuated through so much of Christianity.[5]

More recently, Leonard Nimoy created a photo series called *Shekhina*. *Shekhina* is a Hebrew term for a 'divine presence', which is usually understood as being feminine in nature. Nimoy reframes traditional Jewish rituals by portraying women wearing *tefillin* and *talliths* – and often not much else. A number of more conservative Jewish groups found it inappropriate to combine nudity and semi-nudity with ritualistic practices.

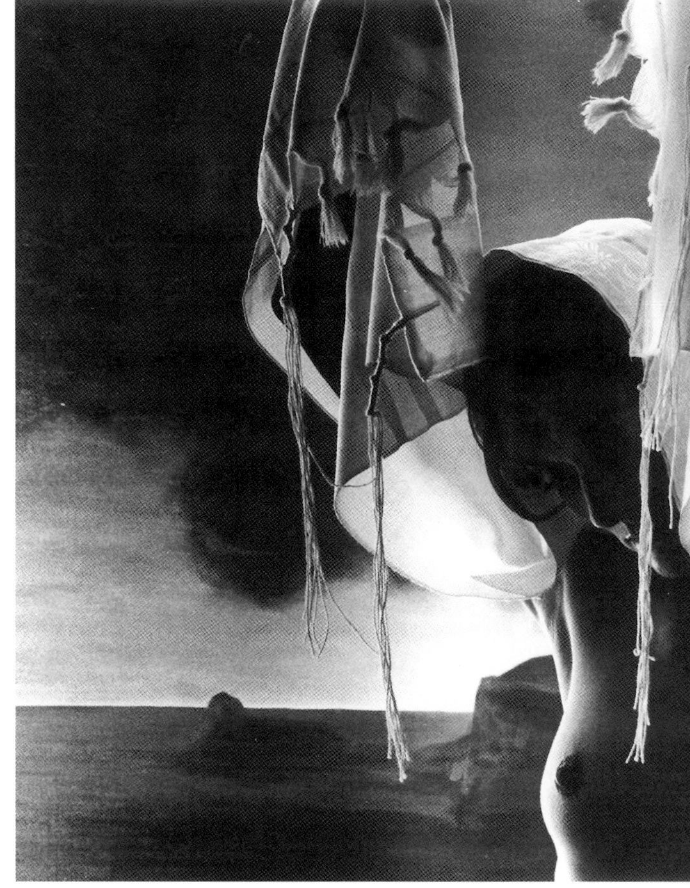

Leonard Nimoy, *The Shekhina Project*, 2002, photographic series, courtesy of R Michelson Galleries (www.RMichelson.com)
In many of Nimoy's images, the *tallith*, a fringed shawl traditionally worn by Jewish men at prayer, is depicted swathed around the nude figure. Likewise depicted are the *tefillin*, the collective terminology for the phylactery: a small leather box containing Hebrew texts on vellum and worn by Jewish men at morning prayer as a reminder to keep the law.

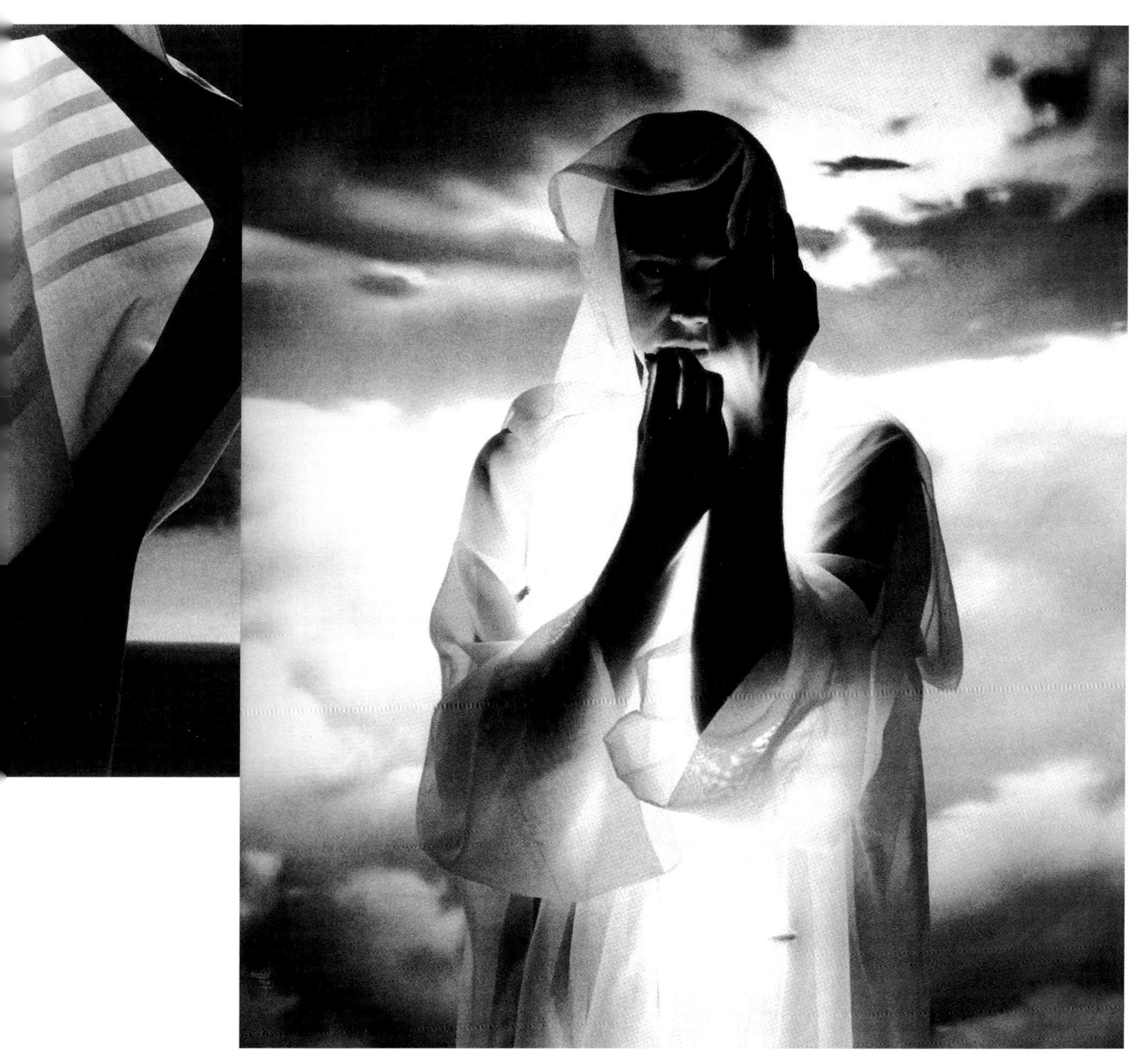

In Christianity the story is somewhat different since Jesus Christ is understood as God incarnate, in the flesh, and biblical passages such as I John 1.1–4 testify that people 'heard', 'saw', and 'touched' the eternal life of Jesus "that was with the Father and was revealed to us". Such passages made the ongoing controversy over the status of the 'god-man' Jesus difficult, and even with the biblical suggestions it took some time for such strange admixtures to become orthodox. The Council of Chalcedon eventually confirmed the 'fully God/fully human' doctrine as orthodox in 451, seemingly making it possible to depict the human part of God. How to do that was another question. Much of the conflation of blasphemy and idolatry stems from the so-called 'Iconoclastic Controversies' that raged between the eighth and tenth centuries in European Christianity. Over several hundred years, various councils were called, gathering bishops together to debate the nature of visual images, especially those of Jesus Christ, Mary, and some of the saints and apostles. One group would rise to power and approve the use of images, then another would condemn them. At the Council of Hiereia in 754 in Constantinople, the synod stated that the *iconophiles* (image lovers) were "Satan-inspired" and that those who actually painted the icons were blasphemous for one of two reasons: they either made an image of the Godhead, or they inappropriately crossed the divine-human border – the humanity of Christ might be depicted, though the divinity cannot. The theological extension of such thinking would suggest that the humanity of Christ cannot be depicted either, since to show only the one side of the dual nature of Christ is also to be heretical. Iconophiles meanwhile fought back with images, as some ninth century psalters show: iconoclasts are here depicted in negative light as they prepare to whitewash an image of Jesus; their actions resonating with the accompanying image of Roman centurions crucifying Jesus. To destroy images of Jesus is to crucify him all over again.

Nicephorous and Iconoclasts, f.27v from Theodore Psalter/Studion Psalter, 1066, illuminated manuscript, courtesy of The British Library

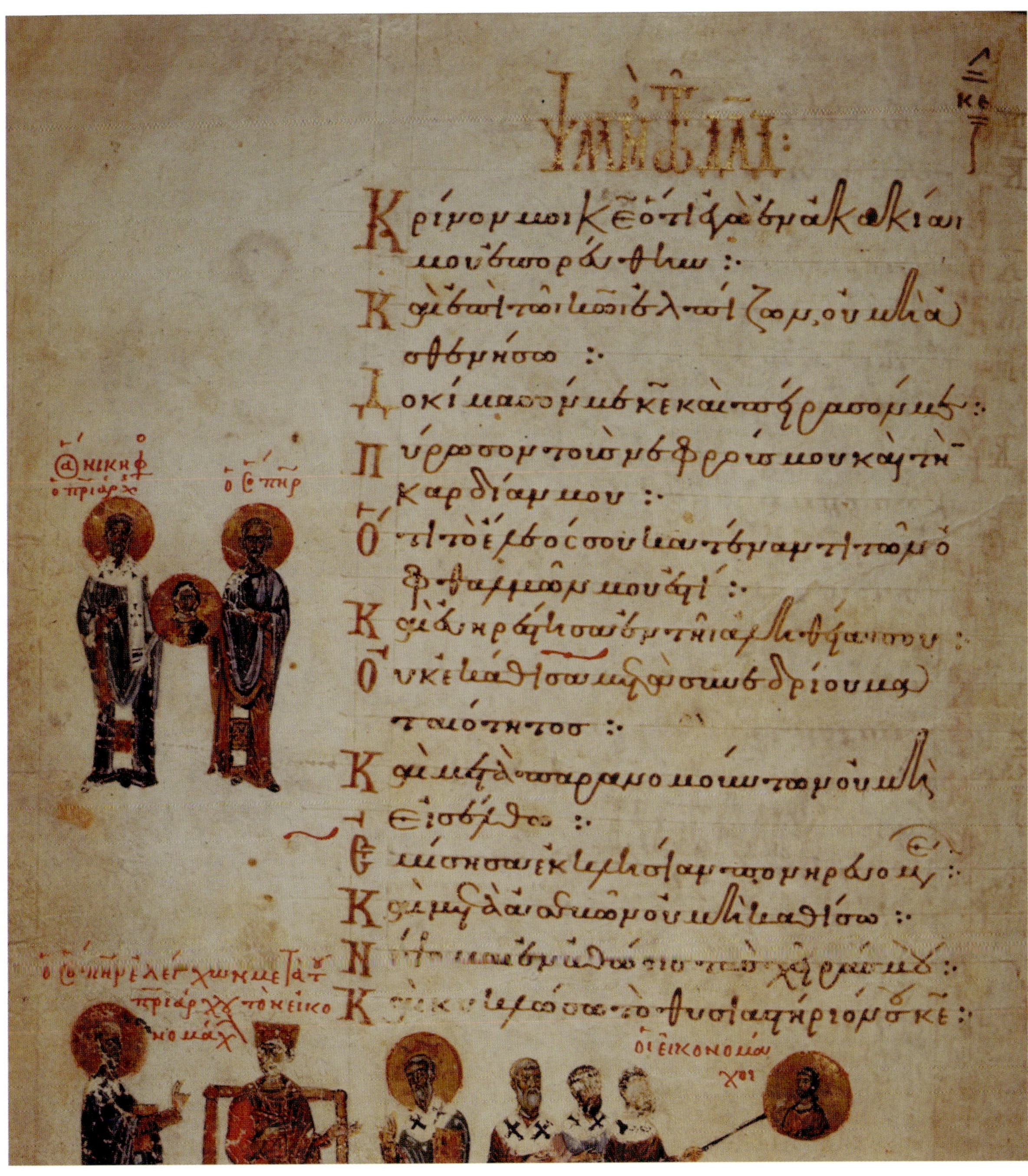

One of the greatest defenders of images in Christian history was John of Damascus who in the early eighth century declared, "I boldly draw an image of the invisible God, not as invisible, but as having become visible for our sakes by partaking of flesh and blood."[6] Especially under John's influence, the Iconoclastic controversy found its high point in the Second Council of Nicea in 787 where images were declared to be orthodox and the worship of them God-pleasing. What becomes apparent after a little reflection on these various councils is that the Church authorities were responding to the already established practices of many Christians. These councils did not come about simply because the leaders had nothing better to do, rather they stemmed from real situations. The point here is that it is ultimately religious practices that produce the need for doctrine and not theologians in armchairs. To understand the Christian tradition, one must see the images as well as read the words.

The articulations of orthodoxy in reference to the Incarnation of Jesus pose great challenges to painters and sculptors. How does one express both the divine and human in an image? Halos worked for a while in the early days, as did Jesus Christ sitting on a great throne. But with the emergence of the Renaissance and its naturalistic emphases, artists found new avenues. Perhaps the most prominent, and most controversial, was the image of a nude Jesus. Many of the greatest Renaissance painters depicted the Holy Family, or Madonna and Child, with a naked baby Jesus. According to the words of Christian theologians and the words of the scriptures, Christ was without sin and therefore like Adam and Eve in their pre-fallen state: naked and without shame. In the Renaissance, then, Christ was portrayed naked, and in his nakedness there was no shame and no guilt. Ironically, once the Renaissance was over many of the paintings of the naked Jesus were again covered up, as loincloths were painted over his private parts, connoting again the battle between religious authority and images.[7]

Andrea Mantegna, *The Holy Family*, c. 1485, oil on canvas, photography Estel/Klut, courtesy of Gemäldegalerie Alte Meister, Staatliche Kunstsammlungen Dresden

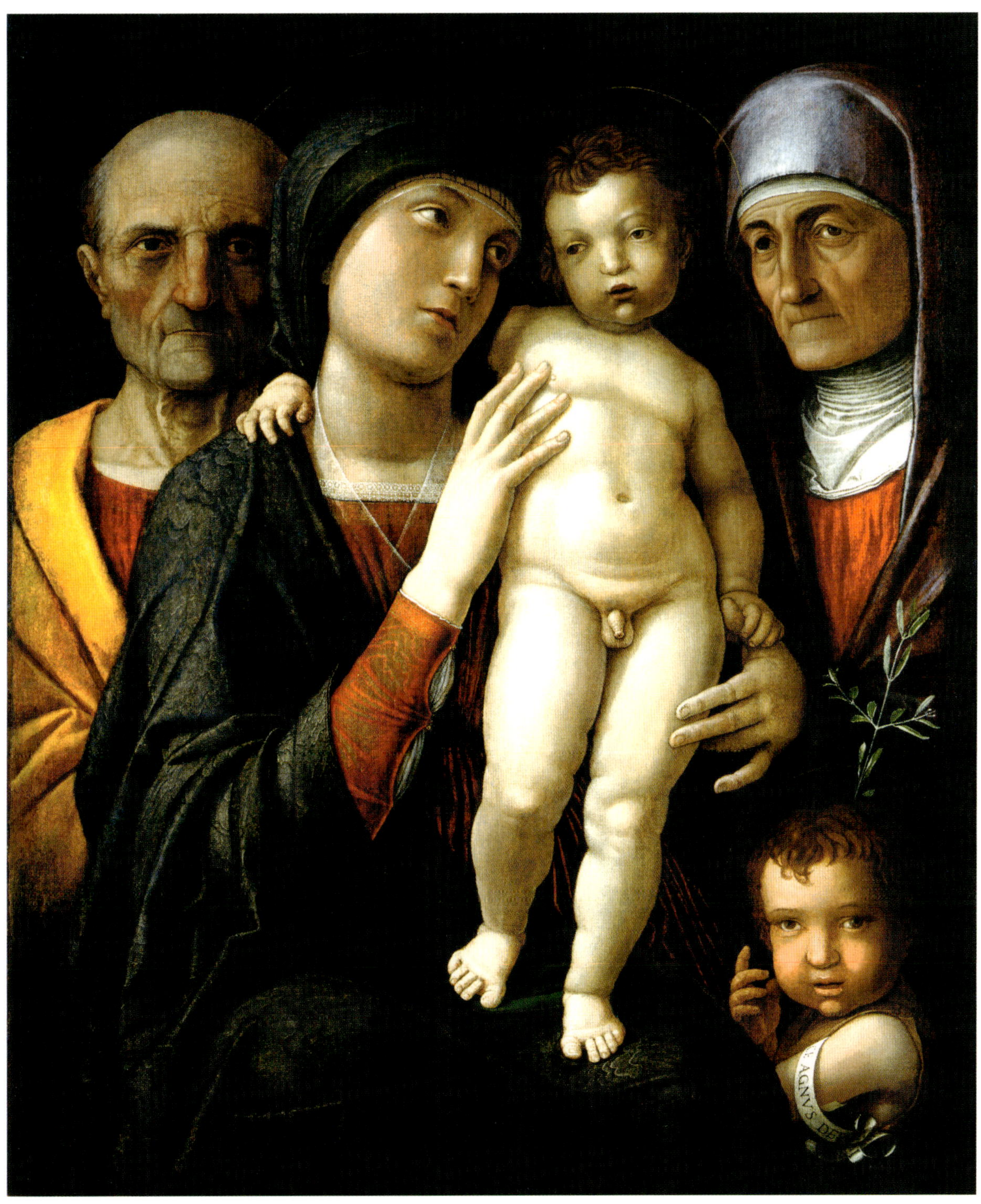
E AGNVS DE

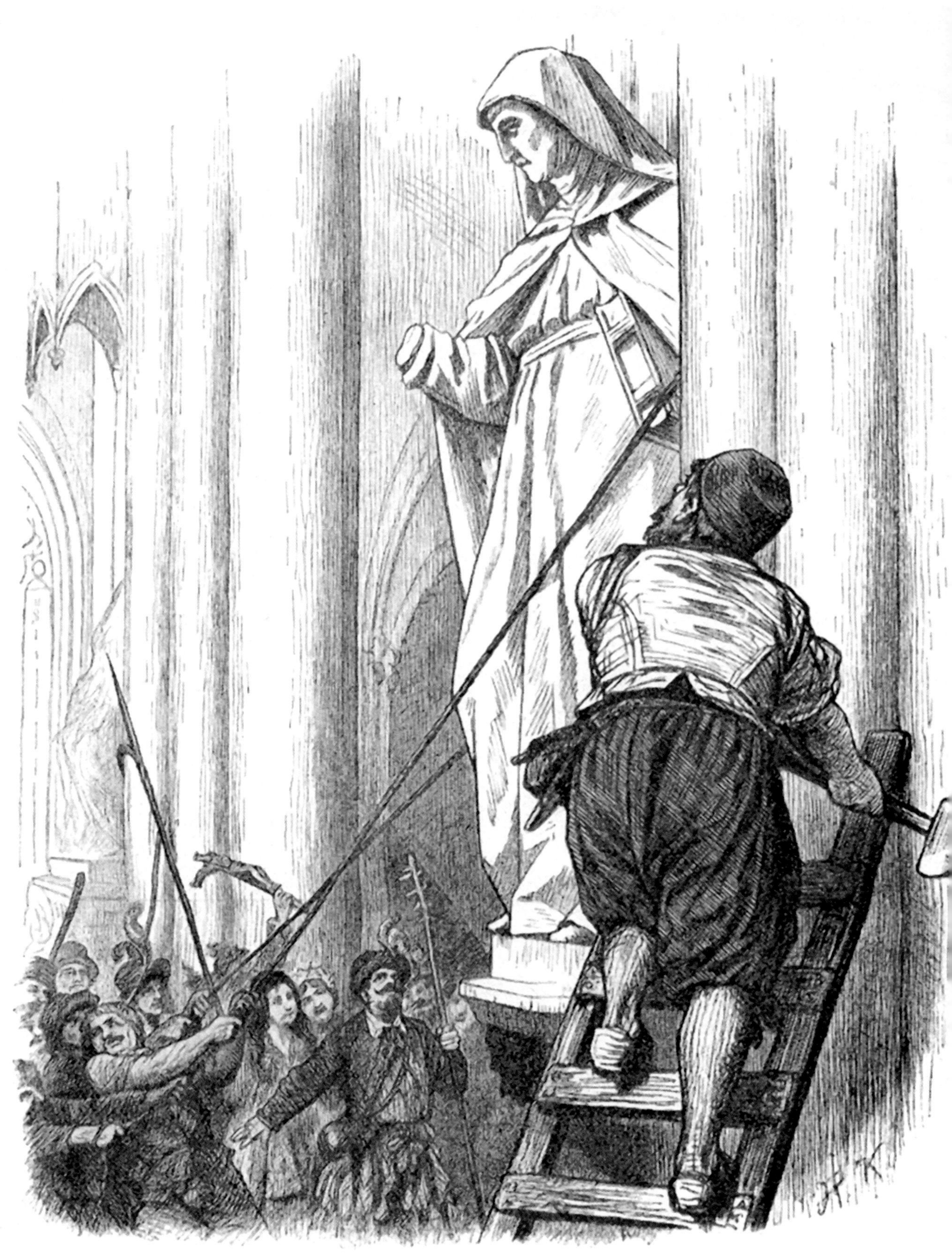

The issue of sexuality and its relation to divinity has continued to trouble theologians, clergy, and laypeople alike. Meanwhile artists have continued to investigate and challenge given assumptions about the sexuality of Jesus, often crossing perceived lines between the sacred and the profane. Work that has come under fire includes Nikos Kazantzakis' novel *The Last Temptation of Christ* and Martin Scorsese's filmic adaptation of it, and Gilbert and George's works such as *Was Jesus Heterosexual?*

Following in the wake of the European Renaissance, the next great split in the Christian church occurred in the sixteenth century. The Protestant Reform movement sought a kind of return to the 'Word of God' (primarily Jesus Christ, but secondarily as revealed in the Gospel and the preached sermon), and it reacted against many of the rituals instituted in the Roman Catholic Church. Martin Luther himself was somewhat tolerant in relation to the use of images, but many of the followers of John Calvin and Ulrich Zwingli went on to destroy a great deal of art. The power of the images that made Reformers apprehensive was not simply based on the belief that they actually harbour some deity within, but often the fear stemmed from the fact that images attract people to them. Such magnetism made authorities worry that laypeople might focus more attention on the earthly, visible details and forsake the true God for a material object. Thus the legacy of the Protestant Reformation is two centuries full of iconoclastic outbreaks, particularly across Northern Europe, toppling statues from church entrances, ripping paintings, smashing stained glass windows. Of course, in a sense it is the iconoclasts themselves who believe the most strongly in the power of images. So strong was their belief that images have power, that in order to establish control, politically and religiously, they needed to destroy what challenged them; in this case, images were a challenge to power.

Image of Reformation Iconoclasm depicting the Dutch Beeldenstorm (Dutch Revolution)

Iconoclasm is described as the destruction of religious icons and other symbols or monuments, usually for religious motives. In Christian circles iconoclasm has generally been motivated by a literal interpretation of the Ten Commandments, which forbids the making and worshipping of "graven images". It is also, on occasion, motivated by Christographical or even political concerns.

Like the mythologies surrounding Moses, God met the Prophet Muhammad in a cave on top of a mountain, speaking to him the great Revelation that would become the Quran (see the first revelation, "Al-Alaq", Quran 96). Yet, there is next to nothing in the Quran about the use of images. There are passages such as "My Lord, make this a peaceful land, and protect me and my children from worshiping idols" (14:35); or, "O Believers, wine and arrowshuffling, idols and divining arrows are an abomination, some of Satan's work; so avoid it" (5.92). But these are a long way from a banishment of images. Besides, there are also Quranic passages that give the opposite impression, such as that of King Solomon commanding the Jinni (spirits) to create "places of worship, statues..." (see 34.12–13). Elsewhere we read of God speaking to Mary, the mother of Jesus, who tells her that Jesus will perform miracles such as healing the blind and lepers, raising the dead, and also creating the 'sign' of creating a bird out of clay, and breathing life into it (3.43). So, in both these instances, God gives power to great prophets to create images.

What have become more important than the Quran are a few passages in the Hadith, a collection of stories and sayings of the Prophet. The key difficulty with figurative images, according to various Hadith, is that the makers of the images are doing creative acts, and *that* becomes a direct challenge to the sole creative powers of God. In the Hadith, there is a story of the Prophet's youngest wife, A'isha, who made (or bought) pillows for her husband that were decorated with images. Upon seeing them, Muhammad became upset and told her that the makers of images will be punished on the Day of Resurrection, and that angels do not enter houses with images of living beings. Then again, there are stories about how Muhammad, having conquered Mecca, rode around the ancient shrine of the Kaba and destroyed all of the Arabian idols there. Except one. Muhammad left an image of Mary and Jesus in place. Not only does this show the high status that Christianity held in early Islam, but also that images are not completely without their purpose.

Gregor Schneider, *Cube Venice 2005 (Ka'aba Mecca),* 2005, digital rendering of unrealised installation/anonymous image from the Internet, courtesy of the artist

Unable to fabricate the work, the artist exhibited a video proposal of his unrealised exhibition which would have been a 50 foot black cube placed in the middle of Saint Mark's Square. The proposed cube was to be constructed of scaffolding covered in black fabric. It is a work directly inspired by the *Ka'aba* in Mecca, the holiest site of Islam.

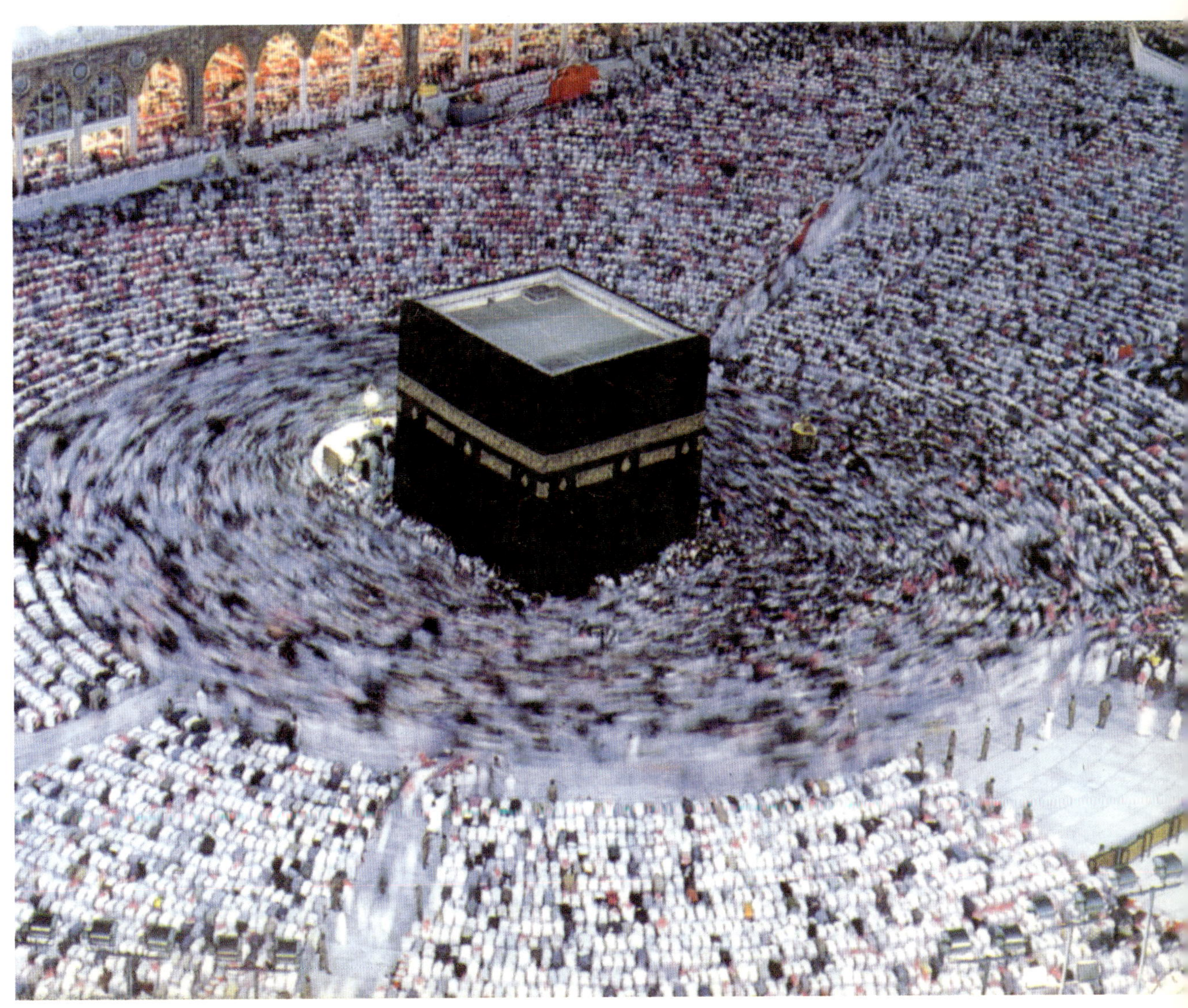

... in order to establish control, politically and religiously, they needed to destroy what challenged them.

Throughout Muslim histories, unlike some Christian imagery, there are probably no visual representations of God. But the Prophet is depicted often enough, though with clear cut regulations surrounding his appearance: very often he is veiled, or is only depicted from behind, though there are some instances of his revealed face even if only in profile. Muhammad is only human – there is no divinity there in a way that Christians understand Jesus – but he is a sacred person and cannot be disrespected. While some contemporary Muslims believe any depiction of Muhammad to be blasphemous, he has been depicted and gazed upon throughout history by pious Muslims.[8]

In terms of iconoclasm, within the Muslim traditions there are many intriguing points of image desecration and ritual de-consecration among illustrations in manuscripts. Finbarr Barry Flood comments on some of these instances, utilising a distinction between *instrumental* and *expressive* iconoclasm: instrumental iconoclasm leaves the image intact yet alters it by various markings – especially by erasing the face, or putting a slash through the neck – to show that the image is not acceptable (even if survivable). Flood suggests that, "all the evidence indicates that iconoclasts in the medieval Islamic world only rarely destroyed images..." and "As the Hadith dealing with images suggests, and iconoclastic practice in the medieval Islamic world implies, this was less an attempt to negate the image than to neutralise it."[9]

Turkish School (sixteenth century), *Mohammed (c. 570–632) Before the Ka'aba in Mecca*, from the *Siyer-i Nebi*, gouache on paper, courtesy of the Topkapi Palace Museum, Istanbul, Turkey/Bildarchiv Steffens/The Bridgeman Art Library

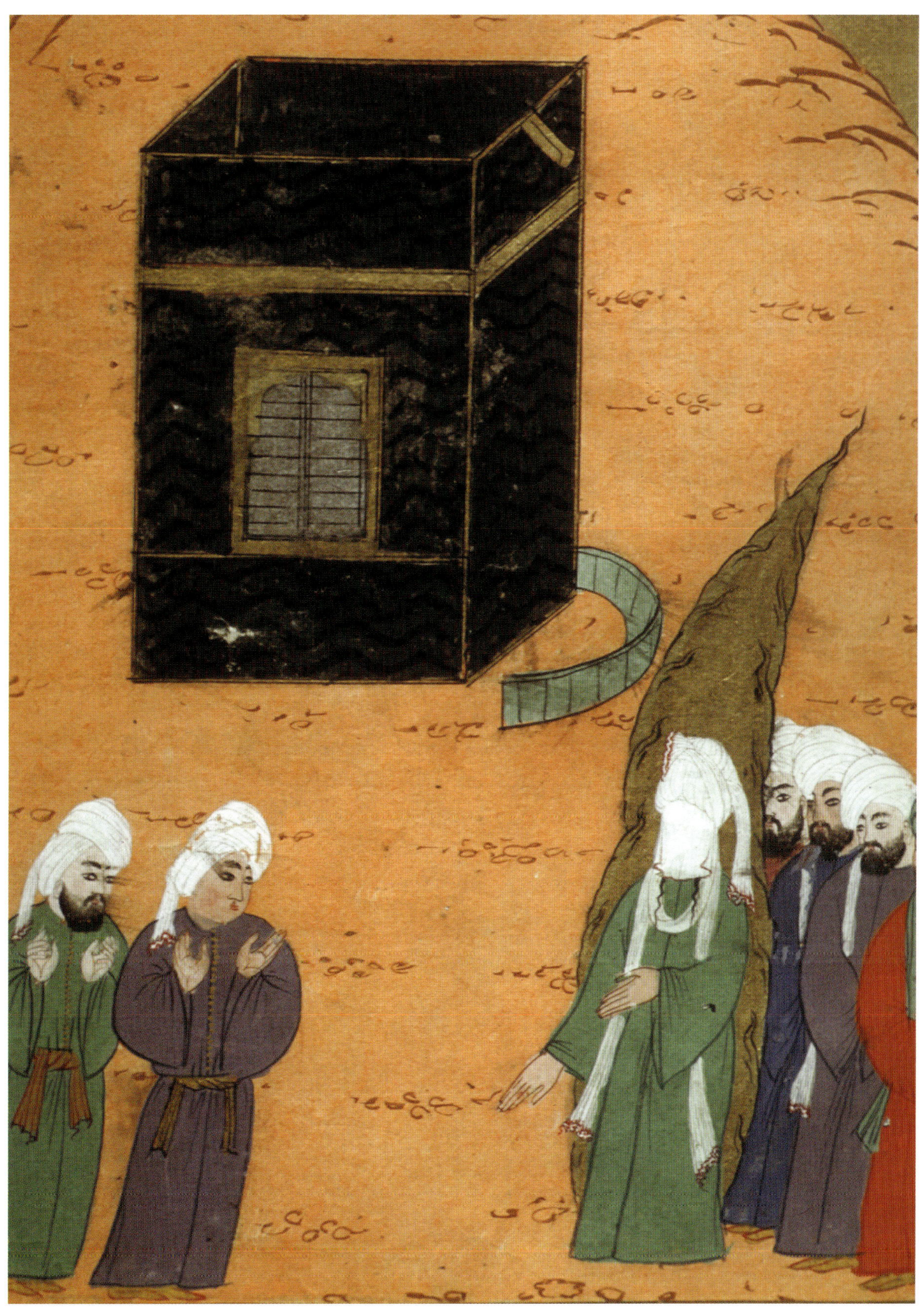

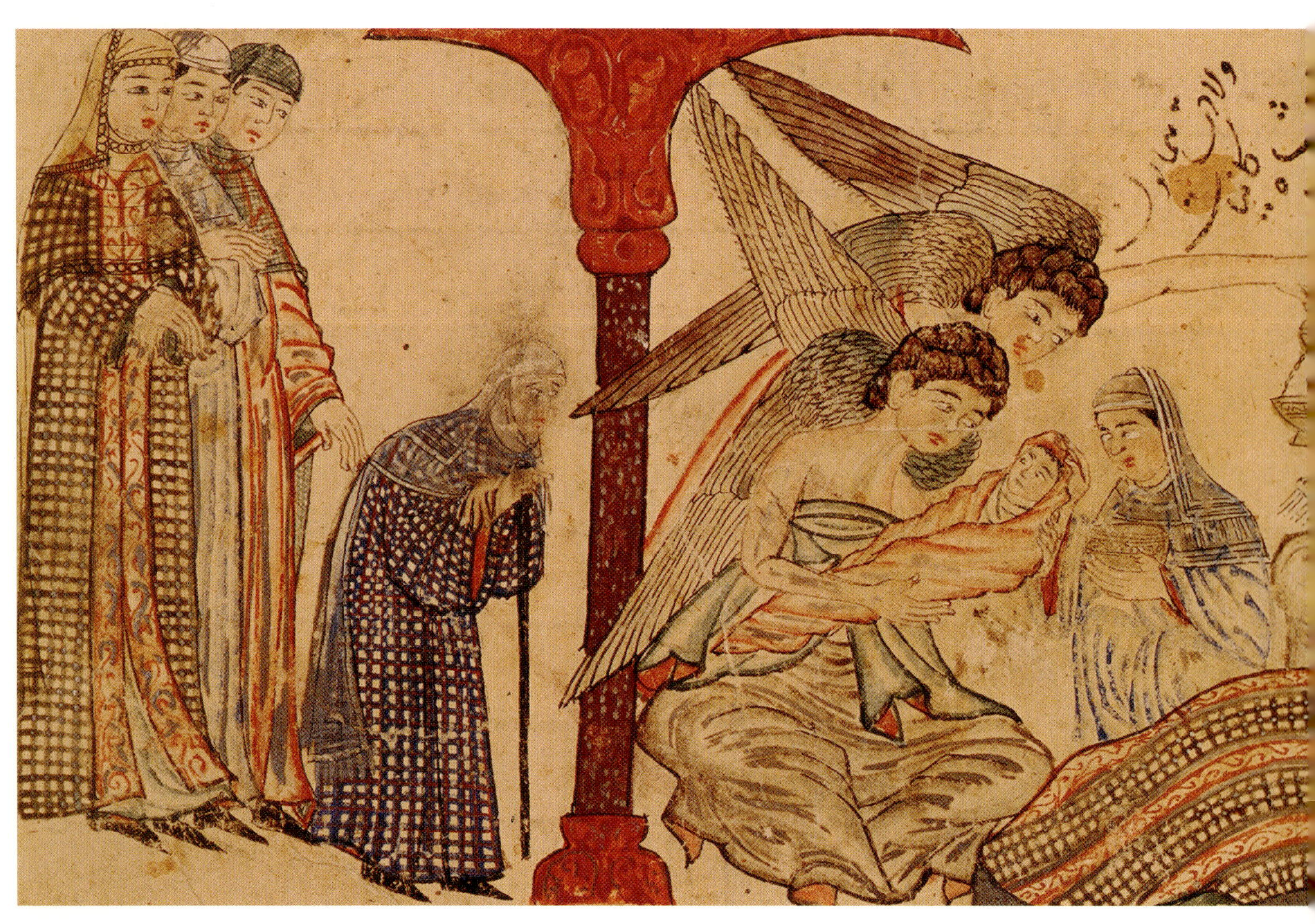

The Birth of the Prophet Muhammad, from *Jami' al-tavarikh* (Compendium of Chronicles), Iran, c. 1314–1315, ink, colours and gold on paper, courtesy of the Edinburgh University Library (MS Arab 20, folio 42r)

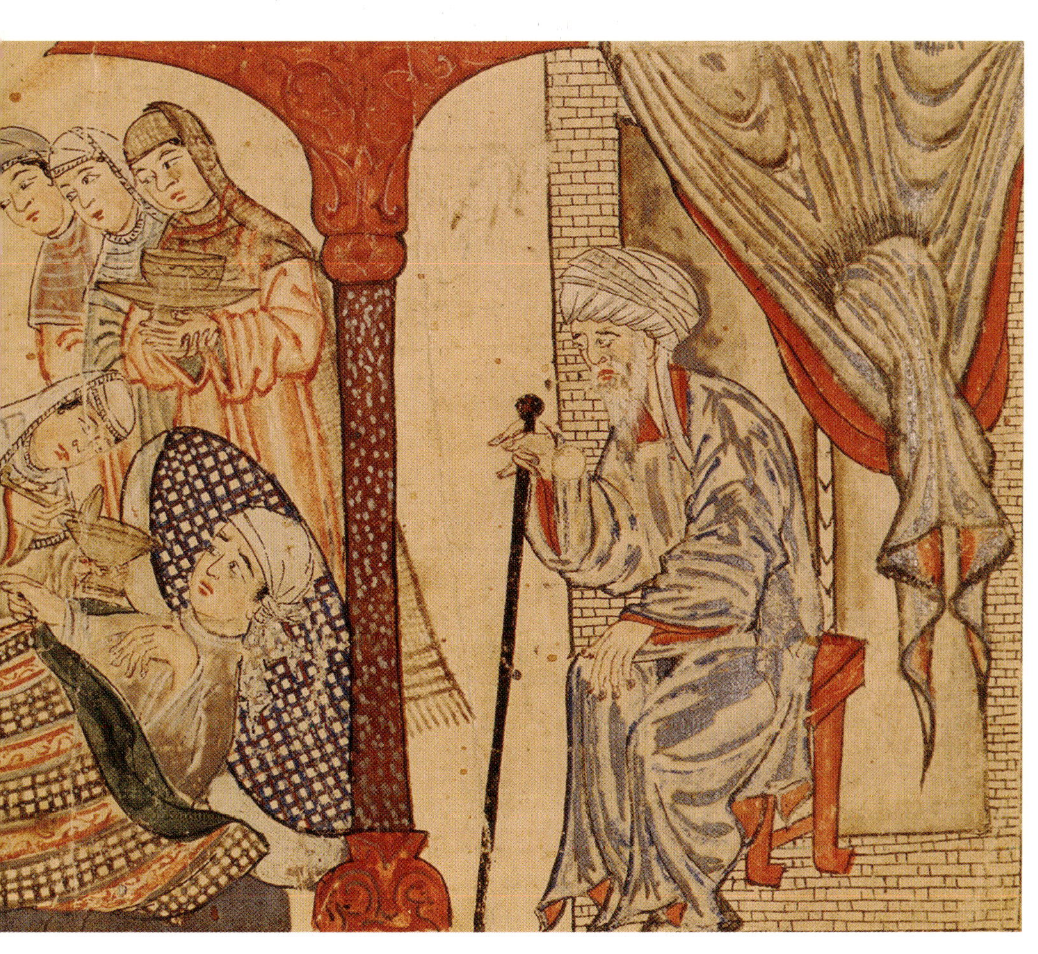

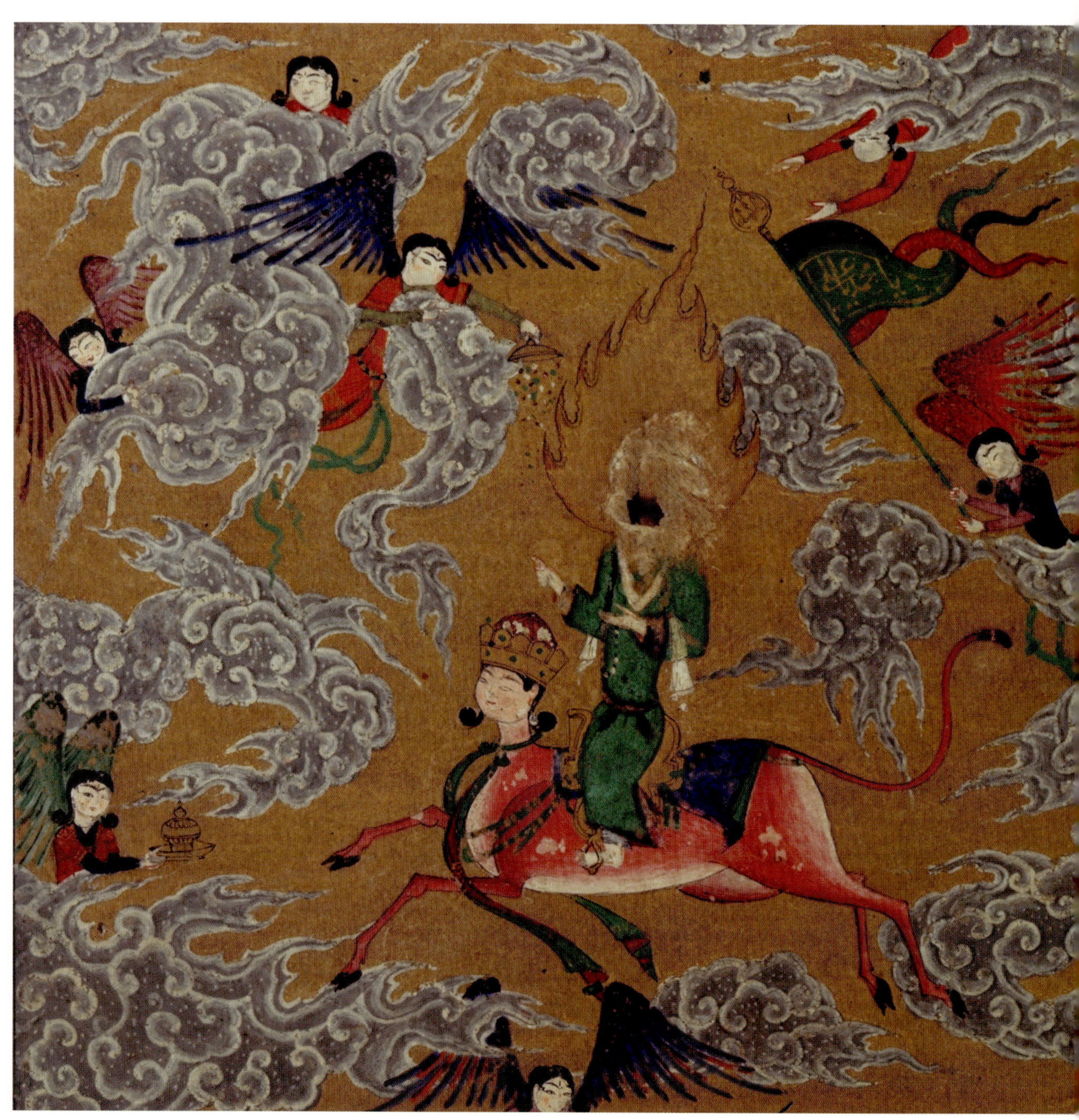

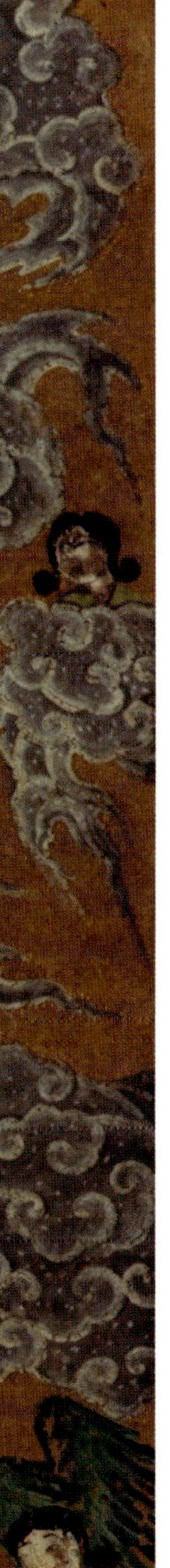

Rarely in the history of Islam has there been as much expressive iconoclasm as that stemming from the rise of Wahhabi Islam in Arabia in the second half of the eighteenth century. At that time, the religious reformer Ibn Abd al-Wahhab joined with the political forces of the Saudi family to establish the First Saudi state. Understanding themselves to be purifying themselves and getting back to the true principles of Islam, the Wahhabis needed to simultaneously show what they were against. And there is usually nothing better than a visual spectacle to proclaim this. Alongside their political activities was an invasion of Iraq in 1801 that led to the destruction of the shrine to Imam Husayn in Karbala, an event that shocked many Muslims throughout the Middle East. A few years later, Wahhabi groups pillaged the very tomb of Muhammad himself in Medina. The British explorer Richard Burton recounts the scene, in ways that indicate again the intimate link between money and morals, iconoclasm and the quest for power, and the perpetually nascent power of seemingly inanimate images, even for those doing the actual breaking of the icons:

> During the siege of [Medina in 1810] by the Wahhabis, the principal people seized and divided amongst themselves the treasures of [Muhammad's] tomb, which must have been considerable. When the town surrendered, Sa'ud, accompanied by his principal officers, entered the Hujrah, but, terrified by dreams, he did not penetrate behind the curtain, or attempt to see the tomb. He plundered, however, the treasures in the passage.... An accident prevented any further desecration of the building. The greedy Wahhabis, allured by the appearance of the golden or gilt globes and crescents surmounting the green dome, attempted to throw down the latter. Two of their number, it is said, were killed by falling from the slippery roof, and the rest, struck by superstitious fears, abandoned the work of destruction.[10]

Wahhabi iconoclastic impulses didn't stop there, but continued well into the twentieth century in their destructions of shrines. In 1925, shrines in Mecca and Medina devoted to holy Imams and Muhammad's family shrines were destroyed. Nonetheless, because of the vast oil deposits found in Saudi Arabia in the 1930s, the group has continued to have British and US support and they continue to the present day in their iconoclastic ways.

Ascension of the Prophet, f.4 from *Khamsa of Nizami*, Iran, c. 1505, courtesy of The British Library

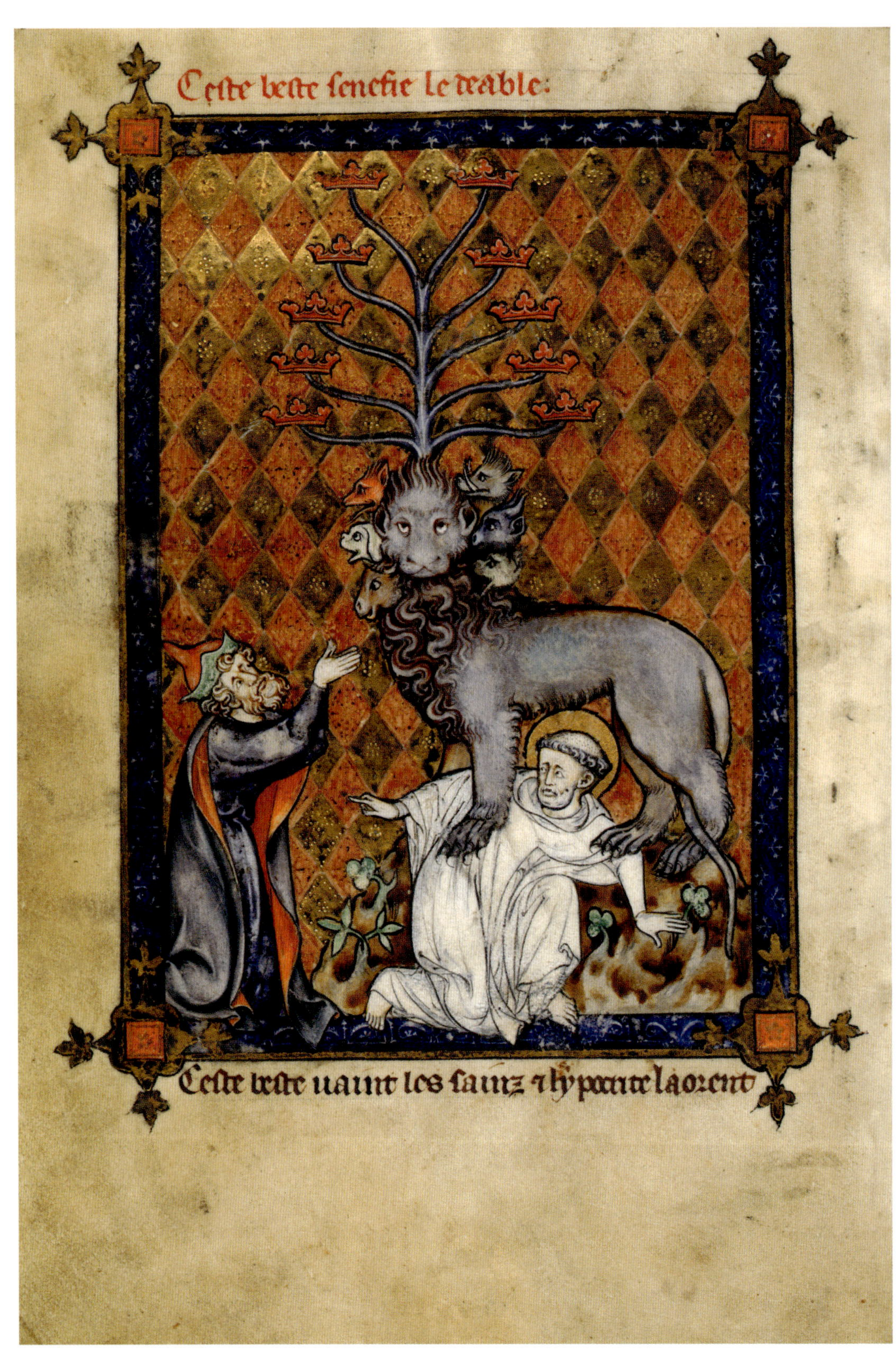
Ceste beste senefie le deable:
Ceste beste uaint les sainz ⁊ ly porte la orent

Idolatry as Blasphemy among the Abrahamic Traditions

What is historically more important than the scriptural and theological proscriptions regarding images is the struggle for religio-cultural identity that all three traditions faced as they each emerged out of polytheistic and other monotheistic cultural environments. To put it in blunt, contemporary terms, religions are in competition with each other and they each have to tell their own stories and develop their own iconologies in order to set themselves apart from each other. Since visual icons were regularly utilised in the worship practices of the polytheistic and pagan backgrounds of the Ancient Near East, Rome, and Arabia (out of which Judaism, Christianity, and Islam respectively grew) the banishment of images within these fledging traditions was an attempt to separate the new tradition from old ones. All three promoted monotheism against polytheism and other monotheisms, and this *exclusivity* made for strict controls on worship practices. This god is/was a jealous God (Exodus 34.14).

But images have also been put to use by people in power in order to maintain power, especially when working against other religious groups. During the medieval period, the lands around the Mediterranean saw constant overlap between Jews, Christians, and Muslims, causing some dramatically vital cultural productions that continue to affect modern life – and not a few clashes. The religious and cultural interchange of the time produced new theologies, advances in science, the arts, and education that have affected all three religions to the present day. Even so, the groups needed, from time to time, to define themselves over and against the others. As a result, there were many clashes between the various groups in the area, with accusations of iconoclasm by Muslims toward Christians and Arab infidels, Jews toward Muslims, Christians toward Muslims, etc.. A plethora of anti-Jewish and anti-Islamic images can be found in Christian illustrated manuscripts throughout history, such as the following two images from Christian cultural texts that depict Jews as idolators, and therefore blasphemers. Many blatantly anti-Semitic images are also found throughout Western history, particularly as modern European nations began to emerge, and the need for an 'other', a scapegoat was made prominent. To define oneself, to create an identity (whether it is religious or political), one must also define what one is *not*.

Beast with Saint and Hypocrite, from *La Somme le Roy*, 1295, illuminated manuscript, courtesy of The British Library
The Beast of the Apocalypse, is witnessed trampling a saint whilst adored by a kneeling hypocrite.

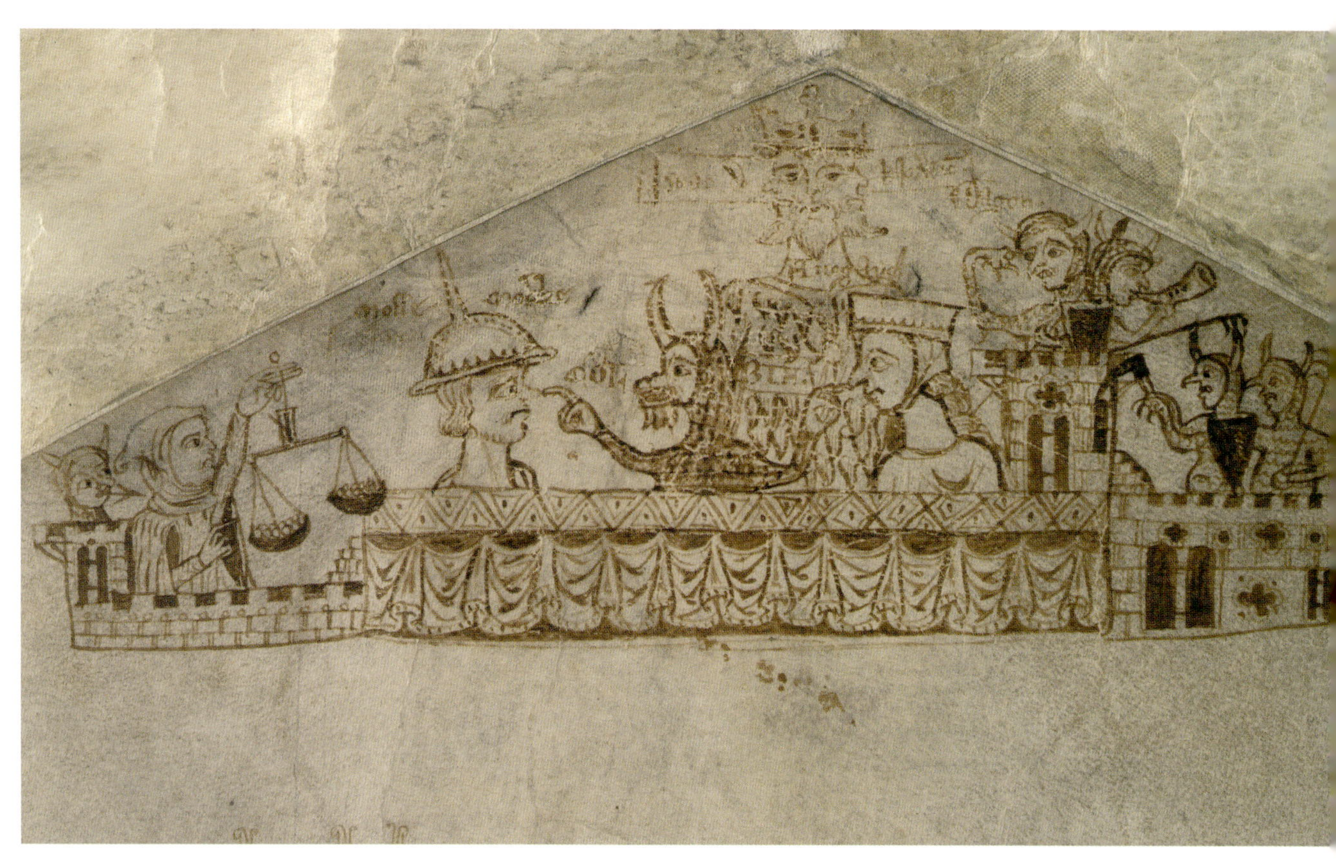

The Idolatry of the Jews of Norwich, *Head of a Roll of the Issues of the Exchequer for 1233*, manuscript, courtesy of the London Public Record Office

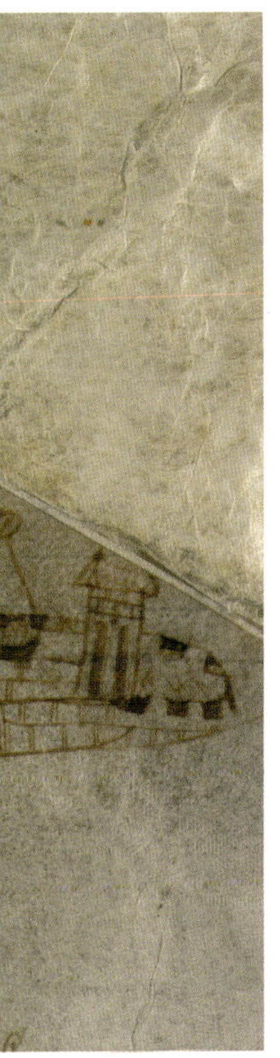

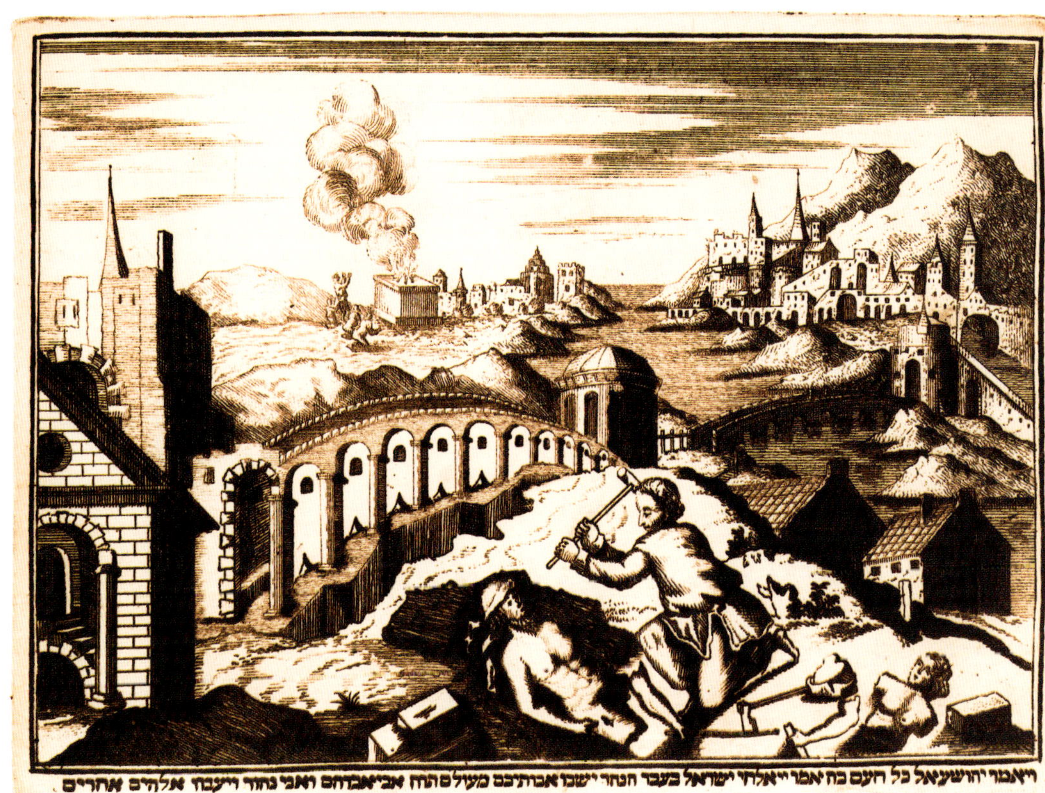

Abraham the Iconoclast, BM675.P4 A3 1712, Haggadah, Amsterdam, 1712, p. 7v, manuscript, courtesy of The Library of the Jewish Theological Seminary, New York

In Judaism, the Haggadah is the text that guides the performance of ritual acts and prayers at the Seder dinner celebrating Passover. The Haggadah retells the story of Exodus, offering commentaries that provide a religious philosophy of Jewish history and supplying answers to the traditional questions asked by children at the beginning of the Seder. More broadly, the term Haggadah can refer to the part of rabbinical literature not concerned with the law (e.g., stories, parables, legends, history, and astronomy).

Nazism was the culmination of hundreds of years of European Christian anti-Semitism, and in a certain twist of fate the Holocaust itself has become an event indelibly marked by taboo. The memory of it, and therefore its representations, have been given sacred status and there are many unwritten, though widely understood and appreciated, rules regarding the memorialising process. Denial, belittling, or making fun of the Holocaust evokes judgments that are parallel to the responses against blasphemers. In 2002, the Jewish Museum in New York City put on an exhibit entitled *Mirroring Evil: Nazi Imagery/Recent Art*. Many of the artworks displayed there came under heavy criticism for their ironic, crude, and sarcastic views of the Holocaust. One of the most prominent artistic themes throughout the show was the conflation of commercialism with events of the Holocaust: Lego concentration camps; a famous image of prisoners at Buchenwald with a Photoshopped Diet Coke in their hands. Here too, we can understand such work to function in a blasphemous way for many, since it too confuses the sacred and the profane.

Alan Schechner, *The Legacy of Abused Children: from Poland to Palestine*, 2003, digitally altered photograph and DVD projection, courtesy of the artist

Schechner's work here explores the links between the Holocaust and the Israeli Occupation of Palestine. The premise of the work stems from the situation where Palestinian/Israeli victims perpetuate the abuse they themselves suffer. The images were used in the project DIALOG: a collaboration with Palestinian artist Rana Bishra.

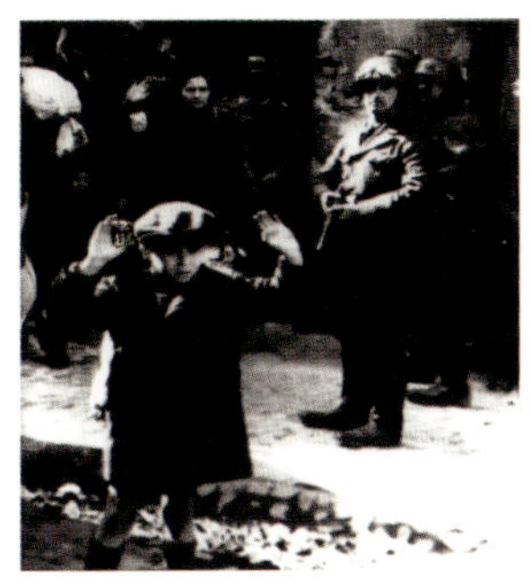

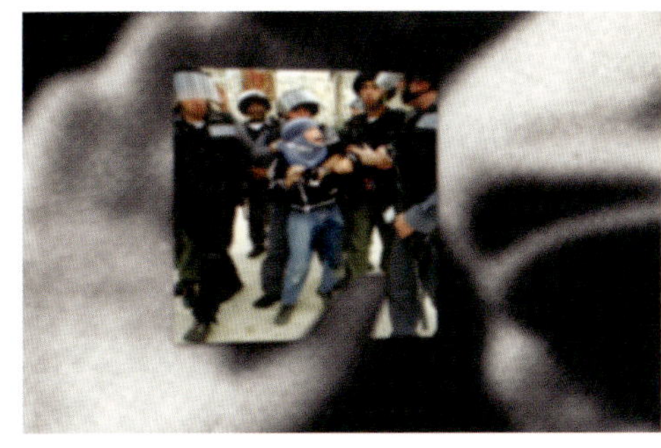

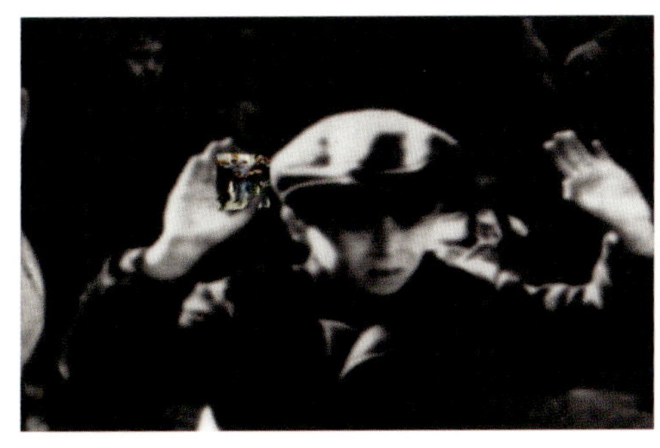

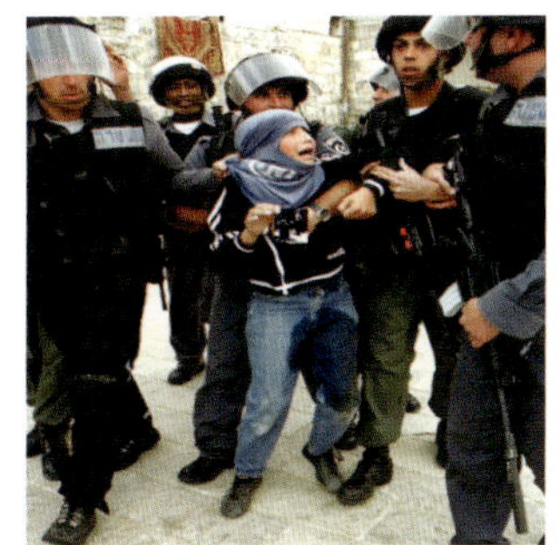

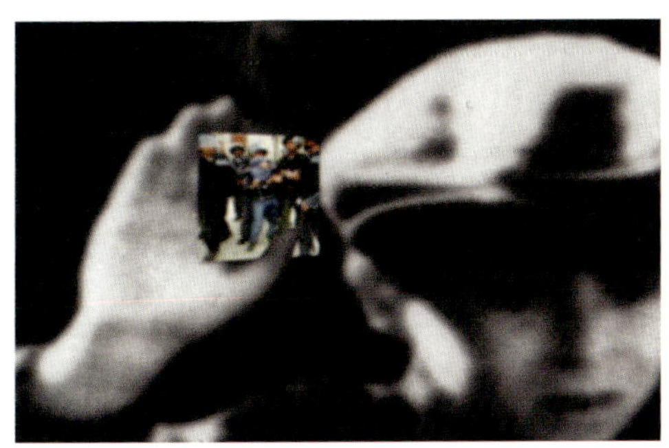

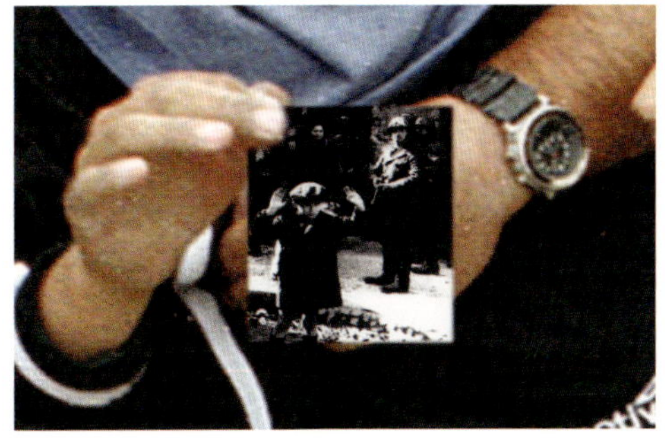

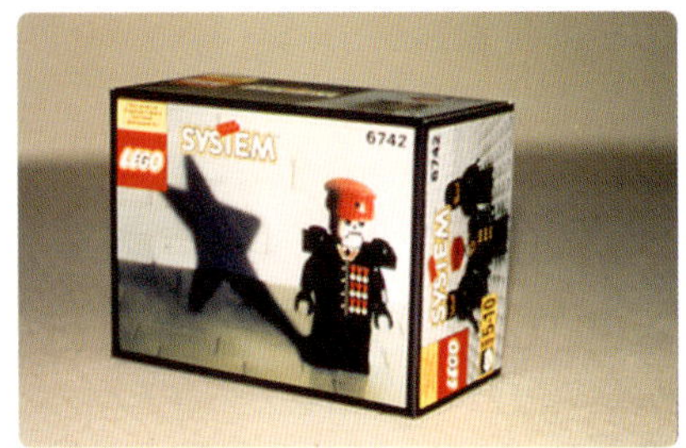

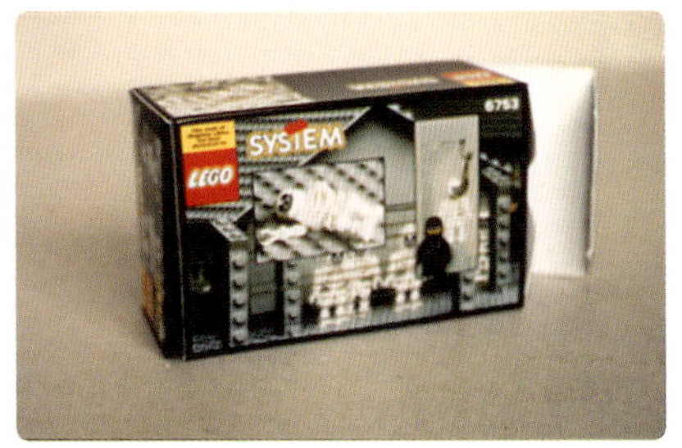

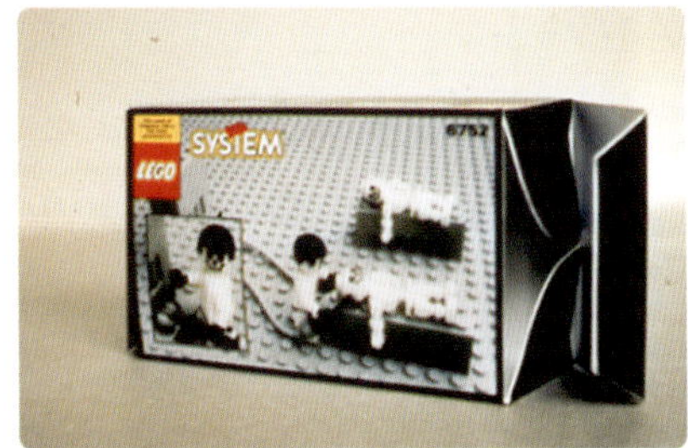

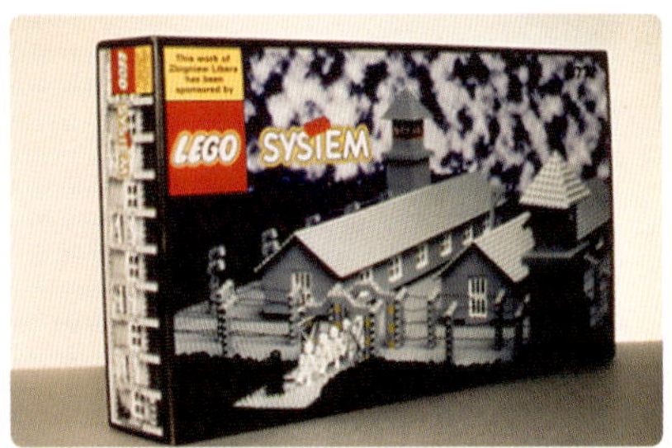

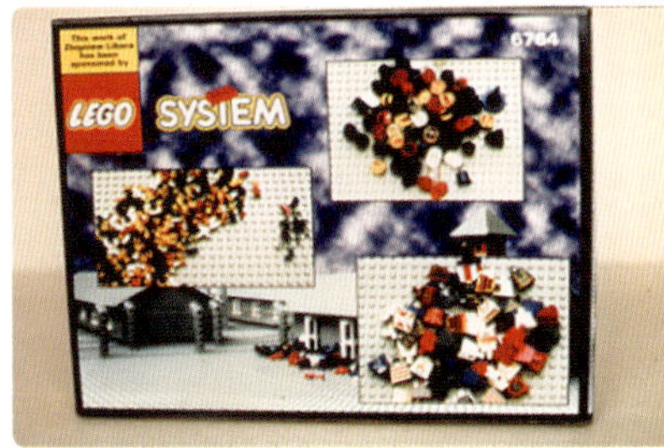

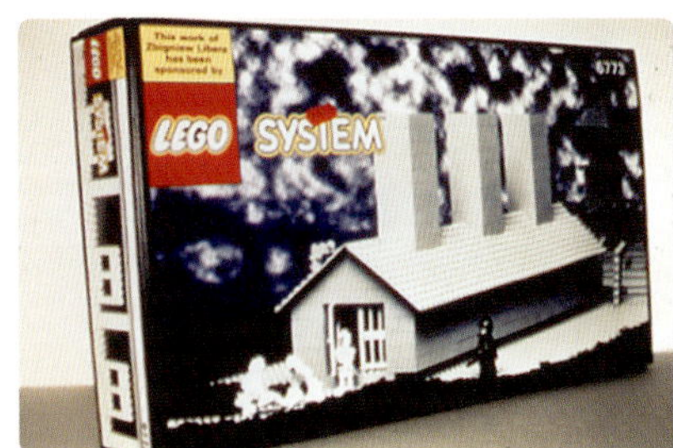

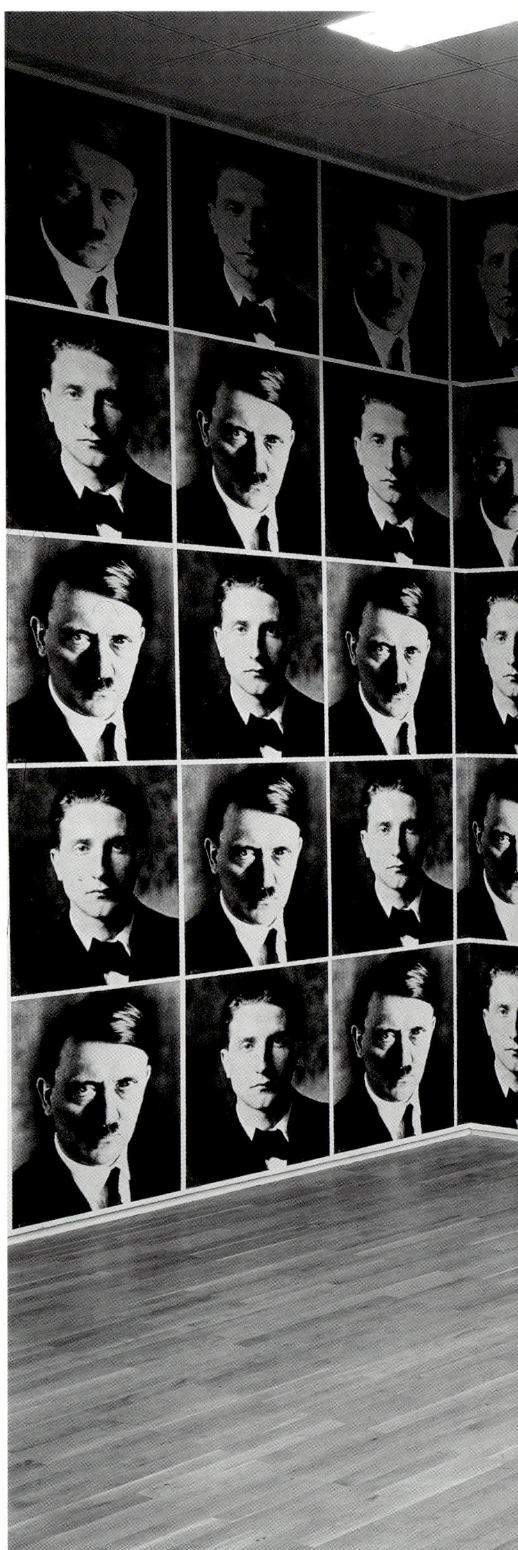

Zbigniew Libera, *LEGO*, 1997, Lego kits wth bricks (boxed editions of three). dimensions variable, courtesy of the artist

Libera has gone well beyond the traditional representational boundaries to create edgy conceptual/pop art about the Holocaust as well as contemporary genocide. His work has raised critical questions as to whether outlandish representations can help understand the Shoah, or whether just the opposite effect is created – an abusive and erroneous vision.

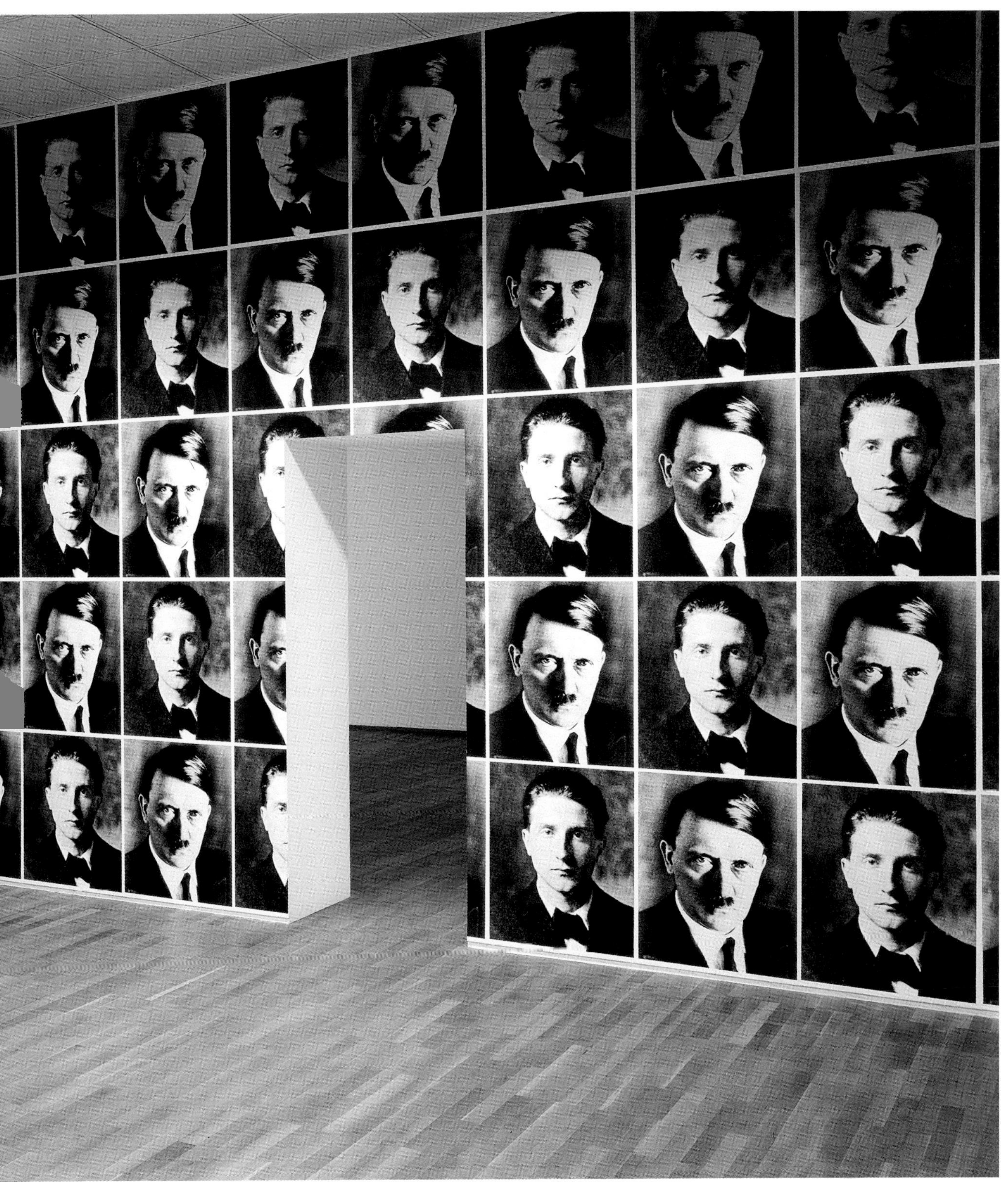

Rudolf Herz, *Zugzwang*, 1995, photographic installation, courtesy of the artist
Herz researched the archive of Hitler's official portrait photographer, Heinrich Hoffmann. He discovered a 1932 portrait of Hitler, and a 1912 portrait of Marcel Duchamp. Herz wallpapers one room of the gallery with these images, repeated like a checkerboard. The title is a chess term describing a position in which any possible move will make the situation worse. The Nazi and the Dadaist stare straight ahead, gentlemen sitting for formal portraits. The lighting and pose are nearly identical; the two men become more alike than different.

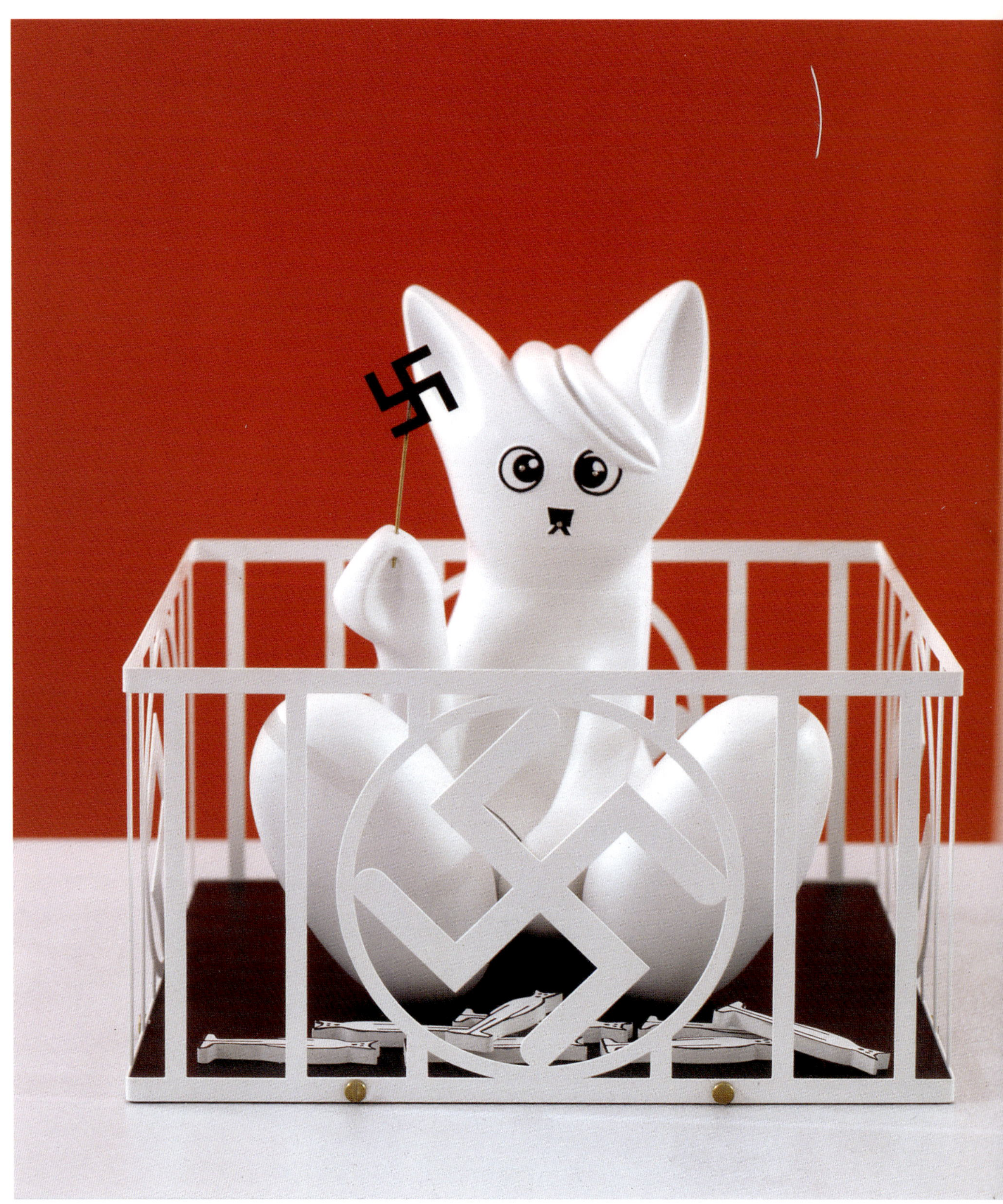

Alain Séchas, *Enfants Gâtés (Spoiled Children)*, 1998, polyurethane mouldings, acrylic, metal, mirror, painted wall (orange), 20 X 20 X 20 cm each, 600 X 250 X 120 cm, the whole, courtesy of the artist

OPPOSITE: **Alan Schechner**, *Barcode to Concentration Camp Morph*, 1991–1993, digitally morphed images, courtesy of the artist
Numbers morph into human faces and the mark of merchandise becomes the dress of affliction, the troubling association of commodification, concentration camps, and digital imaging emerges.

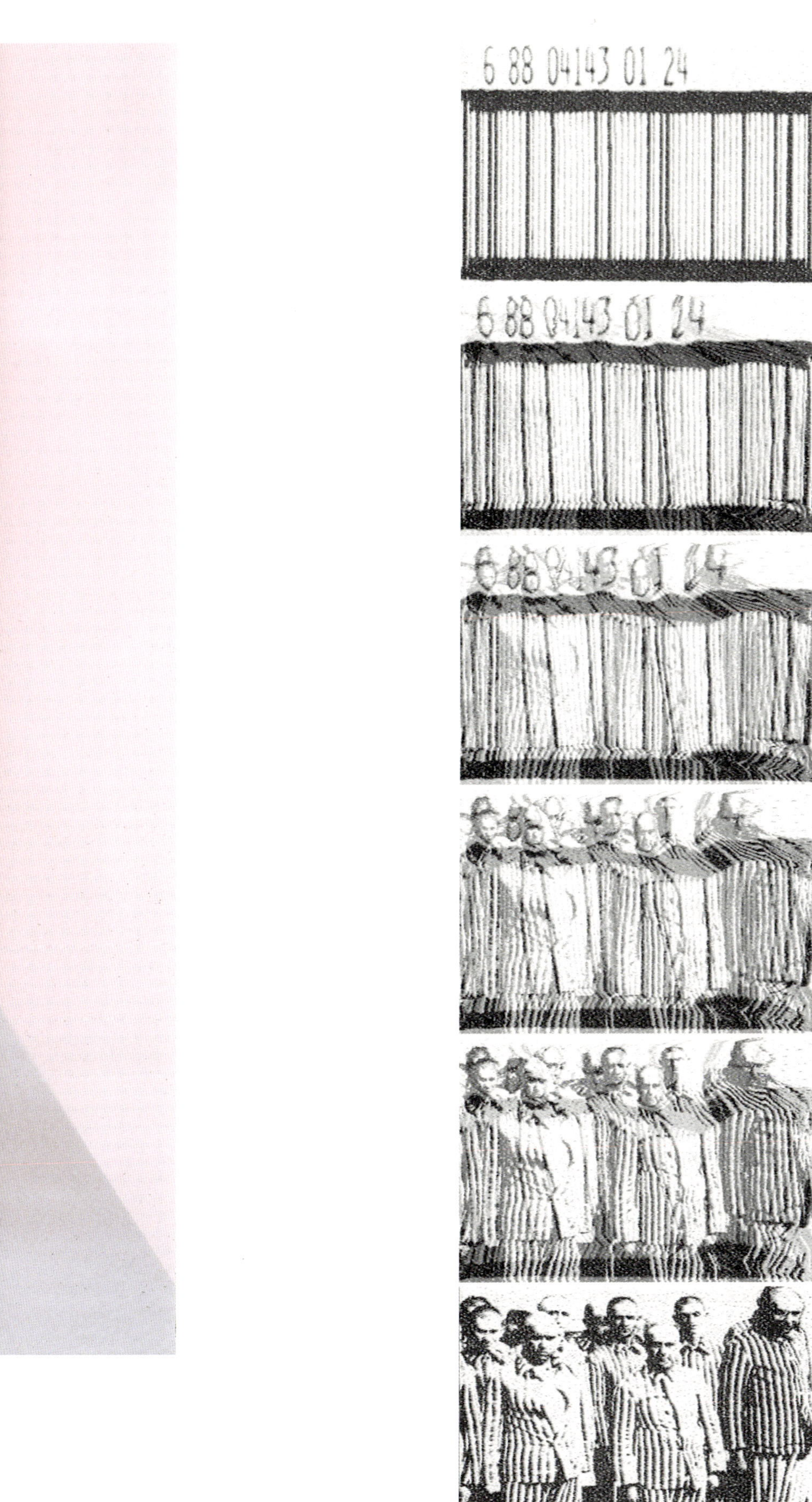
6 88 04143 01 24
6 88 04143 01 24

Meanwhile, at issue with the *Jyllands-Posten* controversy, as many journalists simplistically put it, was the depiction of the Prophet Muhammad, but it was particularly the negative, violent depictions of Muhammad (portrayed with swords, dynamite, and overall violence) that provoked so much ire. Under the influence of, particularly, Wahhabism and Salafism, many contemporary Muslims will suggest that Muhammad cannot be depicted, but as the images above show there is plenty of reason to believe that many Muslims through time have not had problems with these representations. Some of the *Jyllands-Posten* images *were* blasphemous, not in a strict theological view because they simply *represented* Muhammad, but because of the types of representations there were: disrespect of a holy figure. And these are nothing new in Western history. From Italian frescoes, to romantic engravers, to Surrealist painters, Muhammad has been caricatured throughout the predominantly Christian cultures of modern Europe in literature (from Dante's *Inferno* to Voltaire's *Muhammad*) and art.

Denial, belittling, or making fun of the Holocaust evokes judgments that are parallel to the responses against blasphemers.

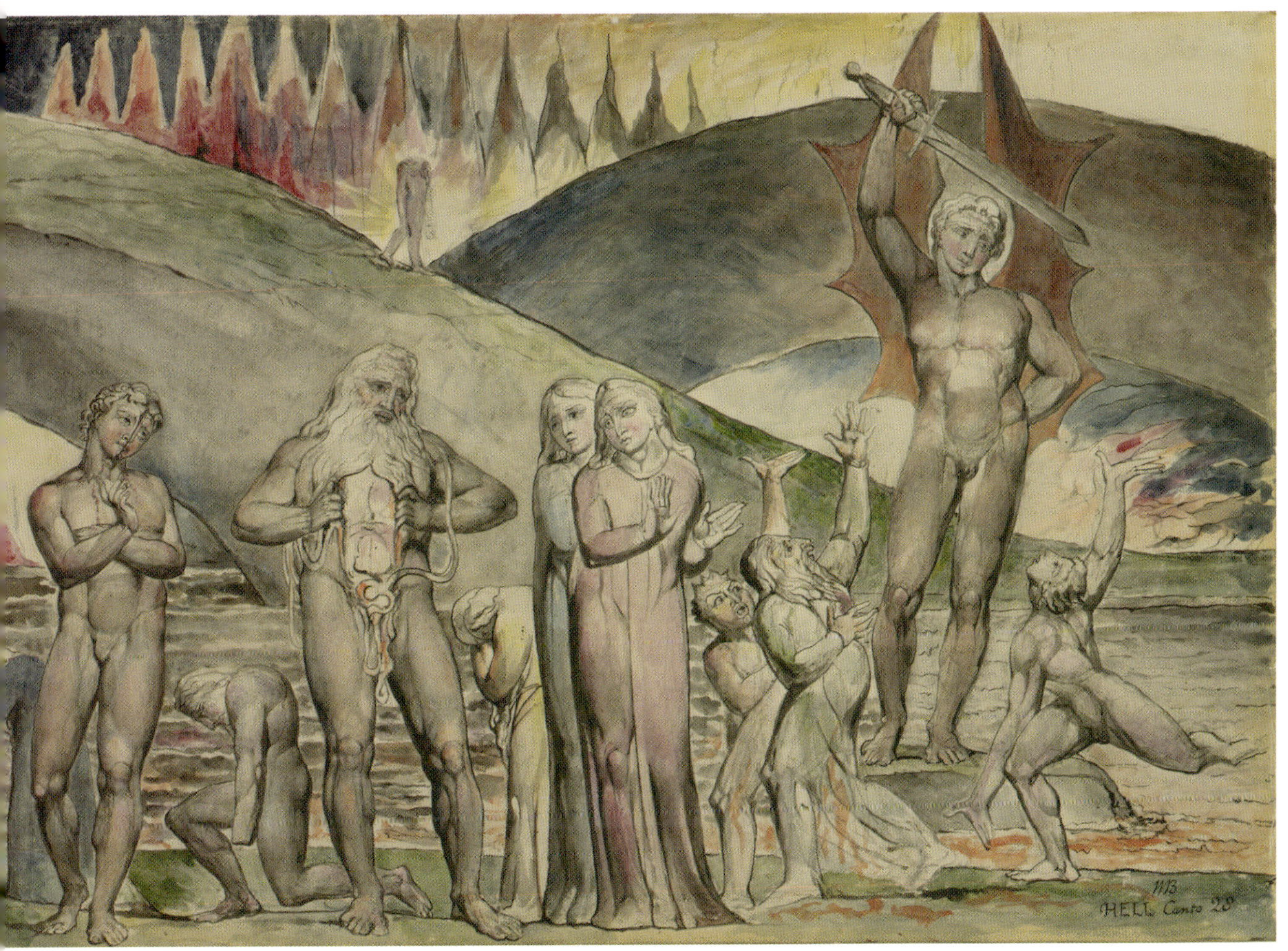

William Blake, *The Schismatics and Sowers of Discord: Mahomet (Inferno, Canto XXVIII)*, 1824–1827, pen and watercolour over pencil, Felton Bequest, 1920, courtesy of The National Gallery of Victoria, Australia

The poets are in the ninth chasm of the eighth circle, that of the Sowers of Discord, whose punishment is to be mutilated. Mahomet shows his entrails to Dante and Virgil while on the left stands his son Ali, his head cleft from chin to forlock. A winged devil with a sword stands on the right. In the distance, behind Mahomet, can be seen Bertrand de Born carrying his head in his hand.

One curious story speaks to an earlier chapter in US history when religious and government relations took on a more nuanced form than they tend to in contemporary 'either-or' society. The Appellate Division Courthouse on Madison Square in New York City was built in the early twentieth century, and decorated with grand friezes, murals, and reliefs inside and out. Around the outside, toward the top, a number of carved mythical figures were placed that allegorically outline the history of law: Moses, Confucius, Justinian, Alfred the Great, and Hammurabi are there, as was Muhammad originally. All were great law-makers and law-givers, religious or not, and barely anyone has had a problem with such a historical treatment of religion and law. In 1955, when the statues were going to be renovated and the images began to be noticed, the governments of Indonesia, Egypt, and Pakistan complained about the representation of Muhammad, and the image was removed. In a poignant ending, John Kifner in the *The New York Times* explains: "Muhammad was lowered by block and tackle, wrapped in excelsior and trucked off to a stone company in Newark. In the last reported sighting – in 1983 – the statue was lying on its side in a stand of tall grass somewhere in New Jersey."[11]

Images have power, and can be used by one group against another, or to stir up emotions within a group whose anger is then taken out on another group. There is simultaneously power in the removal and destruction of images. Their very visibility makes them a focal point for controversy, for something concrete to point to and foist the seeming sins of a society onto, and then ceremoniously banish forever.

There is simultaneously power in the removal and destruction of images.

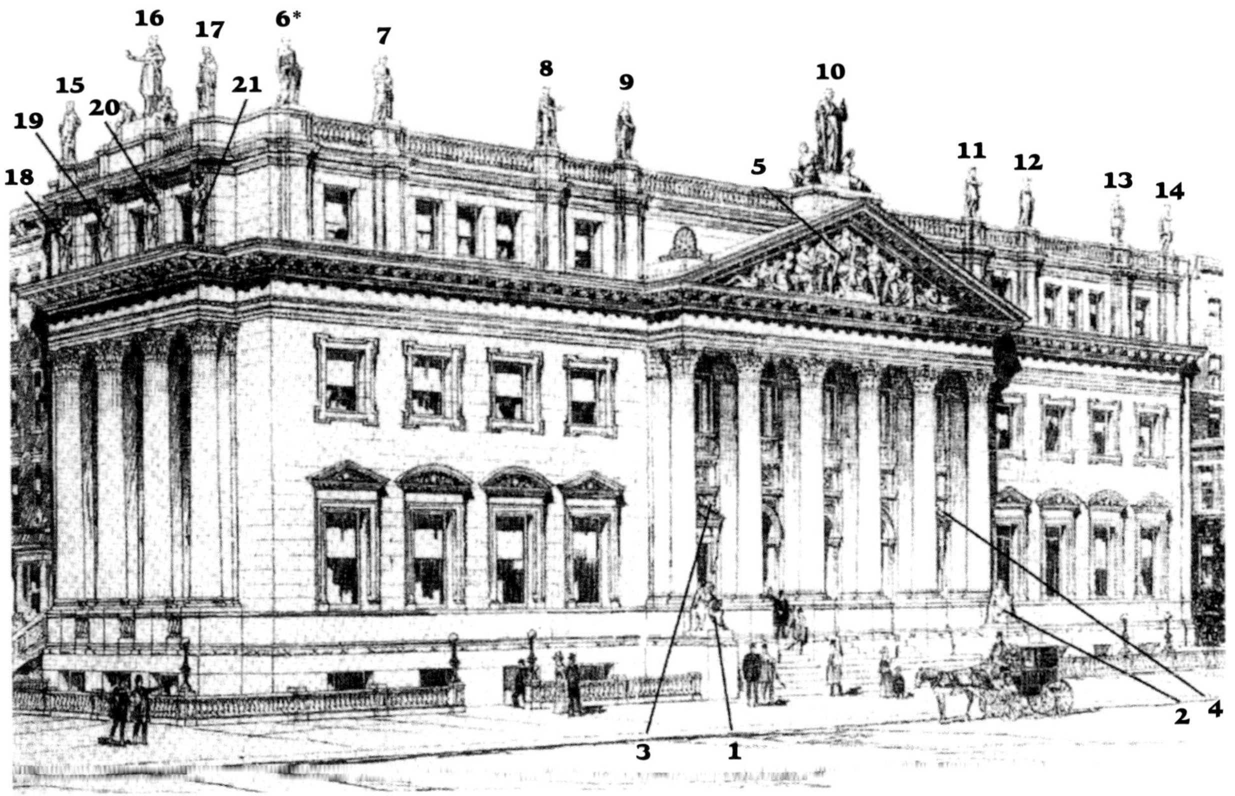

The Appellate Division Courthouse, Madison Square, New York City, *The Placement of the original exterior sculpture*: 1: Wisdom, 2: Force, 3: Morning and Night, 4: Noon and Evening, 5: Triumph of Law, 6: Mohammad (which was removed in 1955), 7: Zoroaster, 8: Alfred the Great, 9: Lycurgus, 10: Justice, 11: Solon, 12: Louis IX, 13: Manu, 14: Flavius Anicius Justinian, 15: Confucius, 16: Peace, 17: Moses, 18: Winter, 19: Autumn, 20: Summer, 21: Spring, line drawing, courtesy of The Appellate Division Courthouse.

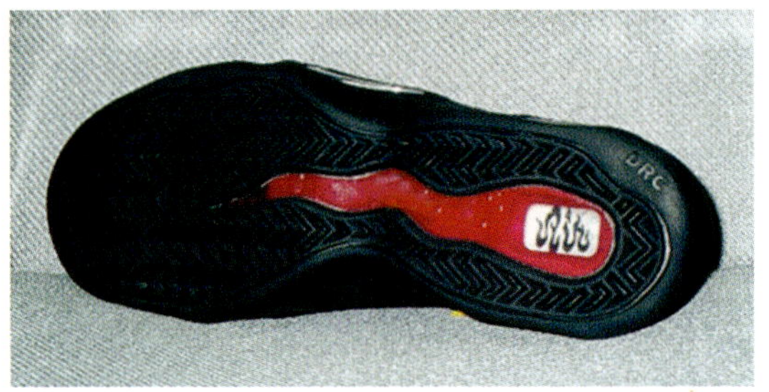

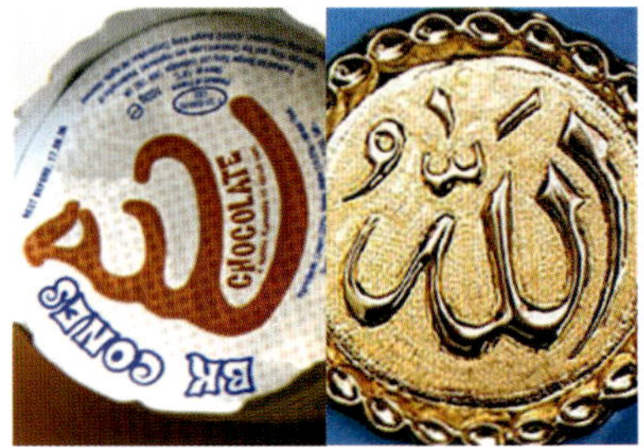

Words and Images, Words as Images

In the late 1990s, Nike unveiled a new line of shoes with a vibrant logo emblazoned around the heel. Wishing to inspire images of fire (the line was introduced in the summer), the company thought they were tapping into a new market. However, when various groups, including the Council on American-Islamic Religions, saw the new logo they suspected foul play since it had an uncanny resemblance to the Arabic script for the name of Allah. Nike quickly recanted and the shoes have been seldom seen since (apparently they have become something of a collector's item). A similar event occurred in 2005, when Burger King put what they said was a 'swirl' design on the wrapper of some of their ice cream cones, though this logo is almost certainly a direct riff on the Arabic Allah. Again, offence was taken, protests began, and Burger King cancelled the use of the design.

Besides the perceived unholy mixture of crass consumerism and the Name of God, what is significant here is the way that a seemingly decorative flourish can be 'read'. The Word of God, as understood by a Jew, Christian, or Muslim, is often thought of as invisible or 'spiritual'; in the practice of religion, however, the Word of God is often *written* and thus made *visible*. Because the writing stands between the invisible-divine and the visible-earthly, the Word of God continues to take part in an incarnational understanding of divine revelation. And therein we realise that written words *are* images, that the difference between words and images is not always so clear.

Because of the sacred status of the Word of God, Western traditions have developed a series of rules and regulations for how this Word might be portrayed: an ice cream cone wrapper in a fast food restaurant is not a sufficient enough surface for the Name of God, nor are people's feet. More than the other two traditions, Islam has developed a highly specialised set of rules for the writing of the Word of God, the Quran. Calligraphy, as a result, has become a predominant art form throughout Muslim history. One of the greatest treatises on calligraphy of all time was Qadi Ahmad's sixteenth century Persian text *Rose Garden of Art*. Therein, he relates several proverbs that were commonly understood in response to the 'word-image' mixing of calligraphy, including, "Excellent writing clears the eyes", and "Calligraphy is the geometry of the soul."[12]

OPPOSITE: Detached folio from a Koran: Sura 53, verses 1–2, Arabic, fourteenth century, ink, opaque watercolour and gold on paper, 37 x 27 cm, courtesy of the Freer Gallery of Art, Smithsonian Institution, Washington DC

OVERLEAF: Detached bifolio, Folios from a Koran, Sura 9: 128–129, Arabic (Egypt), Mamluk dynasty, mid-fourteenth century, ink, opaque watercolour and gold on paper, 41 x 64 cm, courtesy of the Freer Gallery of Art, Smithsonian Institution, Washington, DC

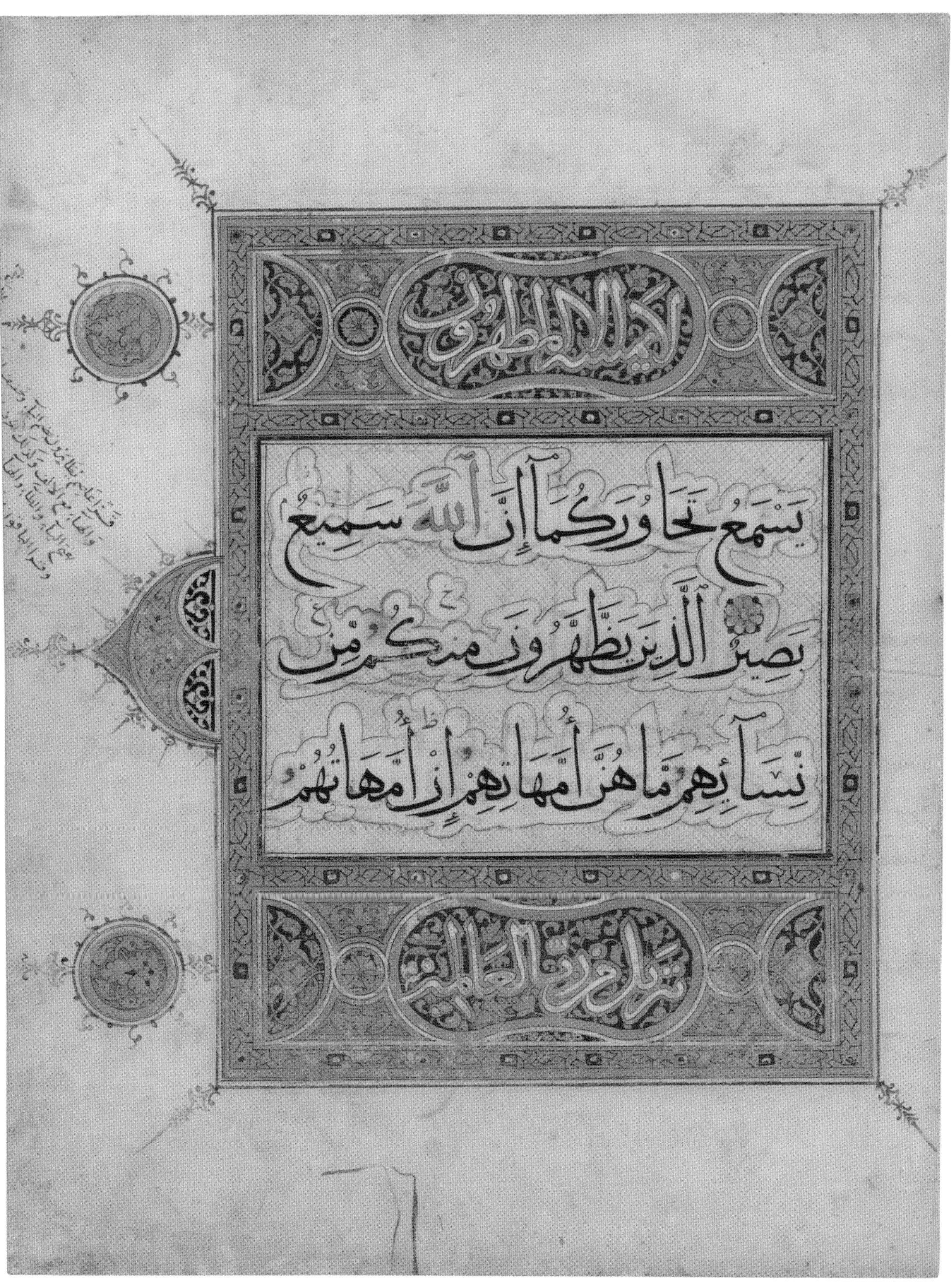

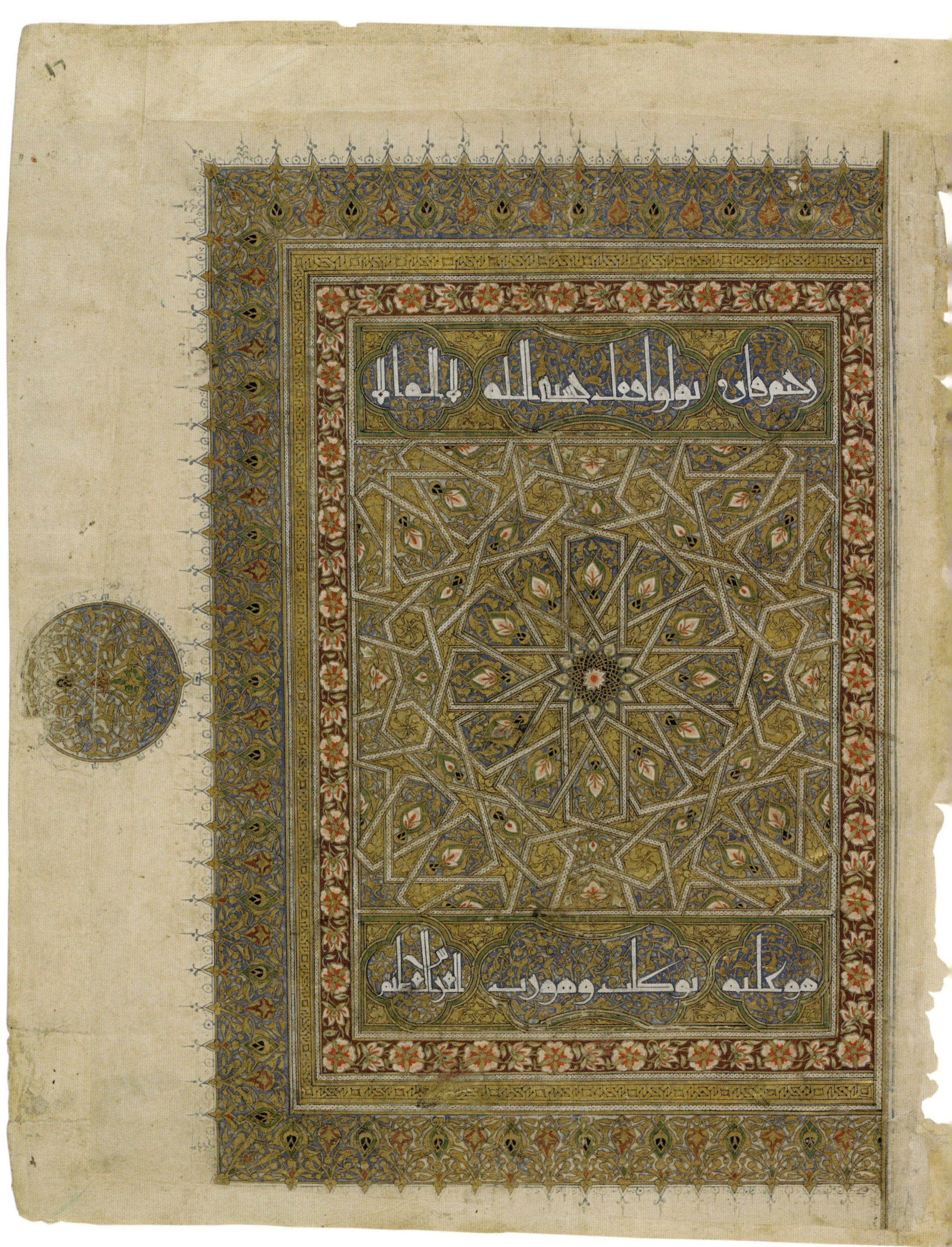

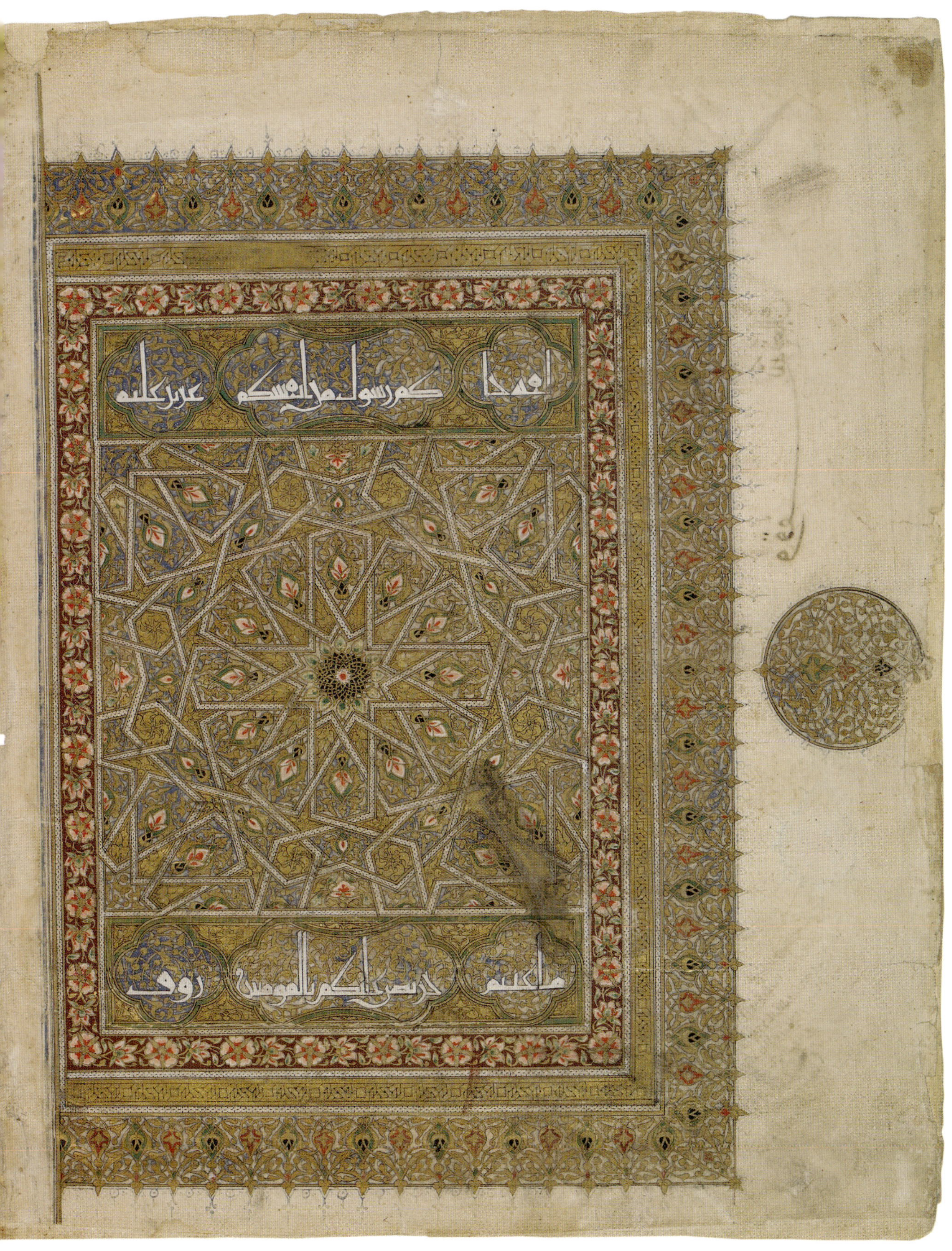
لقد جا كم رسول من انفسكم عزيز عليه
ما عنتم حريص عليكم بالمومنين روف

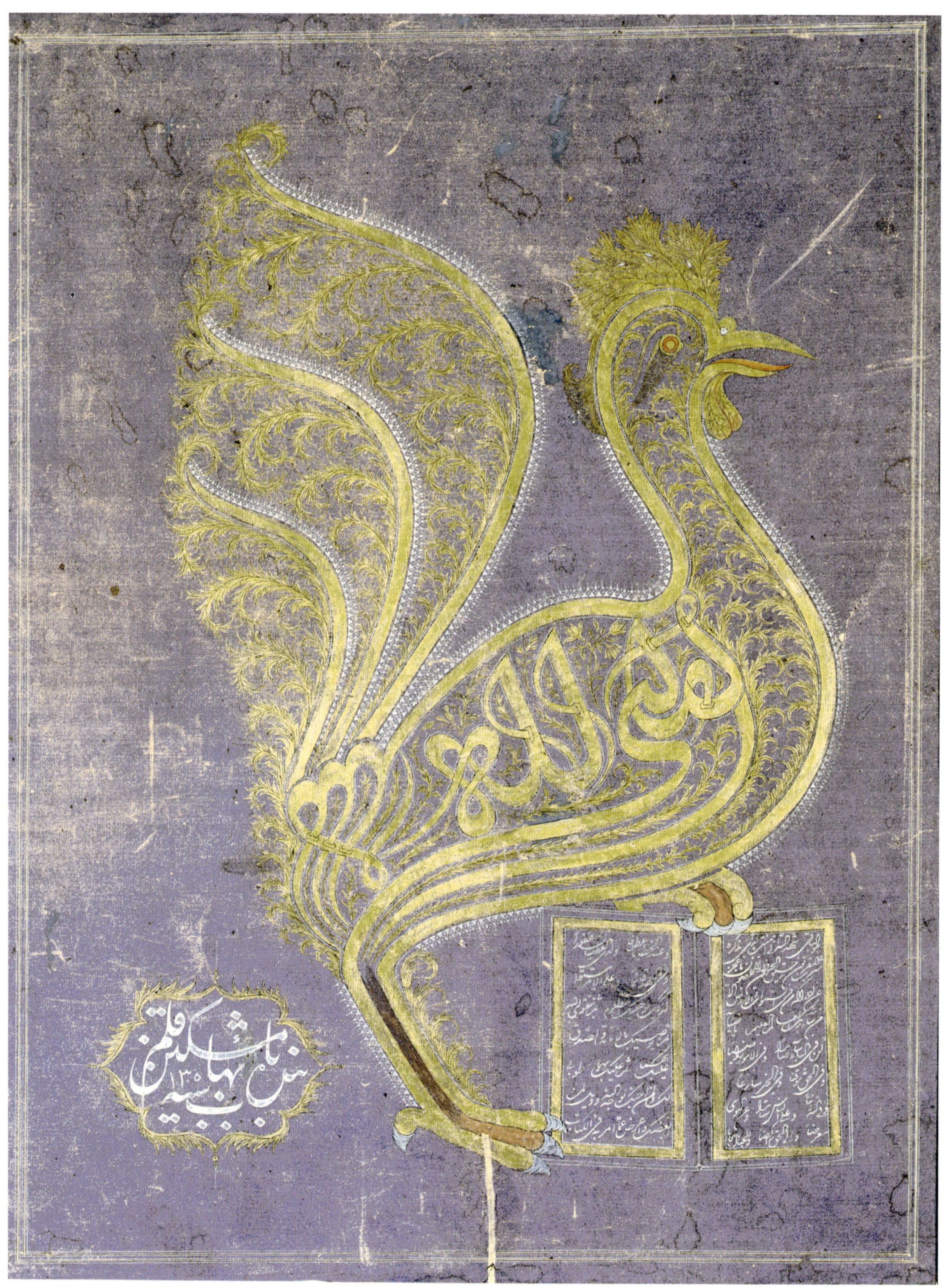

Because of the sacred status of the Word of God, Western traditions have developed a series of rules and regulations for how this Word might be portrayed.

The high value placed on the art of calligraphy, mixed with high value of the Quran, makes it easy to see why the copying of Qurans is considered something of a devotional act itself. This means, of course, that the calligrapher him or herself (there have been many female Muslim calligraphers through history) must be pure. One famous calligrapher is the nineteenth century Persian, Mishkin-Qalam, who was of the Baha'i tradition (formerly a Sufi), and thus considered an infidel by many other Muslims. Mishkin-Qalam was imprisoned as a follower of Baha'u'llah, founder of the Baha'i tradition, and his work considered adulterated. Like other calligraphers throughout history (whether Muslim, Baha'i, or Jewish), his works convoluted the 'word-image' relation by turning words into figural images, a mixture that is perfectly acceptable throughout Islam, but according to the authorities of his day it was not acceptable to mix his impure hands with the writing of the name of God. More recently, Tahir Iqbal was convicted of blasphemy in Pakistan. Iqbal had converted from Islam to Christianity, and was accused by a local Imam of defiling a Quran because he underlined verses and wrote in the margins. He was imprisoned in December 1990 without bail and died two years later. The causes of his death were never ascertained.[13]

Mishkin-Qalam, *The Name of "Baha'ullah" in the Form of a Rooster*, nineteenth century, courtesy of Harvard University Art Museums

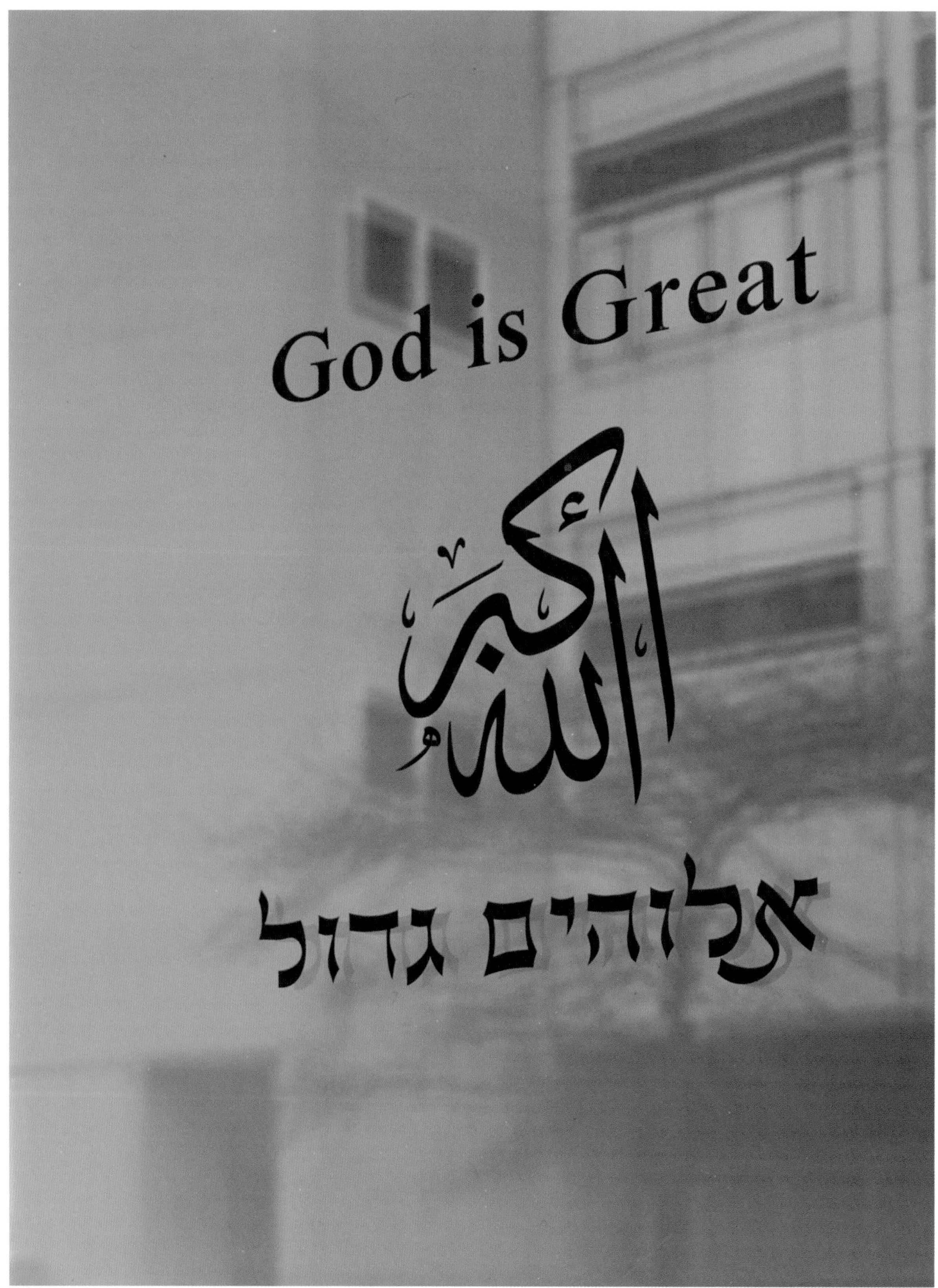
God is Great
الله أكبر
אלוהים גדול

Within Judaism, there are, likewise, Talmudic passages that speak against writings by heretics (Hebrew – *minim*; sometimes used to refer to Christians), and what to do with their texts themselves. One Talmudic comment is interesting for its collection of persons deemed unfit to write the Law: "Rolls of the Law, tefillin and mezuzoth, written by a Min, a betrayer, an idolater, a slave, a woman, a child, a Samaritan or an apostate Israelite, are ceremonially unfit for use."[14] Since even heretical writings, especially by Christians, often mention the name of God, and since heretical writings should be burned, does one also burn the name of God? Rabbi José the Galilean argued that the name of God, wherever it occurred in such texts, be cut out and kept, and the remainder of the texts burned.[15] Likewise, the Babylonian Talmud tractate, *Sabbath* (103b), talks against manuscript decorations, but is not referring to figural images; instead the practice of writing the name of God in gold ink in the Torah is censured.

The written word *is* an image: physical, visible, and full of power, thus prompting the authorities within religious traditions to crack down on the usages of the written language itself. In terms of religious traditions, the Word of God must be incarnated in order for humans to have any relation to the revelation from above. These incarnations (of the body, of the written word) must be holy channels, pure media, at the nexus of the human and divine. If impurities reside, the revelation cannot stand.

John Latham, *God is Great*, 2005, Vinyl text, 43 x 38 cm, photography Dave Morgan, courtesy of the Lisson Gallery and the artist

Blasphemy as Resistance: Race, Gender, and Transgressive Images

To conclude this chapter, I want to take a brief look at the ways in which blasphemous images, statements, and activities become a form of resistance to the powers that be. While this subject would be great subject matter for an entire book, I am merely able to end here, giving a couple examples, especially in relation to struggles of race and gender.

Throughout the seventeenth century, at the height of the Inquisition in Mexico, Afro-Mexican slaves very often denounced God, or carried out some other blasphemous act, almost always in the midst of severe torture from their Christian masters. In this way they would be relieved, at least temporarily, from horrid working conditions and cruel punishment from their masters and placed into the higher hands of the Church; owners could punish for certain 'crimes,' but matters of blasphemy and heresy were under the jurisdiction of the Church. Blasphemous utterances on the part of the enslaved allowed several possibilities: sometimes to be transferred to better working conditions (confessions became ways to speak to the higher authorities about working conditions), or more often to become martyrs, since they would exclaim how their masters' punishments drove them from the faith. Then again, sometimes blasphemous actions were meant to be downright antithetical to the whole Christian social structure: "The use of blasphemy by Afro-Mexicans was both a rejection of the Christian moral order that legitimised slavery and an attempt to survive a violent regime by claiming a Christian identity."[16]

RIGHT AND OVERLEAF: Siddur, (MS 8255), Italy, 1471, ff. 3v, 5v, courtesy of The Library of The Jewish Theological Seminary

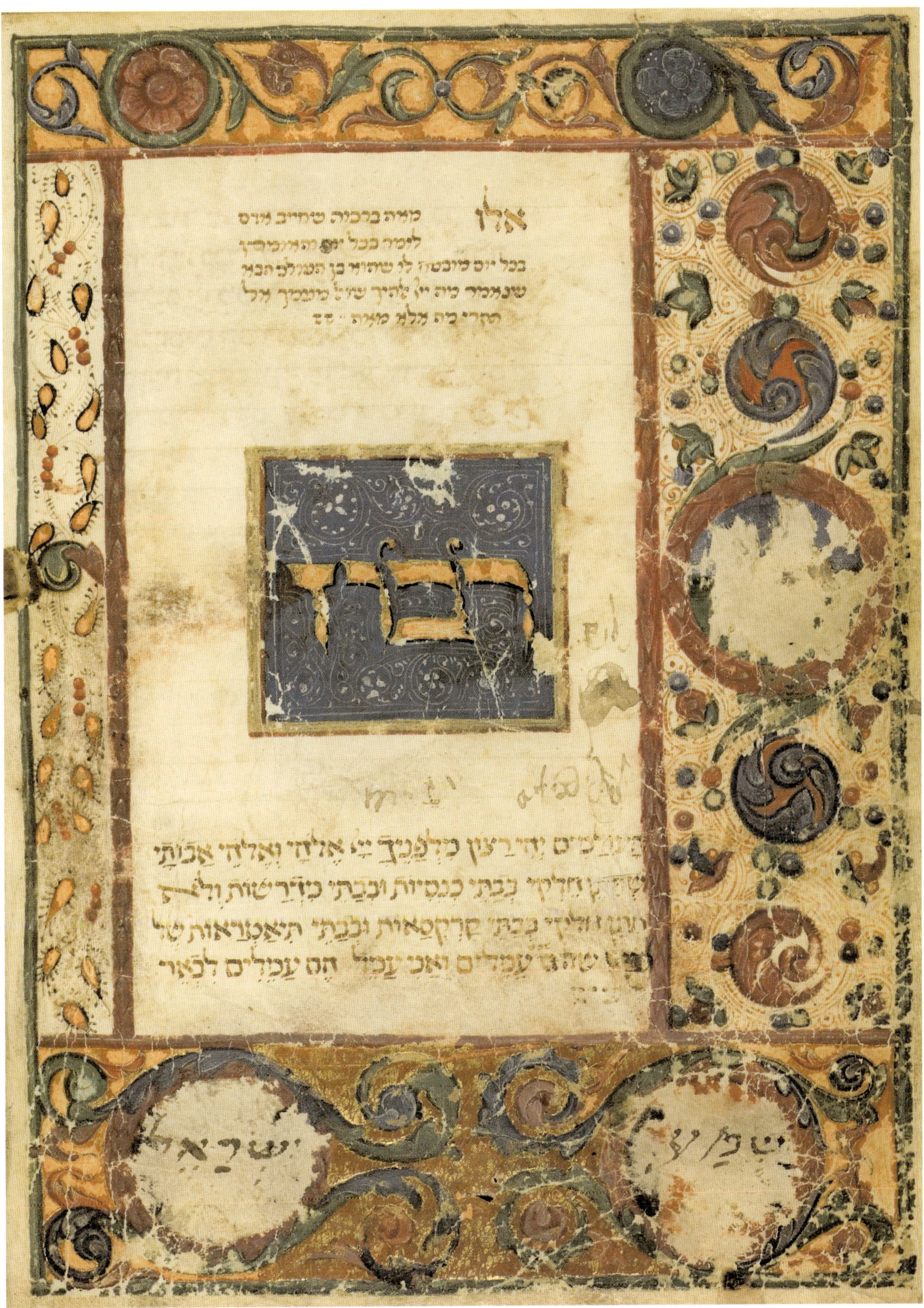

הגומל חסדים טובים לעמו ישראל

באי אתה פוקח עורים

באי אתה זוקף כפופים

באי אתה מלביש ערומים

באי אתה רוקע הארץ על המים

באי אתה המכין מצעדי גבר

באי אתה אוזר ישראל בגבורה

באי אתה עוטר ישרא בתפארה

באי אתה שעשית לי כל צרכי

באי אתה שעשיתני אשה ולא איש

באי אתה שלא עשיתני אמה ושפחה

באי אתה שלא עשיתני נכרית

באי אתה הנותן לשכוי בינה להבחין

בין היום ובין הלילה

באי אתה אקבו על דברי תורה

והערב נא יי אלהינו את דברי תורתך בפינו

ובפיפיות עמך בית ישראל ונהיה

אנחנו וצאצאינו וצאצאי עמך בית ישראל יודעי שמך

ולומדי תורתך באי המלמד תורה לעמו ישראל

באי אתה אשר בחר בנו מכל העמים ונתן

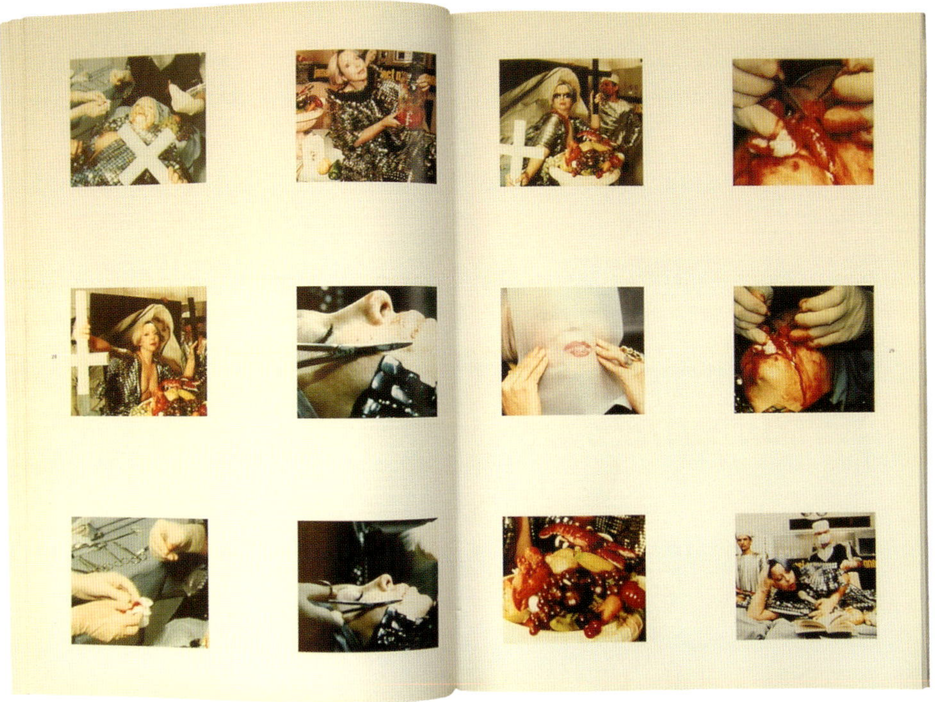

One of the abiding divisions between the sacred and the profane is often seen reflected in the difference between male and female, and it doesn't take a long look at Western religious history to realise how dominant men have been: men have had access to the sacred – books, rituals, beings – in ways that women have not. Nonetheless, to say, for example, that Christianity is wholly patriarchal is like saying Christians don't use images. Some do, some don't, some are, some aren't. The stories and images tell a more complex relation.

In medieval religious practices, as books became mass-produced (yet still handwritten) and therefore accessible to more and more people outside the monasteries and royal courts, women often accessed the sacred through privately-owned books. While the power over the public sacred was still out of the reach of women, book production made possible a private connection with God, even if it was still limited to upper class women. In Christianity, this was particularly done through the Book of Hours, the medieval 'bestseller'. These were small, portable books for the most part, containing biblical passages, calendars, written prayers, and not a few beautiful illustrations that were ostensibly used for private devotional use. There are examples in which the female owners had many of the prayers written with feminine pronouns (not for the name of God, but for the supplicants), and also had their own names written into the texts, and many of the prayers were feminised. Similarly, in Judaism, the so-called Woman's Siddur from fifteenth century Italy, retells traditional Jewish prayers and customs, and one of the morning blessings is a thanksgiving to God for "making me a woman and not a man".[17] On the other hand, the Woman's Siddur shows the continued conflict between male and female in relation to the sacred, since the text has been heavily censored, and images of women from one of the pages have been scratched out.

ABOVE: *Orlan, This is my body... This is my software,* pages 28 and 29, Black Dog Publishing, 1996

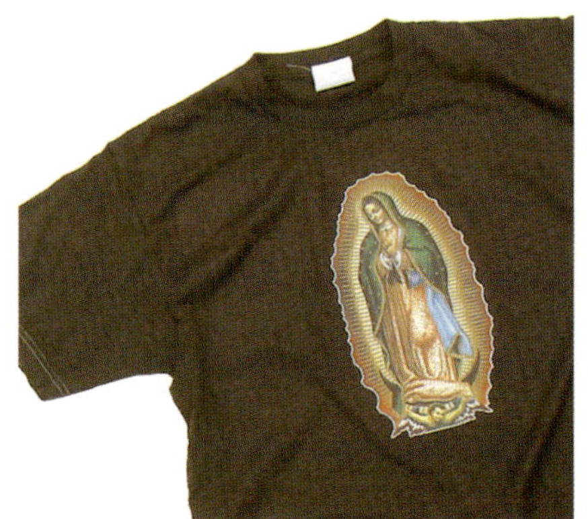

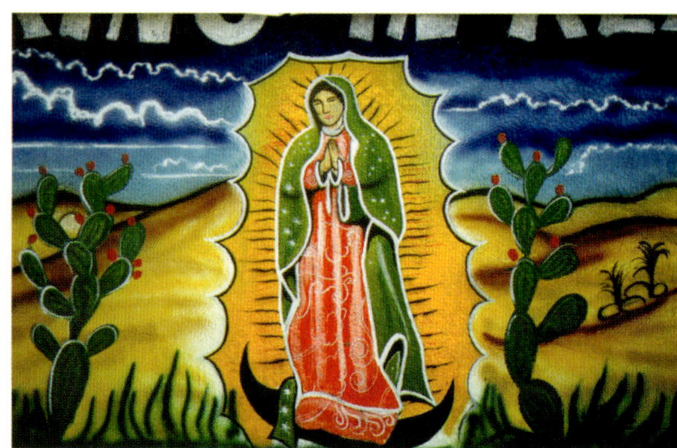

In the modern age, female artists have turned again and again to traditional religious images, revamping them in order to tell their own story. Particularly important is the figure of the Virgin of Guadalupe, who has been used as a symbol for conservativism, but also for liberation. She appears as a symbol of strength on everything from T-shirts to household shrines, lowrider cars to filmic portrayals. In 1978, the US Chicana artist Yolanda López created her *Portrait of the Artist as the Virgin of Guadalupe*, and in 1999, another Chicana artist, Alma López, created her own *Our Lady*, in which López herself stands in the place of Mary, in a sexy and defiant stance. Both Lópezs see in the figure of Mary a powerful feminine, spiritual force that could be tapped into by painting themselves into that imagery. In other representations, Rolando de la Rosa offered a deconstructive take on the Virgin of Guadalupe, by overlaying her face and breasts with those of Marilyn Monroe, and later Manuel Ahumada would do something similar with a Monroe/Virgin collage. All of these works received vehement accusations of sacrilege and blasphemy, perhaps because the artists were tinkering with the sacred symbol of the Virgin of Guadalupe. But probably also because they each dared to challenge the presumed ethnic, gendered, and sexualised divisions of contemporary US and Mexican societies. Indeed, Ahumada's Virgin was eventually destroyed by protesters who broke into a museum and tore it to pieces.

ABOVE: Contemporary commercial images of the Virgin of Guadalupe.

OPPOSITE: **Escamilla Isidro**, *Virgin of Guadalupe*, 1824, oil on canvas, Brooklyn Museum of Art, New York, USA/ Henry L Batterman Fund/The Bridgeman Art Library

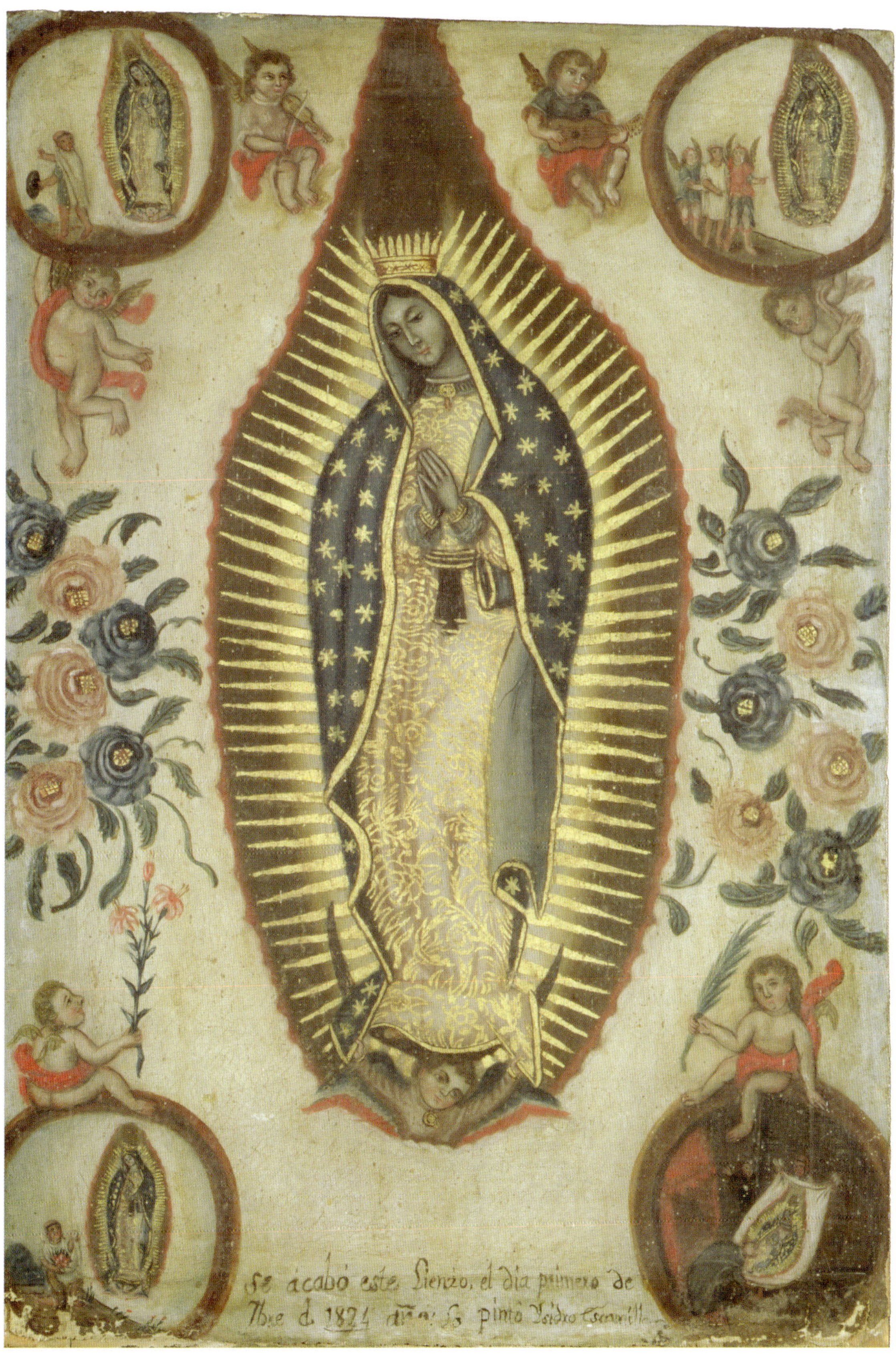
Se acabó este Lienzo, el dia primero de
7bre d. 1824 pintó

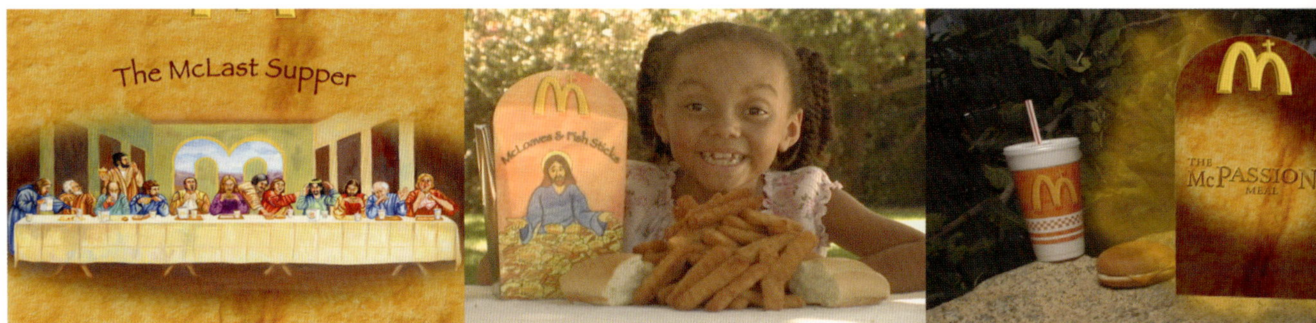

Finally, in another direction, artists have articulated points of resistance in their work by critiquing crass commercialism, showing the ubiquity of advertising and its incessant profanations of religious tradition. Along these lines, one of the more clever recent critiques of consumerist religion is the short film *The McPassion* by Rik Swartzwelder and Benjamin Hershleder. Increasingly sceptical about the commercialisation of religion, and about product tie-ins for 'religious films' (the official website for Mel Gibson's *The Passion of the Christ* sells nails formed into a cross, a 'tear catcher' bottle, and 'official shirts'), they created a little film that hits the issue head-on. Like an extended advertisement for McDonald's, the film tells how kids can get their own McPassion Happy Meal (comes with stigmata stickers or a simulated leather cat-o-nine tails), the McLoaves and Fish Sticks meal, or the Gethsemene Garden Salad. Swartzwelder and Hershleder made the film available for public access during the Lenten season in 2006, and viewers from all over took a look and most had a lot of laughs. Nonetheless, a number of people saw it as sacrilegious or blasphemous, while failing to see the critical commentary. As with Monty Python's *Life of Brian*, the artists' intentions were not about making fun of sacred figures, but of satirising the most base, profane human impulses.

Rik Swartzwelder and Benjamin Hershleder, *The McPassion*, stills, courtesy of the author

Profane materials of oil and canvas, marble and chisels, cameras and photographic paper, can yet produce sacred symbols full of power.

The borders of blasphemy are moveable, changing from religion to religion, culture to culture, specific situation to specific situation. This allows for people involved in power struggles to recast the lines between the sacred and the profane, and level charges of blasphemy against their foes. It also allows points of resistance against established authorities. Harking back to the George Bernard Shaw quote that opened the previous chapter, established truths often begin as "jokes and fancies, then as blasphemies and treason, then as questions open to discussion". But until someone stands up and cracks the joke, exclaims the treason, paints the blasphemous image, the discussion will not open. Through socio-religious history, various people have challenged the given structure, and thereby put themselves in further jeopardy by rethinking the lines between the sacred and the profane. These lines are established due to religious traditions trying to separate themselves from the other, and they are often bound up with perceived differential relations between races and genders.

Profane materials of oil and canvas, marble and chisels, cameras and photographic paper, can yet produce sacred symbols full of power. Because there are shifting borders between the sacred and the profane, and because there are images – both figural and non-figural – that harbour sacred power that enrich the lives of many people, there are a number of proscriptions for what can be imaged, where they can be displayed, and how to view them. These proscriptions are upheld through authority structures (and, concomitantly, authority structures are upheld by these very proscriptions), who must, from time to time, demonstrate their might and sacrifice an image or two. Thus, to understand blasphemy and the weight of religious authority it triggers, it is also necessary to understand the iconoclastic impulses that confront seemingly blasphemous images. Religious authority very often solidifies in the hands and words of an elite few, but these very power relations can then be challenged by those with less power in an ongoing battle of images.

Oleg Kulik, *Bus Stop,* (fragment), 2005, mixed media, 375 x 145 x 285 cm, courtesy of Marat Guelman Gallery

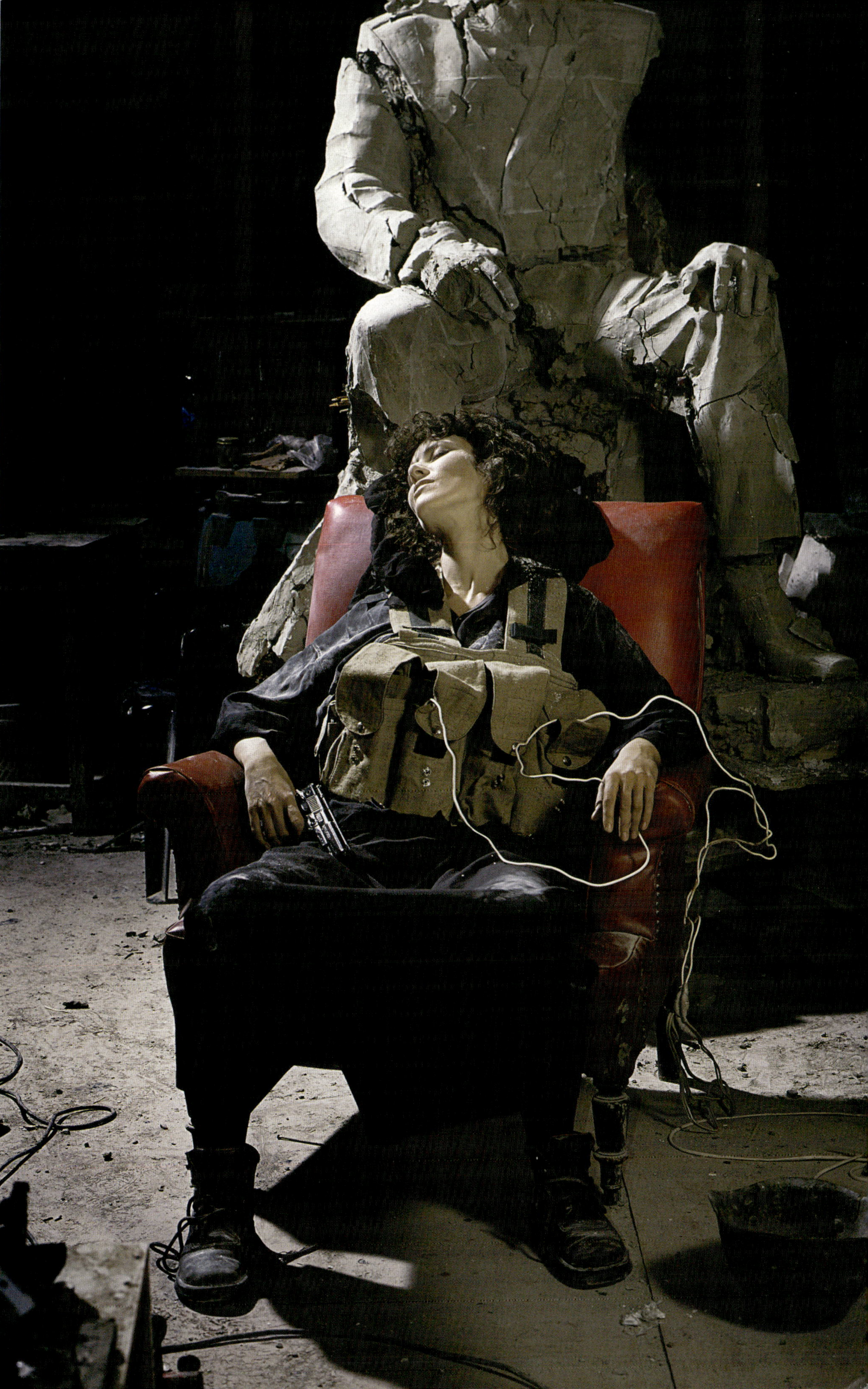

BLASPHEMING THE GODS OF MODERNITY

Chapter Three

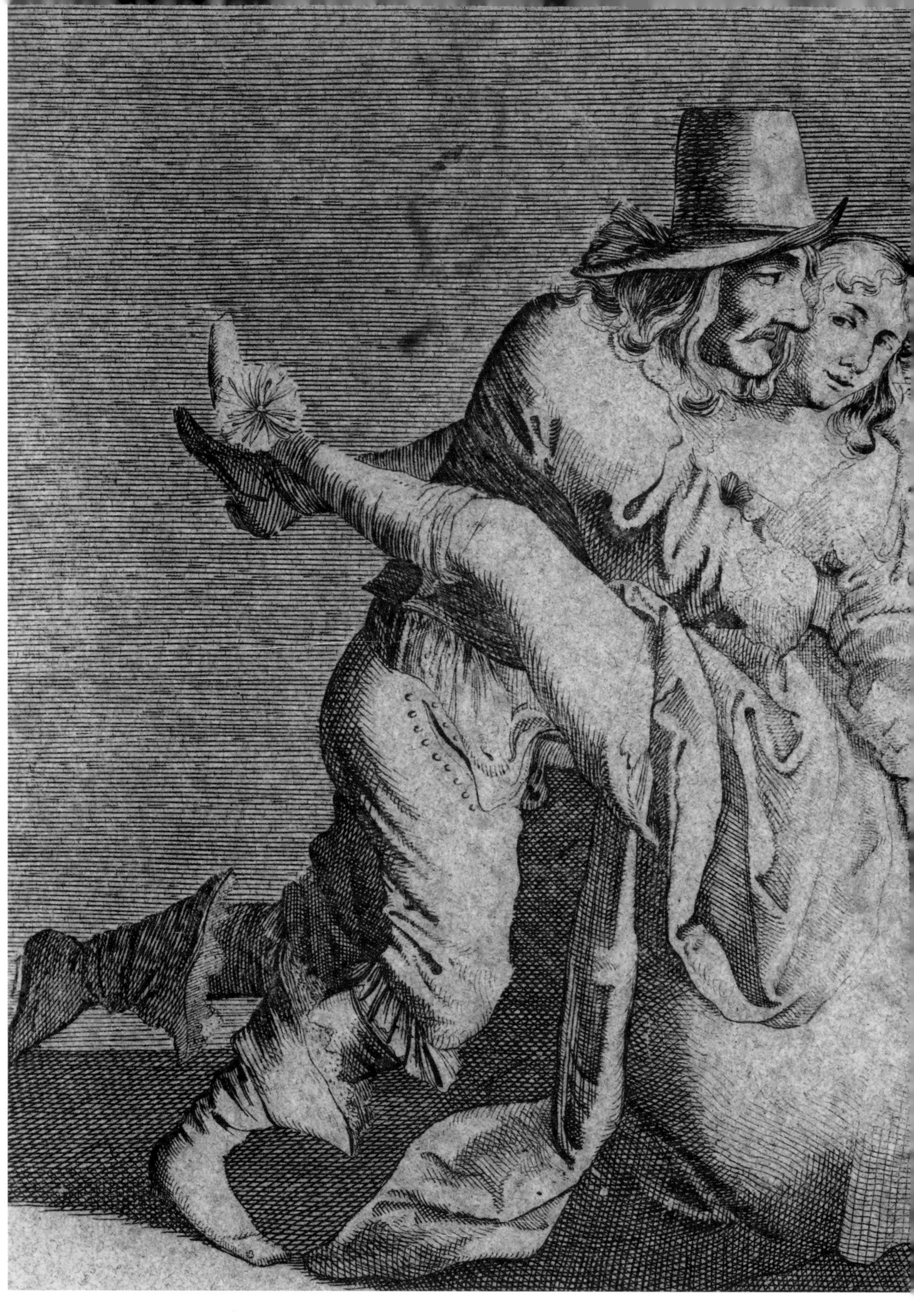

Johannes Torrentius, *Erotic Scene*, seventeenth century, ink and paper, 19 x 14 cm, courtesy of the Rjksmuseum, Amsterdam
One of the few surviving pornographic images by Torrentius.

BLASPHEMING THE GODS OF MODERNITY

Chapter Three

> I think that there is an interesting subject of investigation, for the student of traditions, in the history of Blasphemy, and the anomalous position of that term in the modern world. It is a curious survival in a society which has for the most part ceased to be capable of exercising that activity or of recognizing it.
>
> TS ELIOT, *After Strange Gods*

In 1627, Dutch religious and political authorities physically tortured the painter Johannes Torrentius for creating blasphemous images – mostly pornographic renderings of mythological subjects. They then condemned him to 20 years' imprisonment and publicly burned many of his paintings. In 1989, US Senator Jesse Helms decried Andres Serrano's *Piss Christ* – a photograph of a crucifix submerged in urine – calling it "blasphemy and insensitivity toward the religious community". In a reversal of Torrentius' artistic fate, Helms' accusations, backed up by Senator Alphonse D'Amato's tearing up a copy of Serrano's picture, helped raise Serrano's status as a photographer, prompting both international visibility and an increase in sales of his work. Meanwhile, the Senators' accusations also helped reduce NEA funding to artists. These two historical incidents – and the centuries, differences, and similarities between them – point towards several of the issues raised in this concluding chapter concerning blasphemy in the modern age. Charges of, and punishment for, blasphemy over the centuries have changed; religious and political authorities are often intertwined and confused; despite all the advances of secularism in modern society, artworks are still condemned as blasphemous; and, finally, we run into a confrontation between blasphemy and one of modernity's most sacred values: freedom of expression.

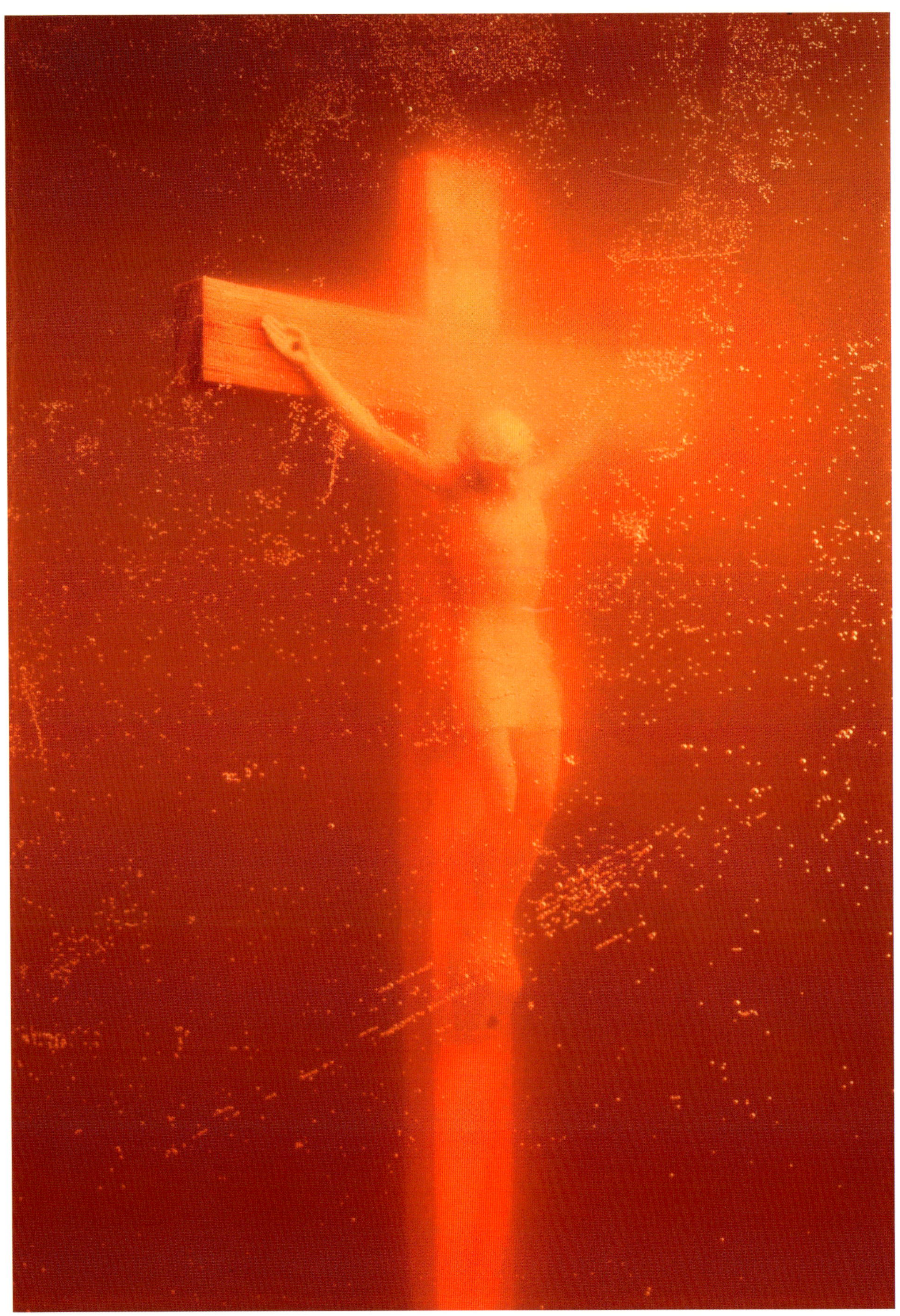

Speaking in the 1930s, Modernist poet and essayist TS Eliot bemoaned a society with nothing left to blaspheme against (i.e. nothing more held sacred): "I am reproaching a world in which blasphemy is impossible."[1] Clearly, he was looking in the wrong direction. We have seen plenty of examples in which blasphemy has continued to be an issue among religious revivalists seeking to purge society from its evil images and 'return' to a purified olden time. Yet, there is another way in which Eliot was looking in the wrong direction: blasphemy has also moved from the realm of traditional religion into modern, secular society and the targets of blasphemy have been redirected.

Around the same time Torrentius was having his works of art burned in Holland, the English philosopher Francis Bacon was championing the empirical sciences. Bacon put great value in education, coining the aphorism 'knowledge is power', and was instrumental in ushering in a modern, scientific worldview, a mode of existence that became increasingly sceptical toward the older religious outlooks, including the power of representational images. Along with these newfound sacred values came a new potential for profanity, even claiming that the Roman statesman Cato was well punished for his *blasphemy against learning*.[2] And in the nineteenth century, the writer Philip G Hamerton continued the advocacy for an intellectual life, though he was writing after the Enlightenment, had seen the limits of rationality alone, and was hence influenced by a Romantic streak. He writes on the value of friendship and suggests that a purely intellectual relationship will not last long but needs a good dose of "feeling". If one wants solely intellectual relations, then one should "arrange a succession of friendships". He stops himself with this arrangement and surmises that "This doctrine sounds like *blasphemy against friendship*; but it is not intended to apply to the sacred friendship of the heart."[3] In the modern age, newer liberal values begin to complement the older religiously-based ones. The Rational and Romantic worldviews both hold up their own sense of the sacred, just as the postmodern age has continued with its fair share of sacred values, rituals, symbols, and myths.

Andres Serrano, *Piss Christ*, 1987, Cibachrome, silicone, plexiglass, wood frame, 152 x 101 cm, courtesy of Paula Cooper Gallery, New York

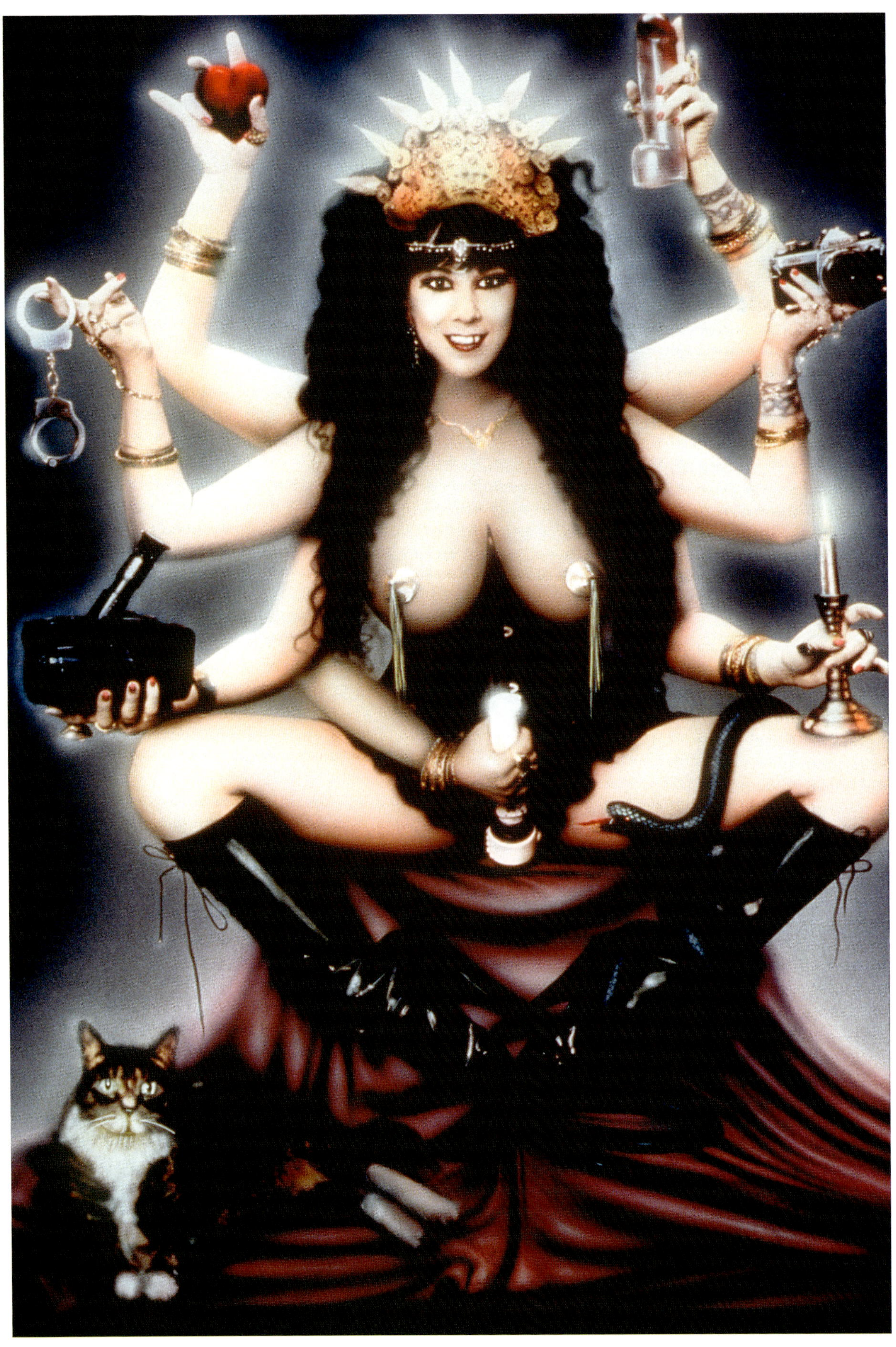

Blasphemy has moved from the realm of traditional religion into modern, secular society and the targets of blasphemy have been redirected.

As we continue to sift through the detritus left over from modernity, there remain at least two ways in which blasphemy continues to be a notable topic into the twenty-first century's postmodern challenges and promises (postmodernity here being understood as an extension of modernity, a condition that arises at the tail end of modernity's exhaustion, and not something wholly separable). The first stems from modernity's *current and future orientation*: it has believed in and is mainly founded upon *progress*. The term 'modern' itself stems from the Latin *modo*, meaning 'just now', and has taken on the connotation of being antithetical to that which is 'ancient' or has gone before.[4] The advances in technology, philosophy, and the arts that ushered in the modern age have made for a way of thinking and being that tends to denigrate the past. In the midst of this, conservative religious revival groups (fundamentalists and others) have reasserted claims to traditional lines between the sacred and the profane, even if that 'tradition' has had to be reinvented. The simple fact is that blasphemous images, and accusations thereof, have not disappeared in recent times. Thus, the first section below briefly discusses the use of blasphemy in the midst of debates between modernists and traditionalists around the role of science.

Annie Sprinkle, *Armed Goddess*, photography Amy Audrey, art direction Leslie Barany, courtesy of the artist
Porn star turned performance artist, Annie Sprinkle is renowned for her provocative exploration of the erotic. In *Armed Goddess*, Sprinkle references the Hindu goddess of destruction, Kali. Rather than traditional weapons such as scythes and knives, Sprinkle depicts herself holding Western icons of erotica.

The final sections of this chapter are then devoted to a second, more subtle way in which blasphemy continues to surface in the modern age. Modern liberal societies *redefine* rather than *banish* the sacred, in spite of their best wishes. Many of these redefinitions spring from the appearance of the nation-state and its ideological enforcer, nationalism, as a major factor in the social construction of the world. Monarchs may no longer hold power over people as they once did, as God's spokespeople on earth, but nationalism emerges in the modern age as its own religious system. As sociologist Josep Llobera suggests, "nationalism has become a religion – a secular religion where god is the nation."[5] The sacred status of the nation is bolstered by foundational myths (e.g. the 'founders of the country'), rituals (annual national holidays, World Cup football), symbols (most importantly for this chapter: flags), and by its own sets of proper, ethical behaviour (usually composed as variations on 'human rights'). The sections below will look at the ways Socialist Realist artwork in the Soviet Union contributed to a national ideology, as well as the dissident work of other artists challenging these ideological creations. Then, turning to the United States, we will look towards the national symbolic significance of the flag and the debates surrounding its display. In parallel with the Soviet dissident artists, a number of US artists have challenged the religious aura that enfolds the flag today. Finally, I conclude with some comments on the ways in which freedom of expression is held up as a sacred value in modern Western societies and how this comes into conflict with blasphemy.

Michael Browne, *Eric Cantona as Jesus Christ and the Manchester United Football Team*, 1997, courtesy of Rex Features
This 305 x 244 cm oil painting shows French footballer, Eric Cantona, as Jesus Christ emerging from the tomb. It was inspired by a fifteenth century painting, *The Resurrection* by Piero della Francesca. The work explores the concept of modern day heroes, and celebrity as religion, and had a mixed reception from members of the British clergy, with some embracing it as a humorous venture, while others took great offence.

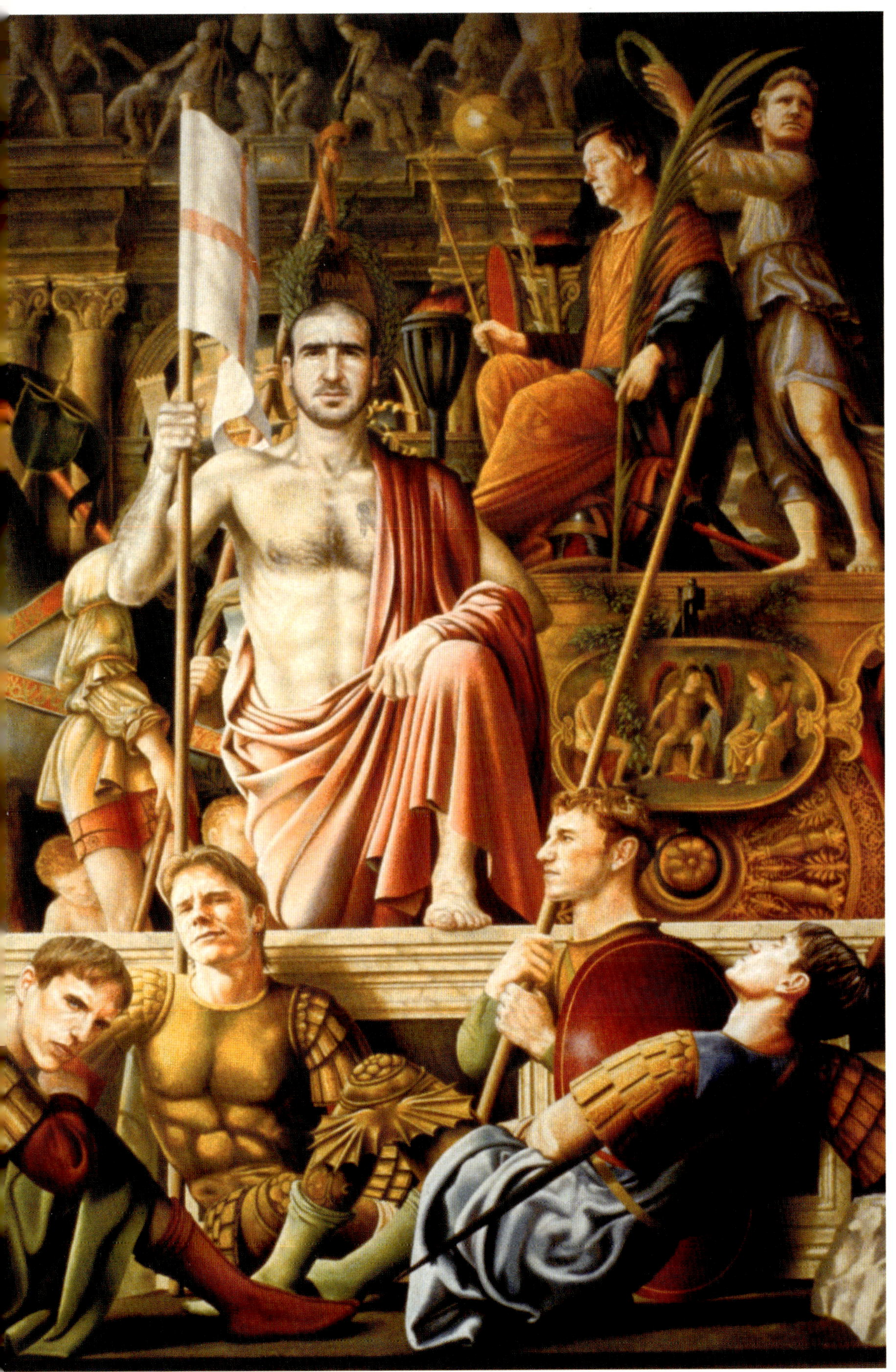

Modernity's Repression

Modernity can roughly be understood as a post-medieval social movement that reached its full expression in the mid-nineteenth century. It is, by and large, a European invention that has been exported to a number of other regions – most prominently, North America – and the term 'developing nation' is synonymous with that of 'modernising nation'. Modernity came about through several interlocking social, political, technological, and philosophical developments, including the Enlightenment and the triumph of scientific worldviews, the Industrial Revolution, and the European colonisation of much of the world. With so many natural and intellectual resources at the fingertips of the colonial powers, with so many new wonders of the world being produced by human sovereignty, it became difficult to remain attached to a past in which God seemed to ordain governmental structures, decide who fell ill with the plague, or spoke to people in their dreams. Science can now answer to many of these.

Yet, modernity can only move toward the future by repressing the past, at least in part, and we all know what happens then: the repressed eventually returns. In this case, modernity's progressive orientation simultaneously unearthed its other: religious revival movements that sought their identity in a perceived past in which God still controlled the events of the world. Amongst a plethora of examples, we see this in the Jewish Orthodox response to the modernising tendencies of the nineteenth century Reform movement; in Christianity in the emergence of Evangelicalism and its more radical nineteenth century offshoot, fundamentalism; and in Islam with groups like the Wahhabi or Salafi that gained momentum at the same time as the Middle East was being reorganised by European colonisers. Each of these conservative, tradition-oriented groups grew out of specific modern environments in which the 'old ways' were under threat, in one way or other. As a result, these religious revivalists had to reinvent the past, to re-mythologise their origins and to claim that the advances of science, technology, and philosophy, not to mention liberal theology and consumer capitalism, were headed in the wrong direction.

Edvard Munch, *Madonna*, 1895–1902, lithograph, composition: 61 x 45 cm; sheet: 86 x 59 cm, The William B Jaffe and Evelyn AJ Hall Collection, © Munch Museum/Munch – Ellingsen Group, BONO, Oslo/DACS, London 2006

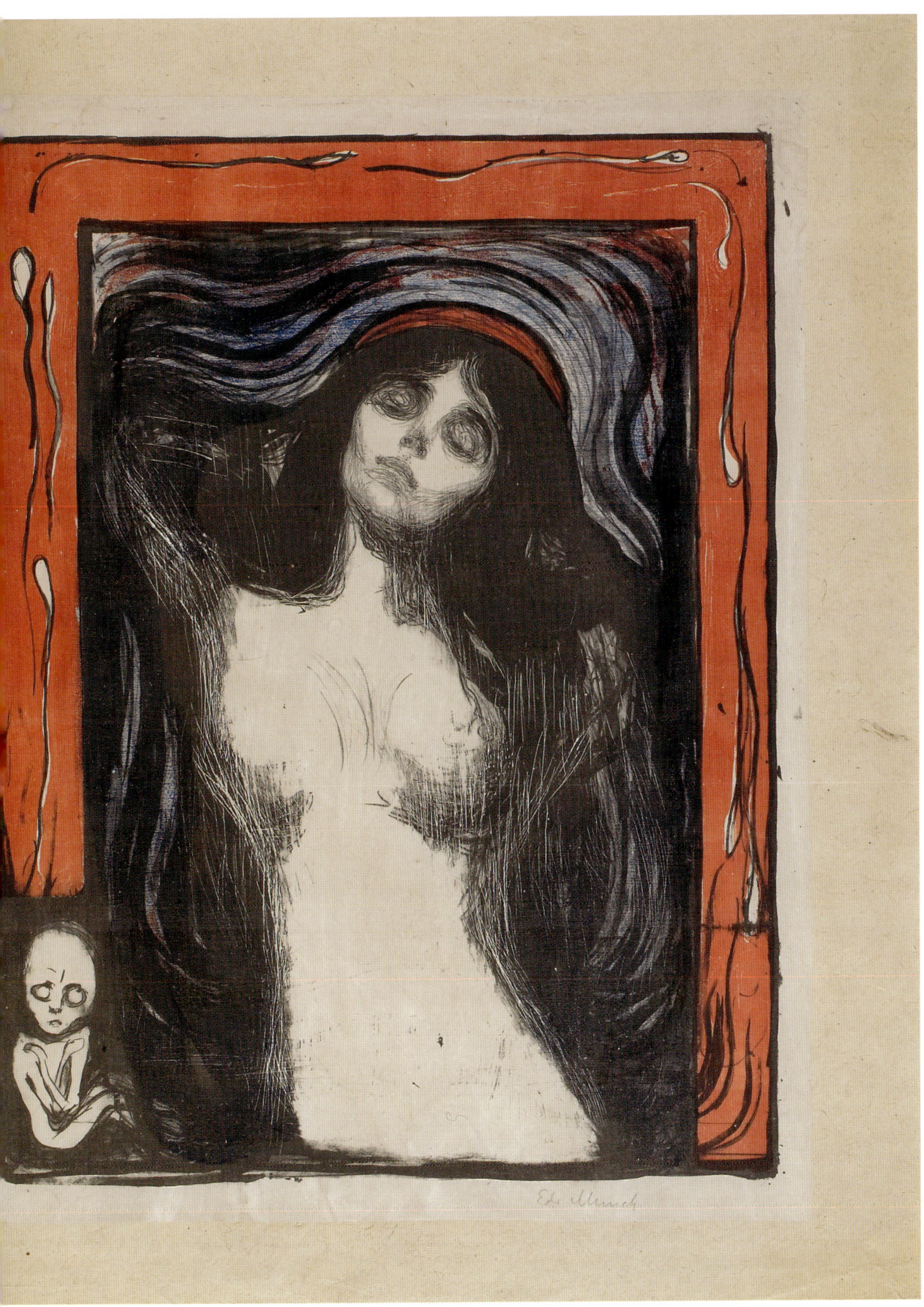

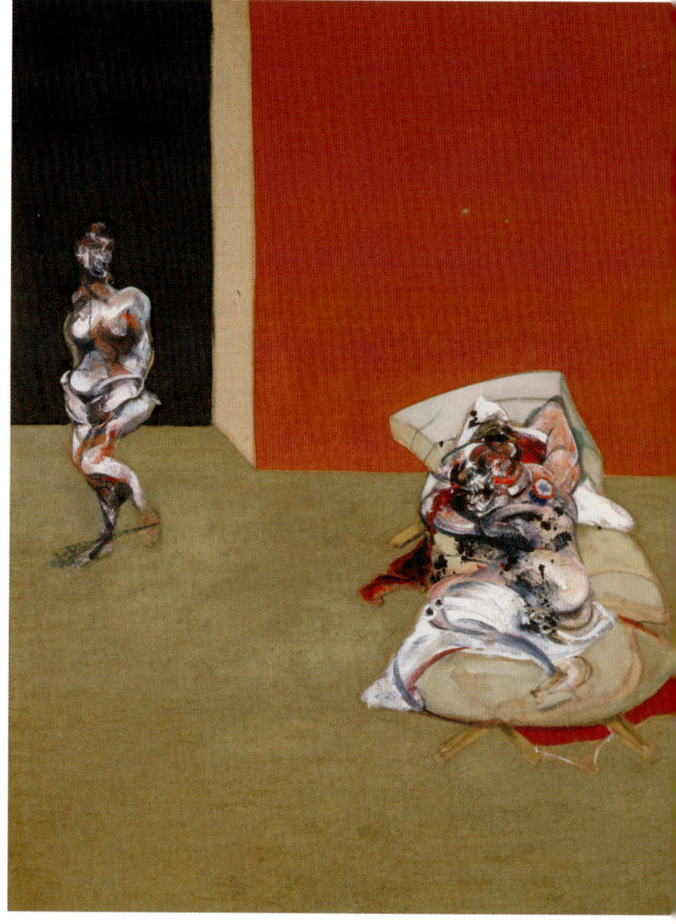

Francis Bacon, *Three Studies for a Crucifixion*, 1965, oil on canvas, each panel 197 x 147 cm, courtesy of Artothek, © Estate of Francis Bacon/DACS, London 2006

The crucifixion is one of Francis Bacon's recurring themes. In this later study, he takes a less emotional approach than in his previous depictions, with cooler colours and a clear, considered composition. On the right, a Michelangelo-esque nude wears a swastika armband, and on the left, a battered male wears a rosette on his bleeding chest. The central panel shows the crucifixion itself, with the form of Jesus looking more like the carcass of a cow than a human figure.

Modern liberal societies redefine rather than banish the sacred, in spite of their best wishes.

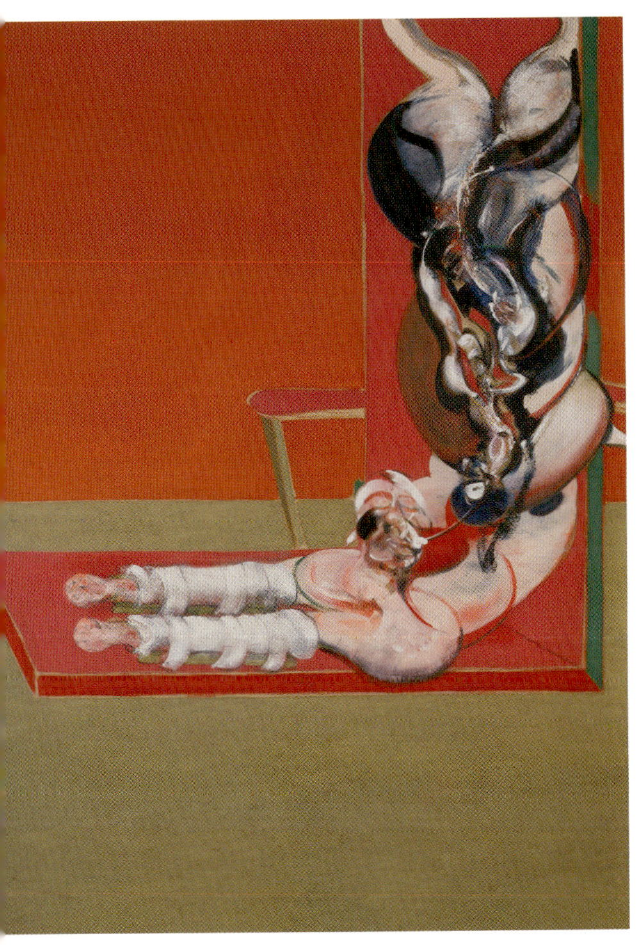

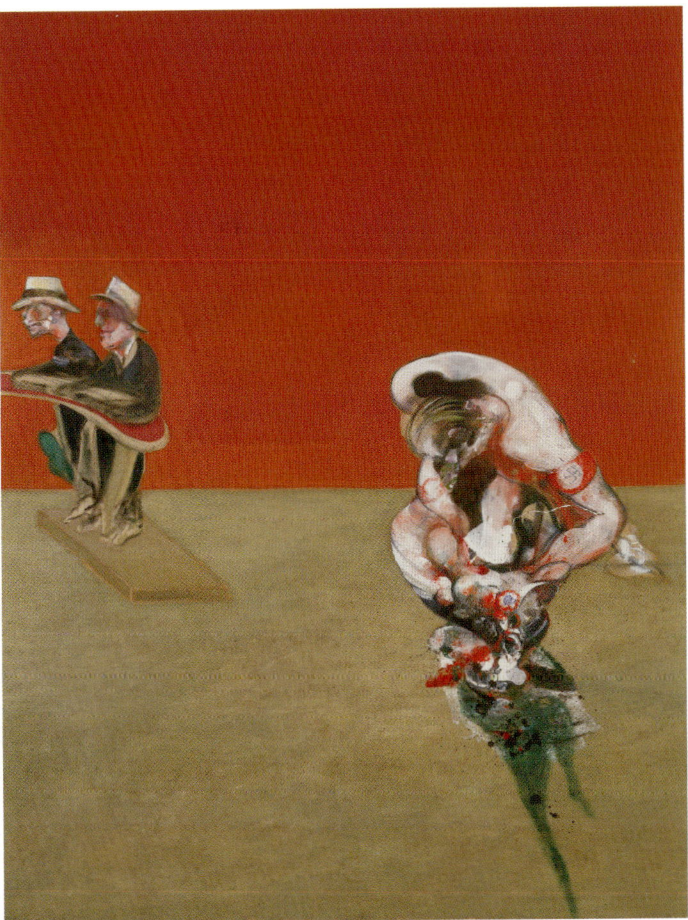

A number of art movements arose from the modern-traditional debate that erupted in Western societies in the nineteenth century, many of them seeming to advocate 'shock for shock's sake', or at least doing all they could to leave the past behind. The writer Anthony Julius renames Modern art as the "transgressive period", in which the making of transgressive art "itself contributed to the definition of the project of art-making."[6] Manet stands at the origins of the period, and in varying ways one can include Kandinsky and Malevich's early experiments in non-figural painting – which were deeply tied to a spiritual optimism based on progressive theosophical views of religion – to the Dadaists and Surrealists turning the perceived world upside-down, and back to the abstract figuration of the likes of Edvard Munch and later Francis Bacon. Certainly, with such figures in the background, blasphemy has become an easy thing to achieve in the contemporary art world, whether the artists intend to be blasphemous or not. And so Gilbert and George put on a show called *SonofaGod Pictures* with one image called *Was Jesus Heterosexual?* and displaying the text: "Jesus Says Forgive Yourself. God Loves Fucking! Enjoy!" The exhibition prompted Conservative Minister of Parliament Ann Widdecombe to label the pictures "blasphemous in the extreme". (Nonetheless, the artists did not consider their own work to be blasphemous and refused to have any images reproduced in this book.) Or, utilising the multimedia capabilities of the internet, the webmasters at www.christonthecrapper.com make it possible to send a 'blasphemy card' that encourages the sender to choose a caption of adolescent humour to accompany images appropriated from children's bibles and other devotional printed matter, and send them to friends.

While webmasters and artists like Gilbert and George find easy targets among institutional religion, other recent artworks have continued in a transgressive mode while simultaneously taking a more critical stance on the modern-traditional divide. Some of these works remain quite serious even when appearing tongue-in-cheek, or simply aim to shock. Most affirm a progressive view of the world in which the past is indeed left behind and we have nowhere to go but the future, though not at all costs.

Examples of 'blasphemy cards' from christonthecrapper.com. This website features religious images with irreverent captions, where one can create one's own bible stories, and play a hangman-style game featuring Jesus's crucifixion.

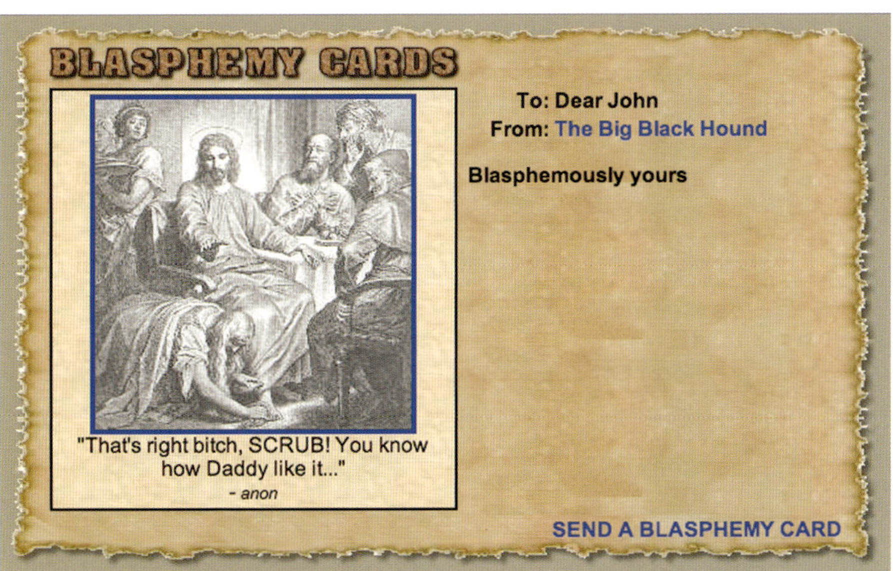
BLASPHEMY CARDS
"That's right bitch, SCRUB! You know how Daddy like it..."
- anon
To: Dear John
From: The Big Black Hound
Blasphemously yours
SEND A BLASPHEMY CARD

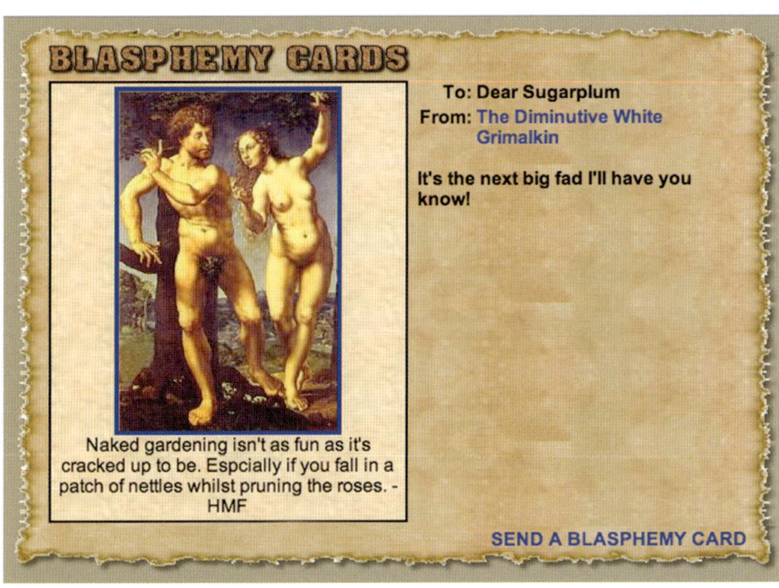
BLASPHEMY CARDS
Naked gardening isn't as fun as it's cracked up to be. Espcially if you fall in a patch of nettles whilst pruning the roses. - HMF
To: Dear Sugarplum
From: The Diminutive White Grimalkin
It's the next big fad I'll have you know!
SEND A BLASPHEMY CARD

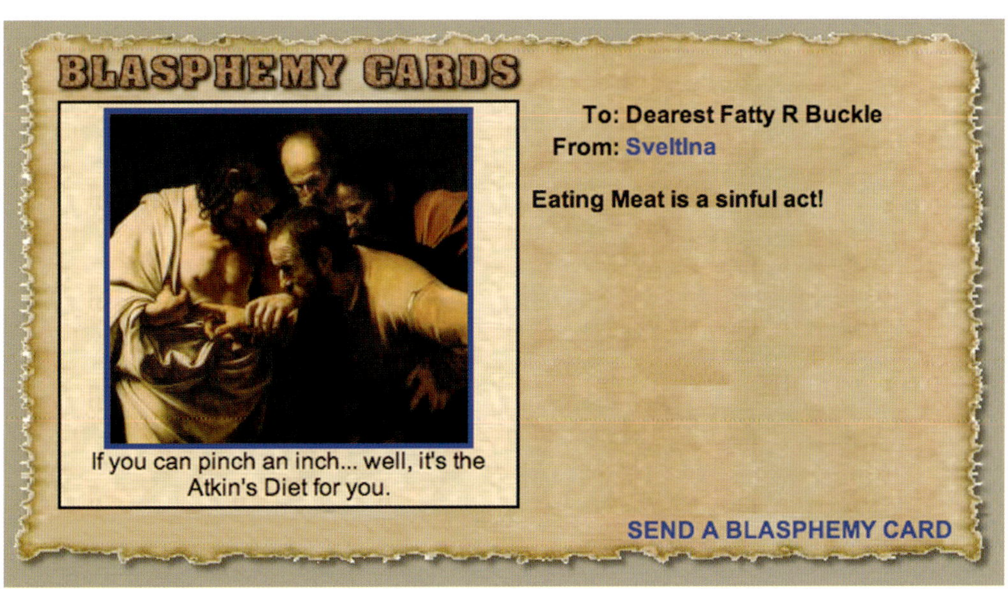
BLASPHEMY CARDS
If you can pinch an inch... well, it's the Atkin's Diet for you.
To: Dearest Fatty R Buckle
From: Sveltina
Eating Meat is a sinful act!
SEND A BLASPHEMY CARD

Many issues in the debates over modernity have been bolstered by a scientific view of the world, beginning with empirical philosophers like Bacon, John Locke, David Hume, and on into the writings of Charles Darwin. The debate between science and religion (from evolution versus 'intelligent design' to euthanasia and genetic engineering) continues to occupy a good deal of political and religious energy into the twenty-first century, and we find artists toying with this debate in their work. To take a couple of examples: contemporary British artists Damien Hirst and Dinos and Jake Chapman seem to work against traditional Western religious outlooks in their art and have often been deemed 'shock artists'. Yet, when exploring more closely their curiously repellent installations on the human/animal body in relation to death and genetic engineering, we find a deeper exploration of the convergence of the scientific and the religious. Of note are Hirst's works such as *The Physical Impossibility of Death in the Mind of Someone Living* (i.e., the 'shark in a tank' from 1991) and *Away from the Flock* (the 'sheep in a tank' from 1994; a piece vandalised when someone poured black ink into the tank). On one level, they are just dead animals in tanks of formaldehyde, but what vexes viewers is precisely a confrontation with death, something that modernity notoriously keeps out of sight. Hirst ultimately offers a meditation on death 'in the mind of someone living' in ways deeply congruent with the traditional contemplative Christian imagery of vanitas still life paintings, passion plays, and Crucifixion images. In a different vein, Dinos and Jake Chapman work uncomfortably within a scientific worldview and show the limits of modern science. The disturbing *Zygotic acceleration, biogenetic de-subliminated libidinal model (enlarged x 1000)*, and their apocalyptic sculpture *Hell*, could both be said to be incisive critiques of modernity: the first by pointing toward a horrific future of genetic engineering, the second by allegorising the end of modernity, the Holocaust.

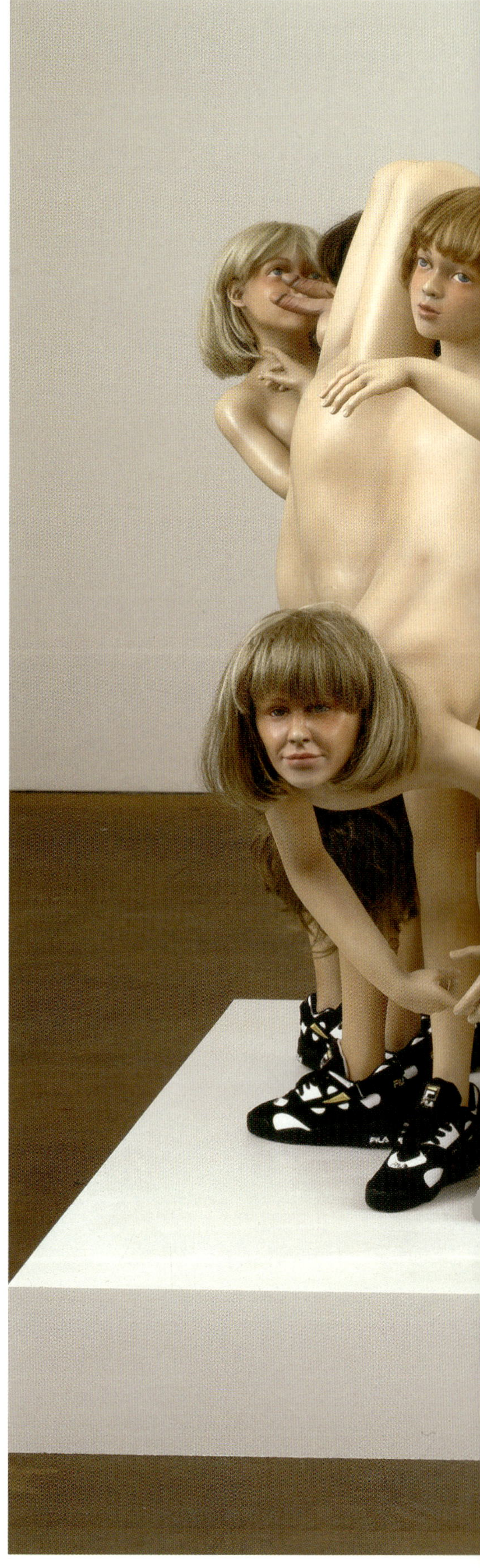

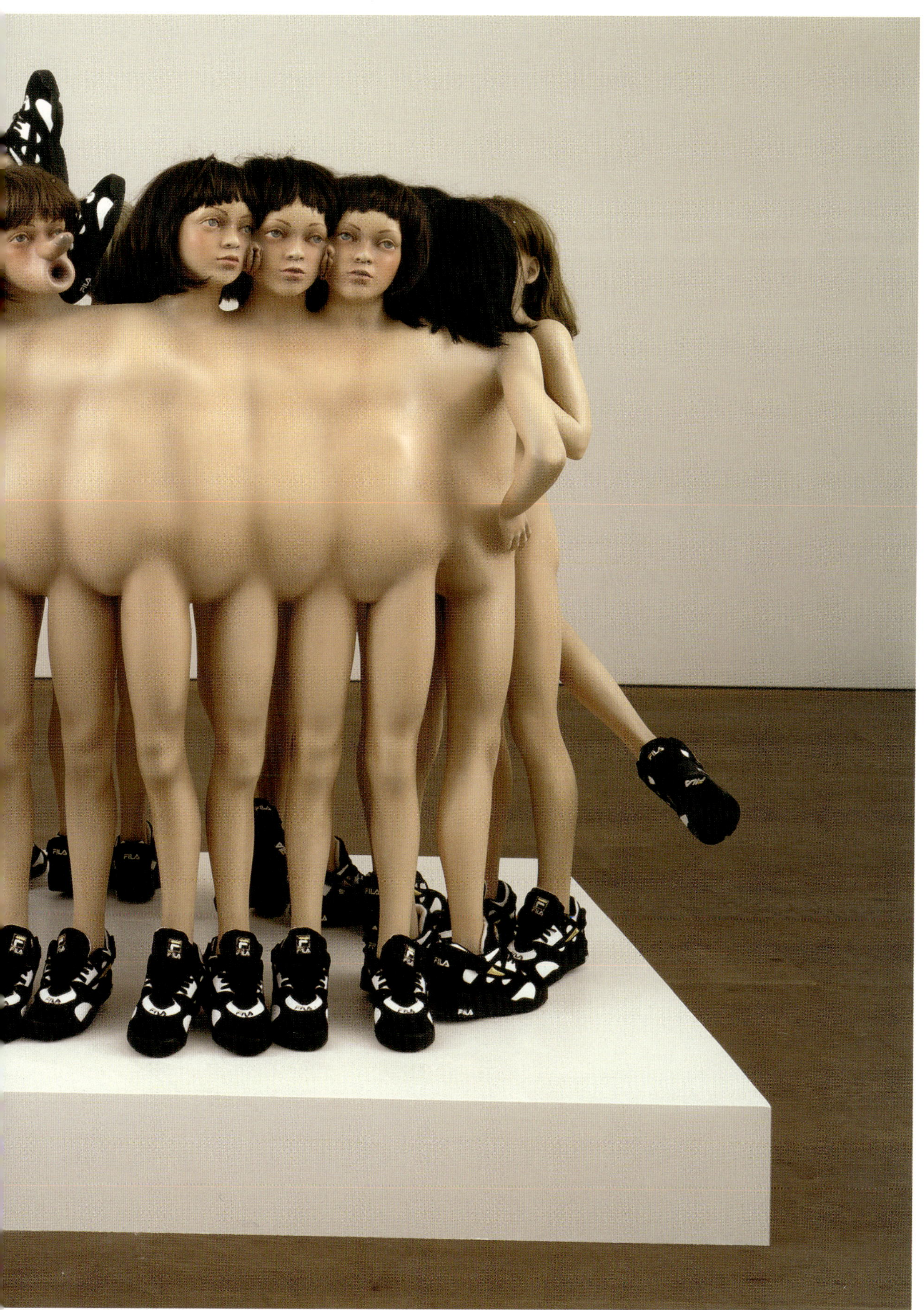
FILA

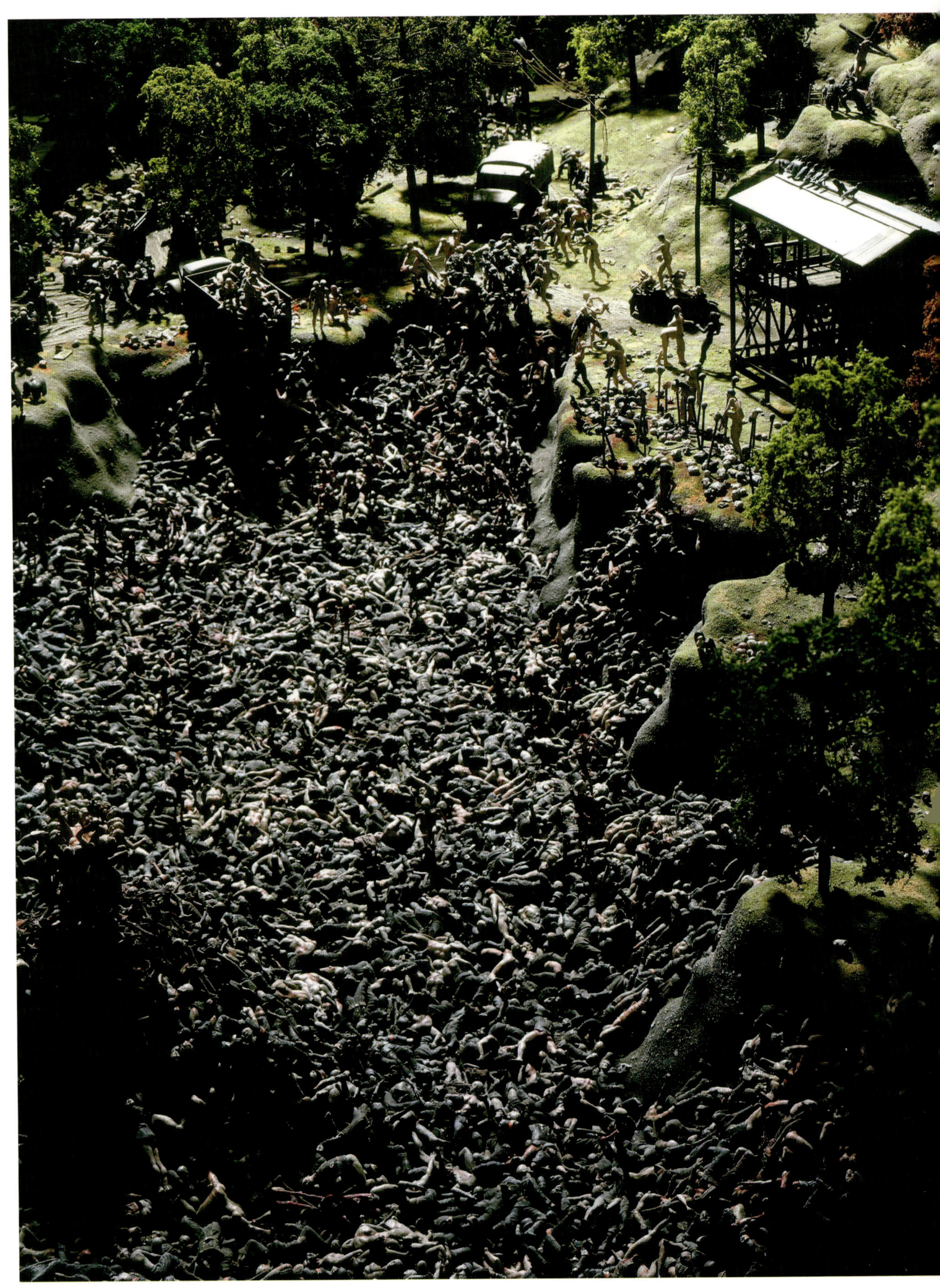

I note these works especially because they were created around the same time that Dolly the Scottish sheep was cloned in 1996, causing a great uproar. The enterprise of cloning was itself called the "ultimate blasphemy" by religious (especially conservative Christian) and other groups.[7] And an op-ed piece in Montreal's *Gazette* borrowed the language as it began by discussing an international treaty that outlawed human cloning, suggesting how "we may desperately want that ban to hold the line against what seems like a blasphemy against the spirit and the flesh."[8] Here again, blasphemy is about transgression, about stepping over a line that some believe is the province of God. In the rhetoric of 'intelligent design', scientific work can transgress the sacred in ways oddly parallel to the Islamic Hadith that forbids image *making* because this would be a challenge to God's sole creative activities. Biology then becomes a kind of graven image that mimics the natural world. While no Christian zealots, Hirst and the Chapman brothers offer a way back into the very design of the animal makeup itself, in an almost reverent *and* scientific way, even when portrayed in apocalyptic fashion. The final twist in this story is that Dolly died prematurely, in 2003, and her body was preserved and put on display in the National Museum of Scotland, looking very much like Hirst's *Away from the Flock*. The Dolly display is particularly targeted toward children who can learn about genetic engineering through interactive tools.

Throughout this book, we have already seen many examples of the ways in which contemporary conservative religious groups brandish the terms blasphemy and sacrilege, and lash out in iconoclastic ways. There is no space for a comprehensive overview here, but one final development in the twentieth century is worth mentioning: the rise of film and television have offered image-makers brand new ways of challenging the accepted social and religious norms, and new ways for people to claim to be offended. The development of new media is never simply about putting the old content into a new format; rather, the media itself can be the message, as Marshall McLuhan suggested, stirring up new passions and leading to newer levels of offence. A short list of films that have provoked the ire of religious conservatives include the already mentioned *Submission* by Van Gogh, *The Miracle* by Rossellini, and *Monty Python's Life of Brian*. There is a much longer list that includes Jean-Luc Godard's *Hail Mary*, Martin Scorsese's *Last Temptation of Christ*, Pier Paolo Pasolini's *Gospel According to Saint Matthew*, Kevin Smith's *Dogma*, and, more recently, *The Da Vinci Code* (which has even been banned in Islamic countries since Muslims have a high regard for Jesus Christ). Each of these prompted conservative religious groups to rise up and condemn the seeming profanations on screen.

PREVIOUS PAGE: **Dinos and Jake Chapman**, *Zygotic acceleration, Biogenetic de-sublimated libidinal model (enlarged x 1000)*, 1995, mixed media, 150 x 180 x 140 cm © the artists, courtesy of Jay Jopling/White Cube, London

OPPOSITE: **Dinos and Jake Chapman**, *Hell*, 1999–2000,Glass-fibre, plastic and mixed media (nine parts), © the artists, courtesy of Jay Jopling/White Cube, London

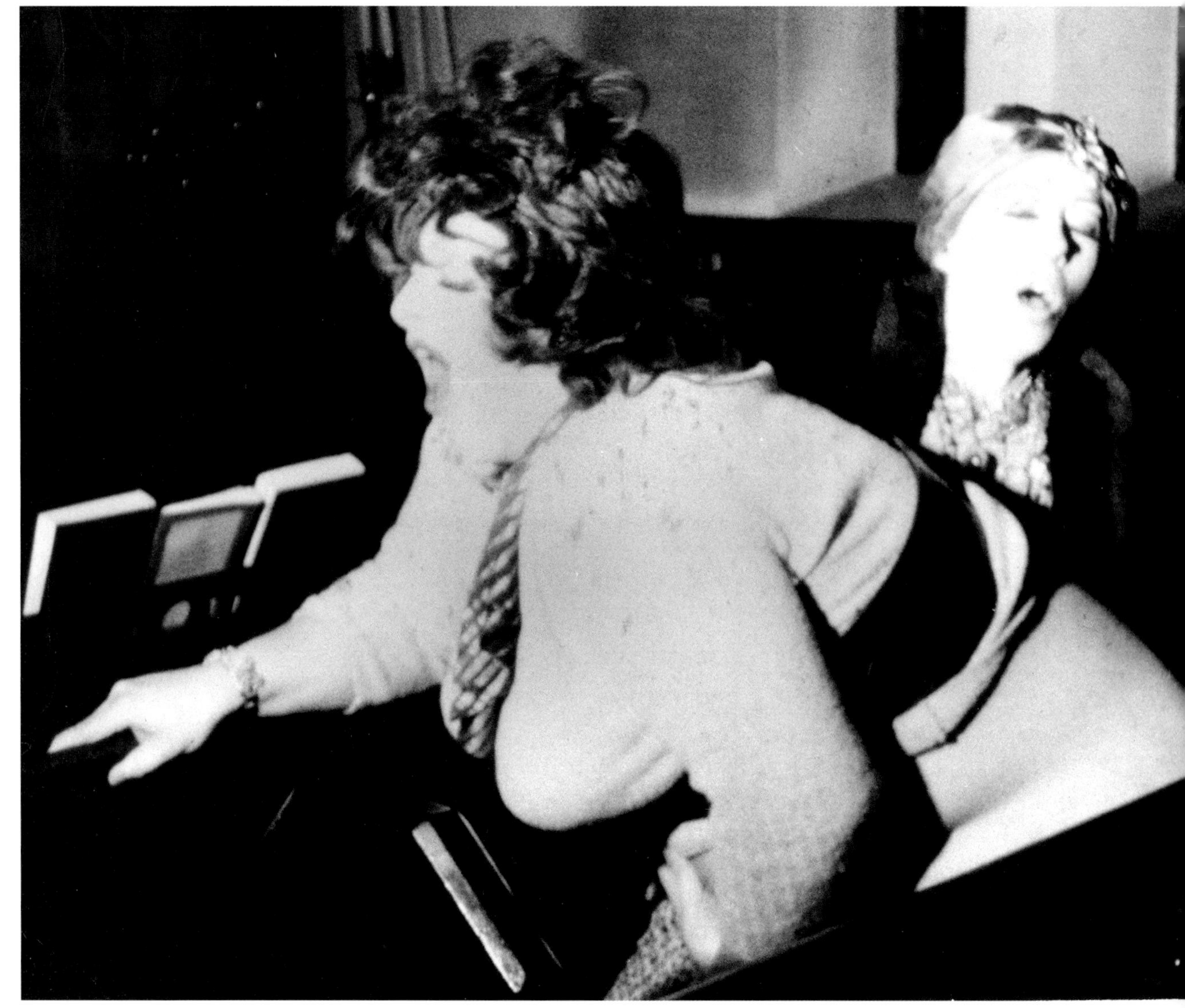

ABOVE: **John Waters**, *Multiple Maniacs*, 1970, film still of the 'Rosary Job' scene, photography Lawrence Irvine, © Dreamland Productions, courtesy of the director

OPPOSITE: **John Waters**, *15th Station*, 1996, six black and white prints, each image: 13 x 18 cm, framed: 94 x 36 cm, edition of eight, courtesy of the artist

This photographic print in filmstrip form draws attention to the sadistic voyeurism with which we view the crucifixion. By assuming to capture this moment on film, Waters depicts Jesus as wholly mortal, the close-up on his face bringing an aspect of vanity to the deity.

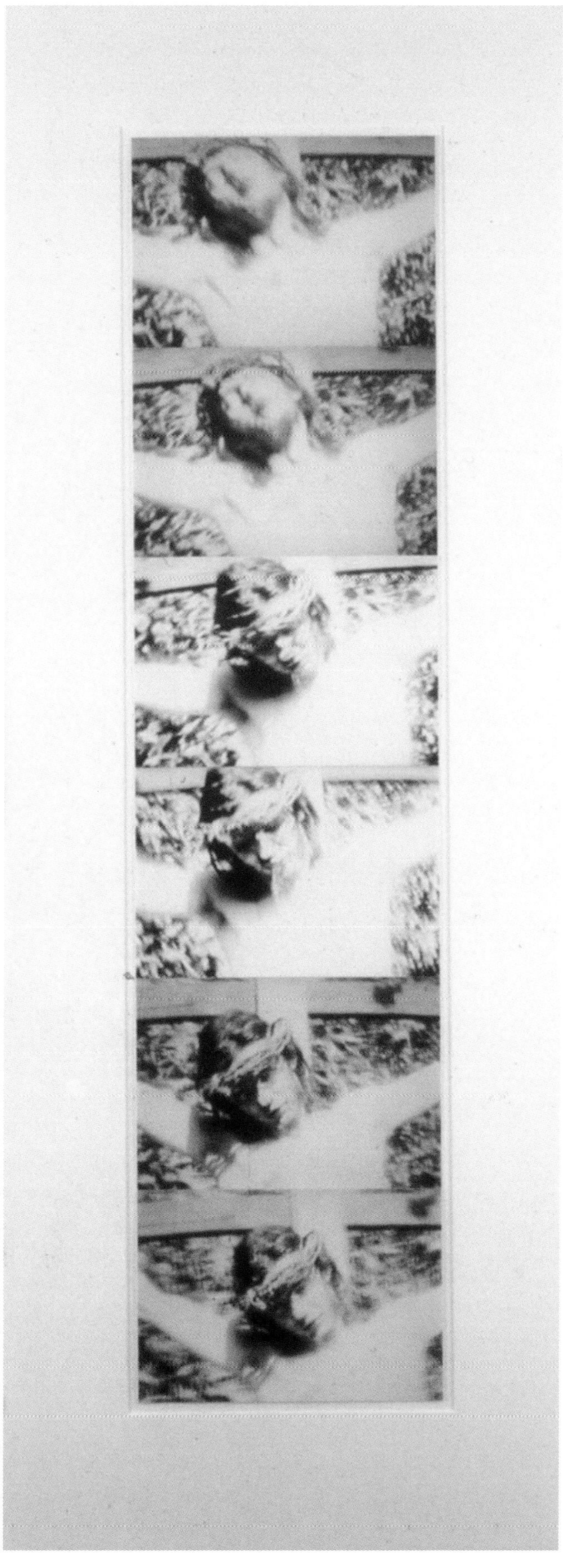

Like its precursors, caricature and cartoons, animation is also a shrewd medium that offers a kind of distance through its drawn or digitised images. Through that distance, animation can actually play with the sacred-profane division head-on. Speaking of caricature, and implying how the Danish cartoons of Muhammad were quite poor, comic artist Art Spiegelman suggests that "Caricature is by definition a charged or loaded image; its wit lies in the visual concision of using a few deft strokes to make its point."[9] (The problem with the Danish cartoons from a technical stance is that most of them had *no* point.) A little abstract distance, and the lines between the sacred and profane can become blurry. Sacrilegious cartoons are not the ire strictly of Islamists either, as many animated television comedies display. Today, shows like *South Park*, *The Simpsons*, and the puppetry of *Spitting Image* have all offered hilarious strikes on religious traditions in recent years, prompting plenty of outrage from religious leaders. This will, no doubt, continue.

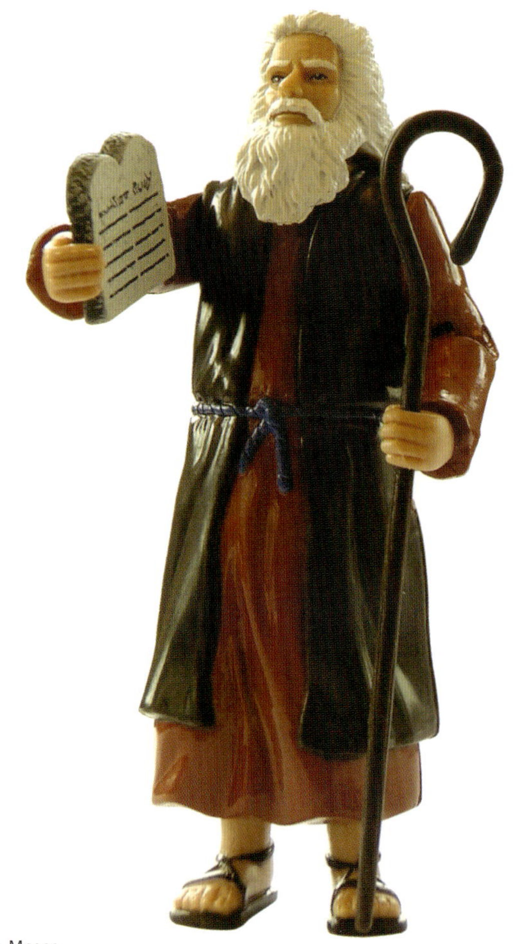

Name: Moses
Age: Lived to be 120 years old in the thirteenth and early twelfth century BC
Occupation: Shepherd/Liberator/Prophet/Lawgiver/Historian
Accomplishments: Lead the Hebrews out of Egyptian captivity, delivered the Ten Commandments
Weapon: Shepherd's Staff/Rod of God
Weapon's Special Powers: Brought ten devastating plagues upon Egypt, parted the Red Sea to allow safe passage for the escaping Hebrews, produced water from a stone to save the Hebrews from dying of thirst in the desert
Courageous Acts: Confronted the Pharaoh with God's demand, argued with God
Fascinating Facts: Is the only person in the Bible to speak face to face with God, revealed God's name (Yahweh) to the Hebrews, had a severe speech impediment, was allowed to see but not enter the Promised Land

Action figures, Top Trumps cards, and cartoons are just some of the formats in which religious figures appear nowadays – a novel way of educating children or merely a blasphemous way of trivialising religion in modern secular society?

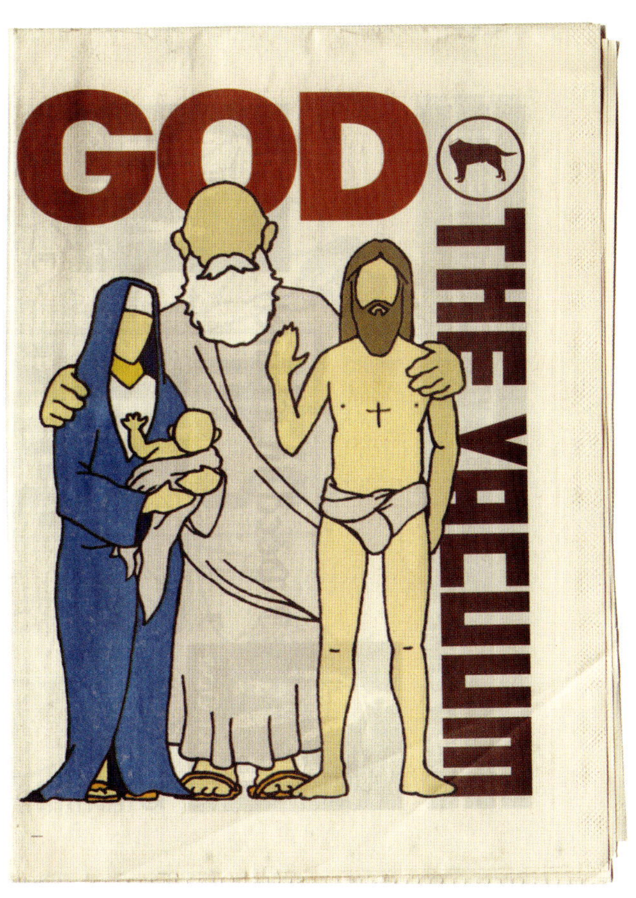

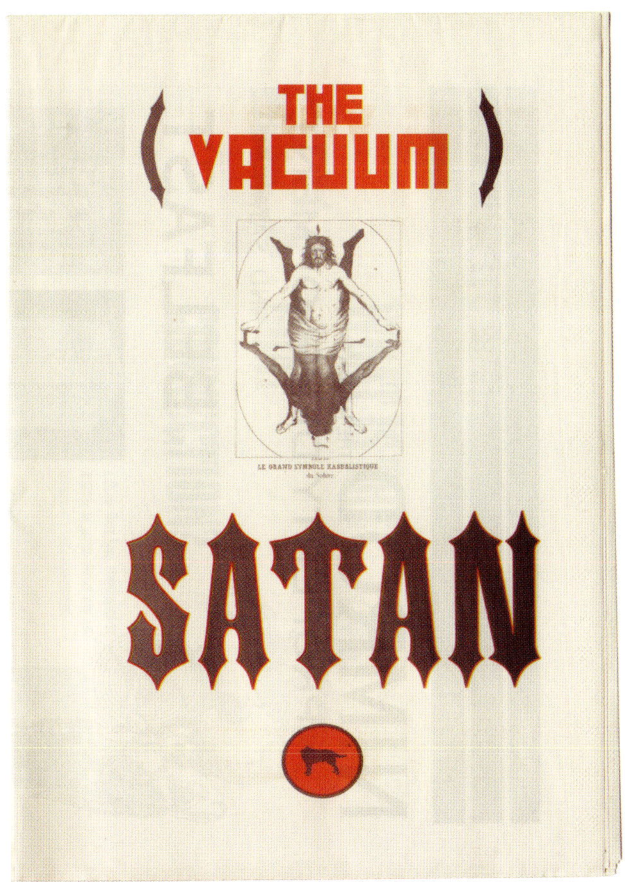

The Vacuum, *'God' and 'Satan'* editions, courtesy of the editors

The Vacuum is a free monthly paper published in Belfast. Each issue is themed and contains critical commentary about broad cultural issues. In June 2004, the publishers, Factotum, produced two issues entitled *God* and *Satan*, and distributed them in bars, cafes and libraries. Belfast Council took offence, and threatened to withdraw funding unless Factotum apologised. This led to a carefully orchestrated (and very tongue-in-cheek) 'sorry day', in which posters and events declared that Factotum were deeply apologetic for any offence caused.

Blasphemous Images and Nationalism

On US Independence Day, 2006, the World Overcomers Outreach Ministries Church in Memphis, Tennessee unveiled the *Statue of Liberation Through Christ*, a rendition of the Statue of Liberty except the hand-held torch was replaced by a cross, and a pair of tablets (conjuring images of the Ten Commandments) are cradled in her other arm (the 'tablets' simply bear the inscription 'The Law of Liberty, James 1.25'). The 72 foot (22 metre) statue was the inspiration of the African-American mega-church's pastor, Apostle Alton R Williams, who wrote an accompanying pamphlet, "The Meaning of the Statue of Liberation Through Christ: Reconnecting Patriotism With Christianity". Mr Williams was concerned about a number of current problems in the United States, such as legalised abortion, a lack of prayer in schools, as well as manifestations of New Age, Wicca, secularism and humanism. The statue was to serve as a symbolic reminder of the links between US nationalism and Christianity. Hundreds of people turned out for the unveiling (the church boasts a membership of 12,000) though many others living and working nearby were not so inspired and described the merging of Christianity and the Statue of Liberty in such a way as "ridiculous".[10]

While contemporary US culture may be experiencing some odd manifestations of it, the fact is: nations and religions have never been far apart. The corollary is that to blaspheme against one is also often to blaspheme against the other. At the point in the narrative of the Hebrew scriptures when the Ten Commandments are unveiled, we read the injunction, "You must not revile God, nor curse a chief of your own people" (Exodus 22.27), and the Psalms suggest "Blessed is the nation whose God is the Lord" (33.12). Much later, speaking of blasphemy law in 1676, England's Lord Chief Justice Hale declared, "Christianity is parcel of the laws of England... therefore to reproach the Christian religion is to speak in subversion of the law."[11] Religiously oriented blasphemy is wrong because it harms secular social stability.

The founders of the United States tried to keep its governance separate from religious moorings. Built into its Constitution is the clause, "Congress shall make no law respecting an establishment of religion, or prohibiting the free exercise thereof ..." a phrase from the First Amendment that is usually interpreted as 'separation of church and state' (though that

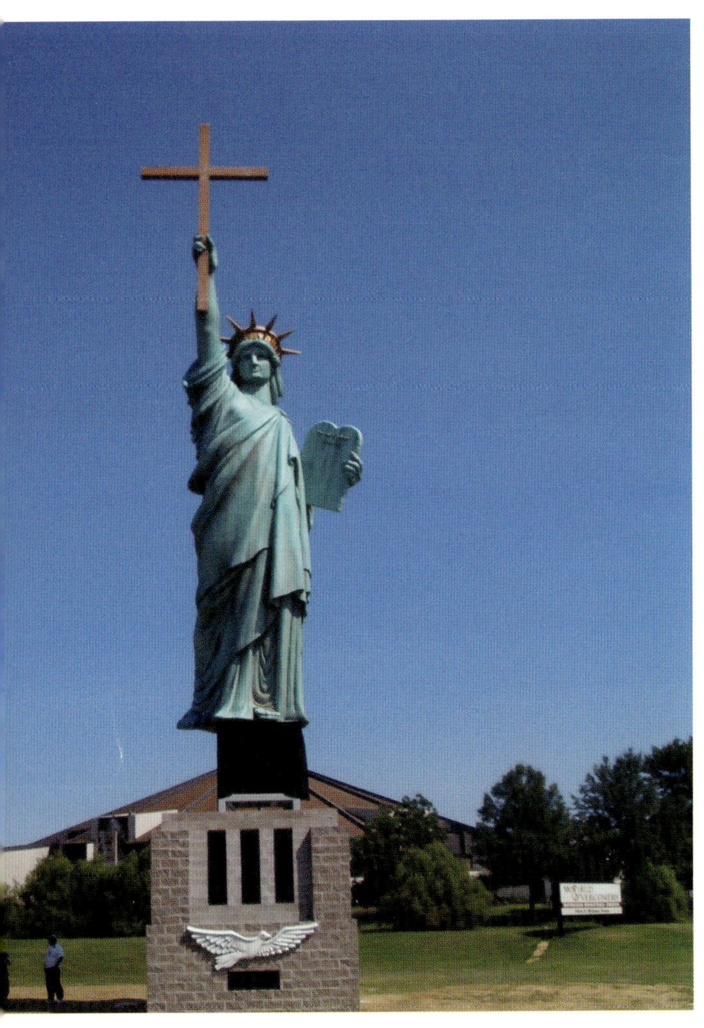

phrasing is a reinterpretation of the original). The United States prides itself on such a radical separation, and yet it is precisely this Constitutional language that has been repeatedly challenged for over two centuries now. The example of the Memphis mega-church's Statue of Liberation Through Christ begins to suggest that there are a number of conservative, especially Protestant, churches working in a revivalist mode, pointing back to some mythical foundation of the country that murkily fuses with religious foundations. Before going further with the United States, however, let us turn to another rendition of nationalism as religion.

If the United States has worked to separate religion and government, the establishment of the Soviet Union worked even harder. Even so, Anatoli Lunacharsky, a key player in the Bolshevik Revolution of 1917, would exclaim a decade previously that "Scientific socialism is the most religious of all religions."[12] And intriguingly, an important collection of essays from 1949 written by intellectuals around the Western world on the problems of Soviet communism is entitled *The God that Failed*. In the midst of a state-sponsored atheistic nationalism promoted by the Soviet Union, there is obviously something ironic in discussing the ideologies of the nation in terms of God and religion.

Statue of Liberation Through Christ,
photography Darren JN Middleton, courtesy of the author

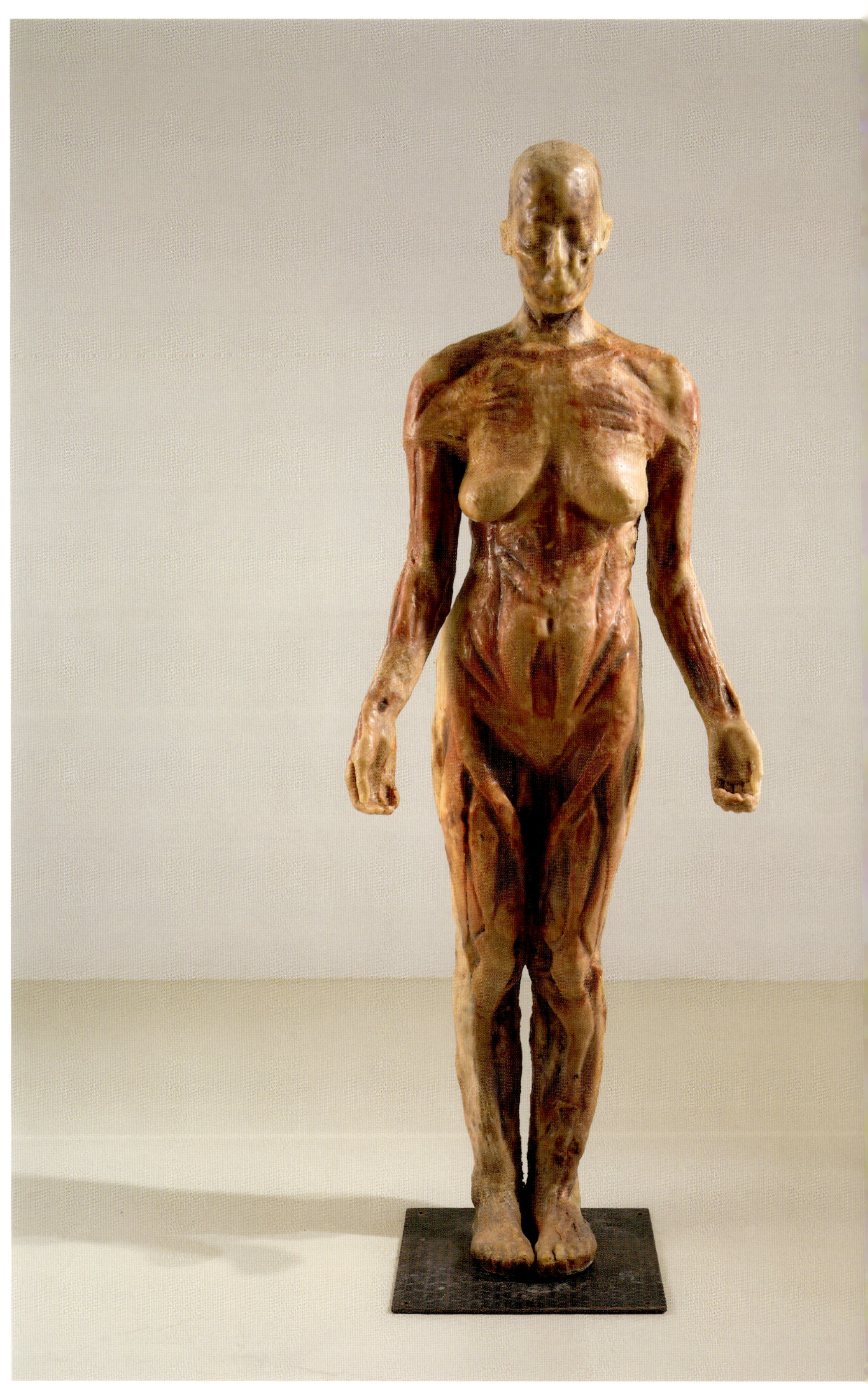

In the rhetoric of 'intelligent design', scientific work can transgress the sacred in ways oddly parallel to the Islamic Hadith that forbids image making because this would be a challenge to God's sole creative activities.

Kiki Smith, *Virgin Mary*, 1992, beeswax, microcrystalline wax, cheesecloth, and wood on steel base 171 x 66 x 37 cm, photography Ellen Page, courtesy of PaceWildenstein, New York
Smith's work focuses on the perception of the body, and feminist reinterpretations of religion and myth. This life-sized wax figure depicts the Virgin Mary flayed of skin, exposing an intricate web of muscles and tendons.

Nowhere is the religiosity of the Soviet system better noted – and critically commented upon – than in the art movement called 'Sots Art' begun in the 1970s. The artistic duo Vitaly Komar and Alex Melamid coined the phrase and meant it as a kind of ironic response to Socialist Realism, shot through with the styles of the US-based Pop Art ('sots' being the first syllable of 'social' in Russian: *Sotsialisticheskiy*). "Irony is the faithful companion of unbelief and doubt; it vanishes as soon as there appears a faith that does not tolerate sacrilege," writes Abram Tertz (the pseudonym of Soviet dissident, Andrei Siniavsky).[13] Socialist Realism was this faith that did not tolerate sacrilege, as it symbolically propped up the religious system of Soviet Communism. It was a kind of hyper-idealism of larger than life proportions: straightforward, leaving little space for second-guessing, and certainly no room for irony. Especially championed by Josef Stalin's regime (Stalin himself actually had little interest in art), its aim was, in the words of Andrey Zhdanov, one of Stalin's cultural spokesmen, "to depict reality in its revolutionary development".[14] Yet even with its supposedly progressive interests, Socialist Realism borrowed on Russia's painterly past, and lighted on the rich tradition of Christian Orthodox icons as a way to praise the worker and Soviet leader as hero/saint. J Hoberman paraphrases this mode, suggesting, "The saint is axiomatic in Socialist Realism; the figure of the so-called positive hero or heroine is the brave, steadfast, selfless, and allegorical personification of Bolshevik ideals, the embodiment of history's "forward trajectory".[15] During Stalin's reign, even more than Lenin's before him, the leader's own visage became a national icon, postered ubiquitously, with giant statues in public spaces to remind the workers how they got there and what they should aspire to; a desire not unlike the functions of the rituals and symbols of religions.

Komar and Melamid worked alongside – even if underground – Eric Bulatov, Alexander Kosolapov, and Leonid Sokov, as Socialist Realism operated above the surface, in the government-sanctioned art spaces. In the shadow of Socialist Realism, Marc Chagall, who had initially been appointed Commissar of Fine Arts in Vitebsk 1918, was removed from his post, and by 1922, he was in exile. Throughout Soviet rule, several of Chagall's works were destroyed or censored, just as they were in Nazi Germany. Fellow artists like Wassily Kandinsky and Kasimir Malevich were particularly rough on Chagall, though their work, too, would eventually cease to fare well in the Socialist Realist-dominated artistic culture of Soviet Russia.

Komar and Melamid, *Souls Inc.*, 1979, advertisement
Komar and Melamid, *We Buy and Sell Souls, "Fine Quality Souls for Every Taste"*,1978, photo offset poster, 61 x 51 cm
Komar and Melamid, *We Buy and Sell Souls, "Bring us your tired souls yearning to be free"*, 1978, photo offset poster, 61 x 51 cm
Komar and Melamid, *We Buy and Sell Souls, "Your Soul is in Good Hands with Us"*, 1978, photo offset poster, 61 x 51 cm, all courtesy of Ronald Feldman Fine Arts, New York and the artists

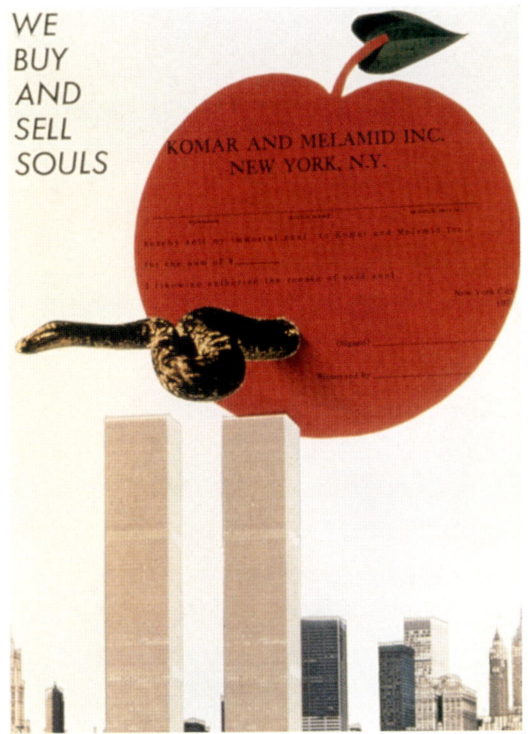
WE
BUY
AND
SELL
SOULS
KOMAR AND MELAMID INC.
NEW YORK, N.Y.

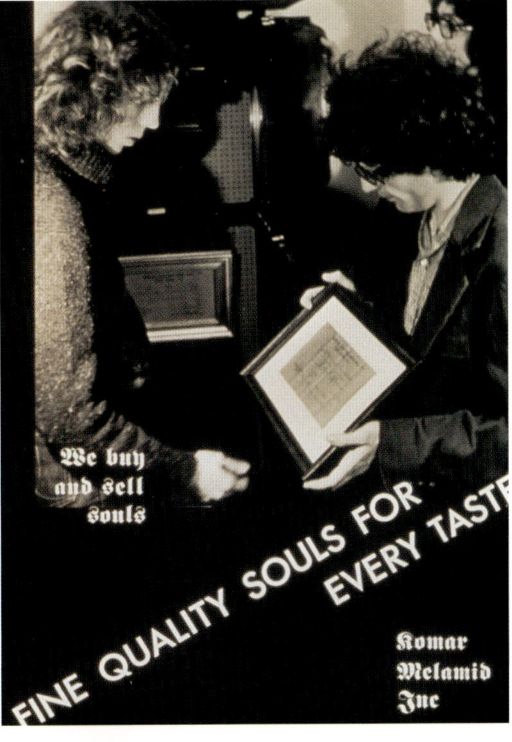
We buy
and sell
souls
FINE QUALITY SOULS FOR
EVERY TASTE
Komar
Melamid
Inc

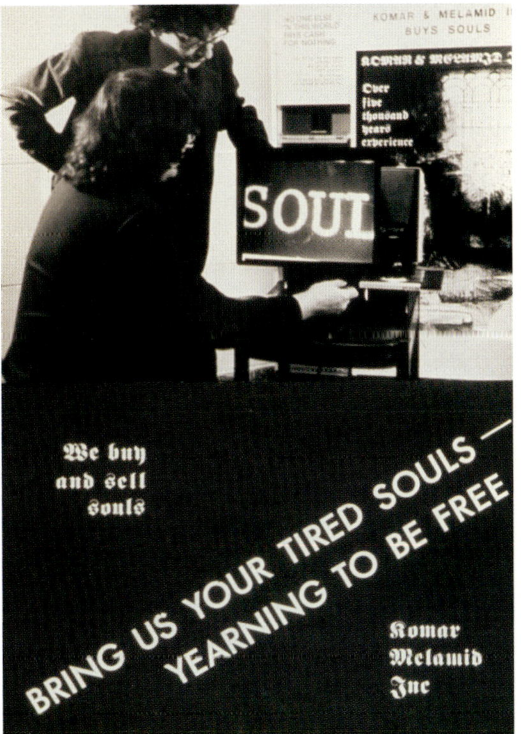
BUYS SOULS
Over
five
thousand
years
experience
SOUL
We buy
and sell
souls
BRING US YOUR TIRED SOULS —
YEARNING TO BE FREE
Komar
Melamid
Inc

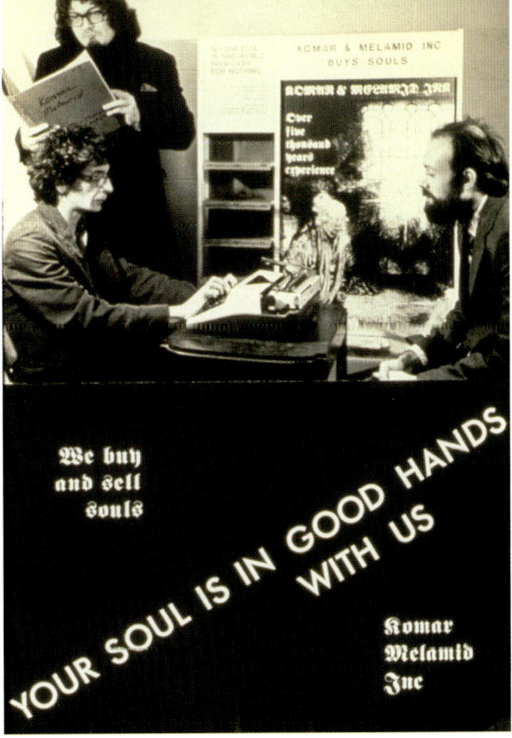
KOMAR & MELAMID INC
BUYS SOULS
Over
five
thousand
years
experience
We buy
and sell
souls
YOUR SOUL IS IN GOOD HANDS
WITH US
Komar
Melamid
Inc

In response to the stifling mode of this official art, the work of so-called 'non-conformist' artists (including the Sots Artists) wedged irony into the literalness of Socialist Realism, attempting to prove how nothing really is as it seems. It was precisely the sacred status of Soviet nationalist ideologies ('that do not tolerate sacrilege') that made it possible for artists to work against the system, and produce what became another instance of blasphemy as a form of resistance. The works of these 'non-conformist' artists did not go unchecked by Soviet authorities and a number of well-noted exhibitions were shut down. Perhaps the most famous was the *Bulldozer Exhibition* in 1974, which "was held on a deserted street in Moscow for as long as it took the police to hose down, bulldoze, and destroy as many works as possible".[16] Alongside this, artists from the 1950s–1980s were regularly suppressed, had their jobs taken away, were sent to labour camps, or made to leave their country.

Among the various works of Sots Art, Komar and Melamid's *Origins of Socialist Realism* plays on the iconic or, depending on your point of view, idolatrous, status of Stalin, while mocking the 'spiritual' processes of idol-making: the muse traces a literal silhouette of Stalin's profile, thereby proffering the 'origins' of Socialist Realism. As with much of Sots Art, "In its ironic over-eagerness, it undermines what it purportedly celebrates."[17] Meanwhile, Bulatov paints photorealistic images of landscapes, and then overlays them with Soviet political slogans, thus taking two 'realistic' images and juxtaposing them to create an ambiguous, highly-charged meaning – a method not unlike that used by the great Soviet filmmakers of the 1920s: Eisenstein, Vertov, and Kuleshov. Within the works of Bulatov, Komar and Melamid, the so-called 'reality' of Socialist Realism is deconstructed. As Bulatov says, art is "a rebellion of man against the everyday reality of life.... A picture interests me as some kind of system, not hermetically sealed, but opening into the space of my everyday existence."[18] The works of the non-conformists take literalist (even 'fundamentalist') images to their extremes, showing the strange situations of excessive glorification of an ideological system that poses as reality.

Komar and Melamid, *The Origin of Socialist Realism*, 1982–1983, oil on canvas, 183 x 122 cm, courtesy of Ronald Feldman Fine Arts, New York and the artists

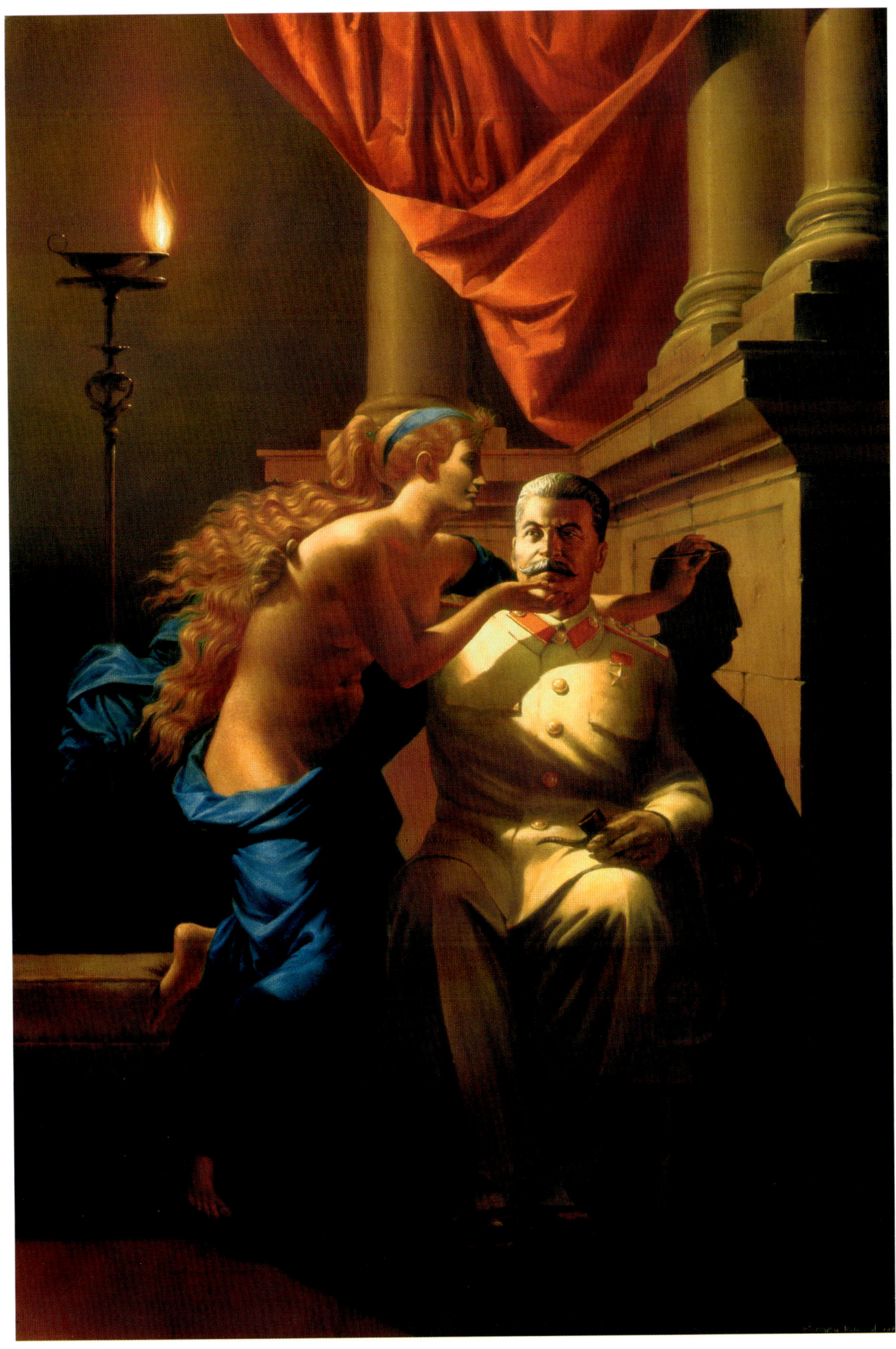

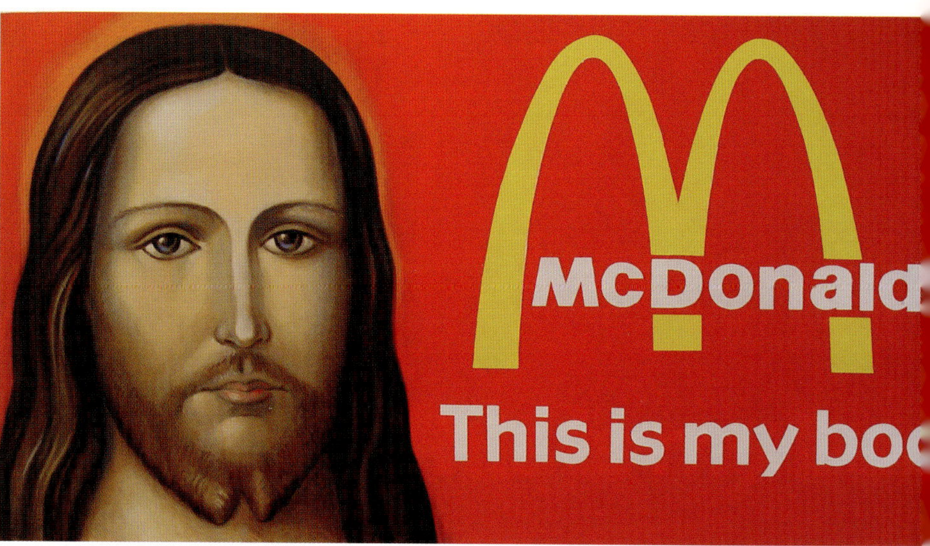

Alas, as the Soviet Union has disbanded, we come to yet more ironies in the struggle for freedom of expression. The Sots artists were sometimes called "dissident artists", along with one of the most famous Soviet dissidents, the physicist Andrei Sakharov, who had been sent into exile for his critical views of the Soviet Union. When the Communists were ousted from power, a new wave of artistic expression became possible, and tolerance levels even allowed for a new museum to be named after Sakharov. The Andrei Sakharov Museum was opened in 1996 as something of a memorial to the victims of the repressive Soviet regime, as its permanent exhibits include a history of repression in the Soviet Union. In 2003, the museum mounted an exhibition called *Caution! Religion!* Several of the artists adopted a Sots Art style, but instead of being directed toward Socialist Realism, they reapplied their irony to the two most imposing, social-constraining voices in post-Soviet Russian life: Orthodox Christianity and capitalism. As Komar and Melamid compared the production of consumer goods in the United States with the production of ideology in the Soviet Union, artists like Alexander Kosolapov followed through in the post-Soviet age, juxtaposing the

ABOVE: **Alexander Kosolapov**, *This is My Body*, 2002, acrylic and canvas, courtesy of the artist

OPPOSITE: *This is My Body* destroyed whilst on display at the *Caution! Religion!* exhibition, 2003.

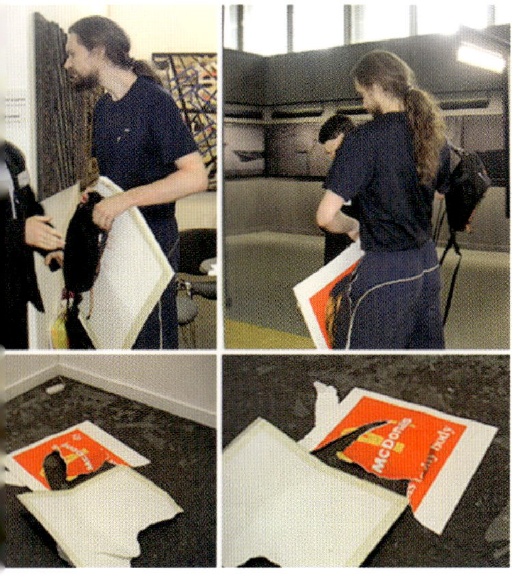

As Komar and Melamid compared the production of consumer goods in the United States with the production of ideology in the Soviet Union, artists like Alexander Kosolapov followed through in the post-Soviet age.

icons of Soviet Communism with the icons of consumer capitalism, the McDonalds, Coca-Cola, and Marlboro cigarettes that came rushing into Moscow with the fall of Communism. For Kosolapov, Lenin is a hero in his subconscious, just as the Marlboro man represents for him the "last American hero."[19] And his work, *My Blood,* situates the offerings of Coca-Cola alongside the Eucharistic offerings of the Christian church.

As if attempting a bad parody of the former Soviet system, government authorities, prompted by the Orthodox church, shut down the *Caution! Religion!* exhibit after only four days, and members of a local Orthodox church vandalised many of the artworks. More importantly, charges of blasphemy were eventually brought by a Moscow court against the director of the museum and curator of the show, Yuri Samodurov and Ludmila Vasilovskaia. The prosecutors worked to have them each imprisoned for a few years, but the courts ultimately decided on a hefty fine, and the chances seem slim that they will be able to work in Moscow's official art world again. None of the individual artists were charged, even though some of their works were destroyed.

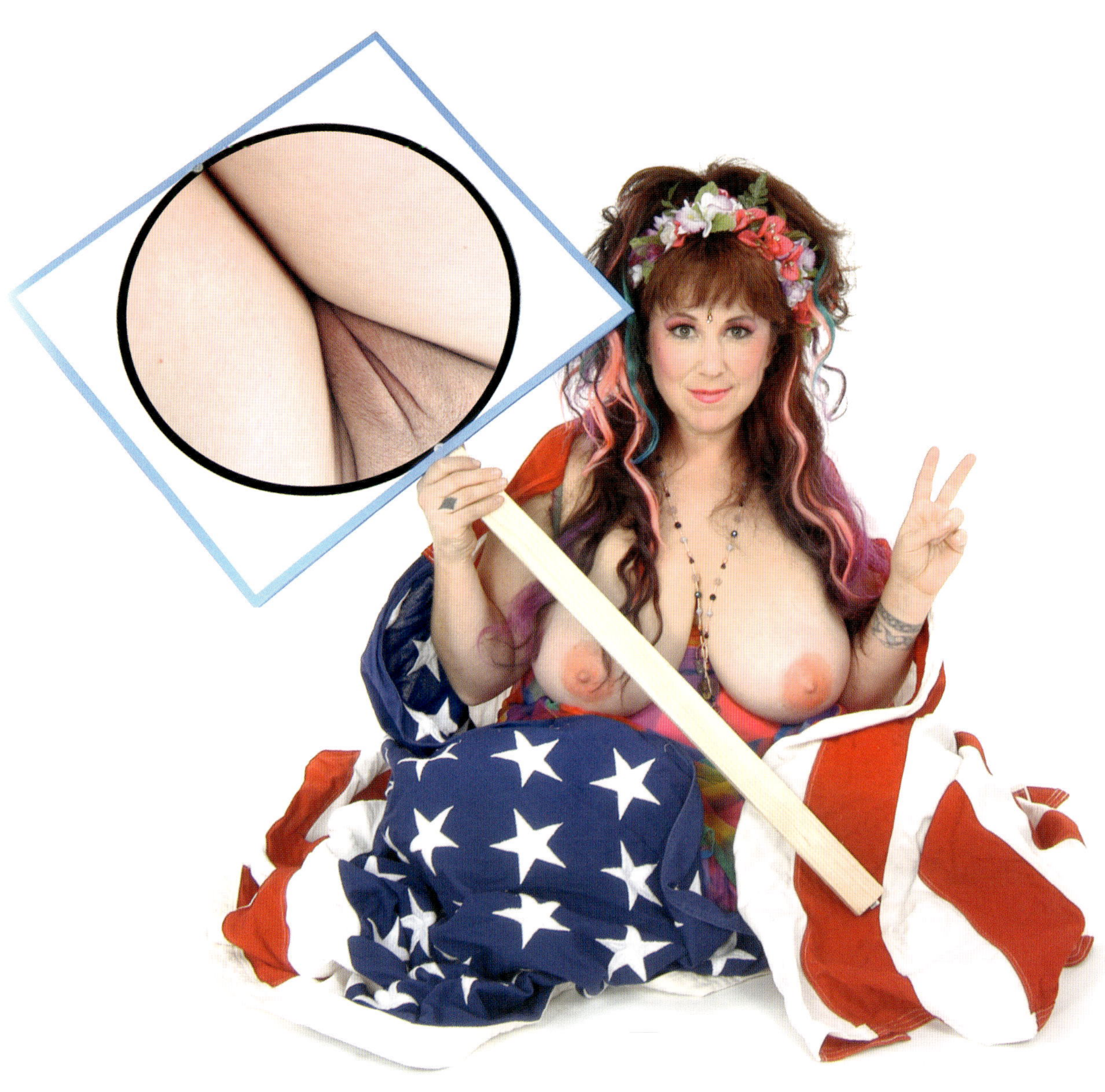

Annie Sprinkle, *Peace Sign*, photography Julian Cash, courtesy of the artist

A Nation Wrapped up in a Flag

Nations, like religions, do not develop, reform, and sustain themselves by abstract doctrine alone. Rather, they construct myths, symbols, and rituals to buttress the system. With regard to nationalism, one of the strongest symbols is that of the flag. In the United States in particular, the flag has become what anthropologist Sherry Ortner labels a "summarizing symbol" that 'sums up', just as it 'stands in for' the whole system. Summarising symbols represent for the participants,

> in an emotionally powerful and relatively undifferentiated way, what the system means to them. Among other examples is the flag, particularly that of the United States: the American flag, for example, for certain Americans, stands for something called 'the American way', a conglomerate of ideas and feelings including (theoretically) democracy, free enterprise, hard work, competition, progress, national superiority, freedom, etc.. And it stands for them all at once. It does not encourage reflection on the logical relations among these ideas, nor on the logical consequences of them as they are played out in social actuality, over time and history. On the contrary, the flag encourages a sort of all-or-nothing allegiance to the whole package.[20]

Stemming from the Civil War era, factions within US politics have worked to enact laws prohibiting *desecration* of the flag. The current language attempting to get a constitutional amendment for such a prohibition reads: "The Congress shall have power to prohibit the physical desecration of the flag of the United States." The Oxford English Dictionary defines desecrate as: "To take away its consecrated or sacred character from (anything); to treat as not sacred or hallowed; to profane." Here, of course, we are looking at a national symbol, a political entity, that is considered by many to be sacred.

From the late nineteenth century politicking of Colonel George T Balch and Charles Kingsbury Miller, to the late twentieth century congressional debates over adding a new Constitutional amendment that would make flag desecration a punishable offence, the US flag has been raised, burned, scorned, prayed to, argued over, and turned into what can only be called a 'national icon'.[21] Making the religious connotations even more apparent, in an address in 1898, Miller claimed the flag "should be kept as inviolate as was the Holy of Holies in King Solomon's temple".[22] And in almost every scholarly book on the subject, authors note the religious nature of adherence to the flag in the United States.

Artists working in the United States from the 1950s to the present day have, like their Soviet non-conformist counterparts, challenged the symbolism of a monolithic national image. Jasper Johns' 'flag' series in the 1950s began, in a subtly postmodern way, to query the representational status of the image of the flag. Is it still a 'flag' if it is just an oil-on-canvas painting? What if I took my child's red, white, and blue crayons and drew a flag on a piece of scrap paper: would it be illegal for me to crumple it up and throw it away?

Issues raised have ranged from the theoretical to the economic, as the US flag has been pasted, printed, and stamped onto all manner of sellable items. As with the post-Soviet challenges of free-market capitalism, the United States too is awash in an admixture of the iconic flag with consumer product icons. There is an extensive US Federal 'Code' (i.e. not a 'law' and therefore not enforceable by punishment) that lists a number of guidelines regarding the proper display of the flag. Like anything sacred, there are proper ways to care for and be in relationship with it. Within the code are general guidelines such as not flying the flag at night without a light, and that no other flag should be flown above it. Along with these ritualistic codes of display are others: "The flag should never be used for advertising purposes in any manner whatsoever" and "The flag represents a living country and is itself considered a living thing." Indeed, akin to Talmudic proscriptions regarding the life of a Torah scroll, the flag, when no longer usable, should be destroyed in a dignified way, preferably by burning. Burning in a dignified way (though what this means is ambiguous) *de*consecrates the material of the flag, ritualistically carrying it from the realm of the sacred to the realm of the profane. Burning the flag in an 'undignified' way would be mere desecration, an improper crossing from the sacred to the profane.

To think about this modern, nationalistic confusion of the sacred and the profane, compare Alan Schechner's juxtapositions between Holocaust icons and consumer items such as Diet Coke, Alexander Kosolapov's merging of Soviet and Christian icons with the McDonalds logo, and post-September 11 advertisements by companies that capitalised on a feverish need to display flags and ended up creating flag-bedecked underwear, bikinis, key chains, lighters, and every manner of profane, sellable object. Schechner and Kosolapov were accused of profaning the sanctity of the Holocaust and the Christian sacrament, respectively, while, in a strange reversal of the sacred and the profane, companies have attempted to *sanctify their goods* through the inclusion of a flag on their products or in their advertisements. Even so, in the wake of the 2001 terrorist attacks in the United States, nationalist lines between the sacred and the profane have been redrawn. A Coca-Cola spokesman acknowledged that "sensitivities have changed", and an article in the marketing publication *American Demographics* stated, "Coke was caught in the same bind that constricts many of the advertisers these days, especially those as iconic as the beverage industry leader: how to touch on Americans' newly awakened patriotism to promote their products, without seeming to exploit a national crisis."[23] Here we find advertising firms tip-toeing around the border that keeps the sacred what it is in all societies: separate from quotidian life, full of power, and only capable of being touched through strictly set rituals.

Marc Morrel, *Crucifiction*, Papel flag, Christian flag, Episcopal flag, American flag, cord, wood, 200 x 160 cm, courtesy of the artist

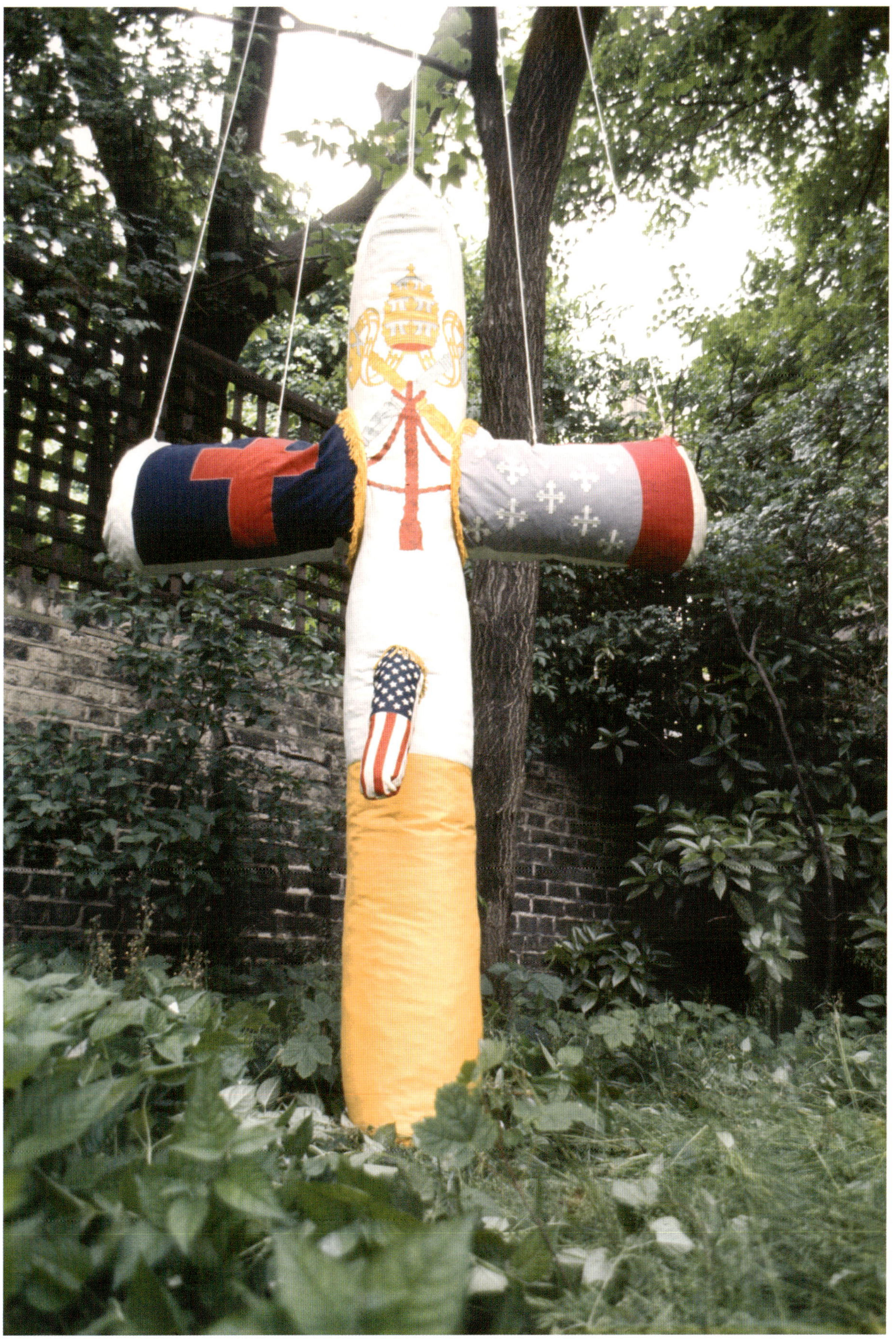

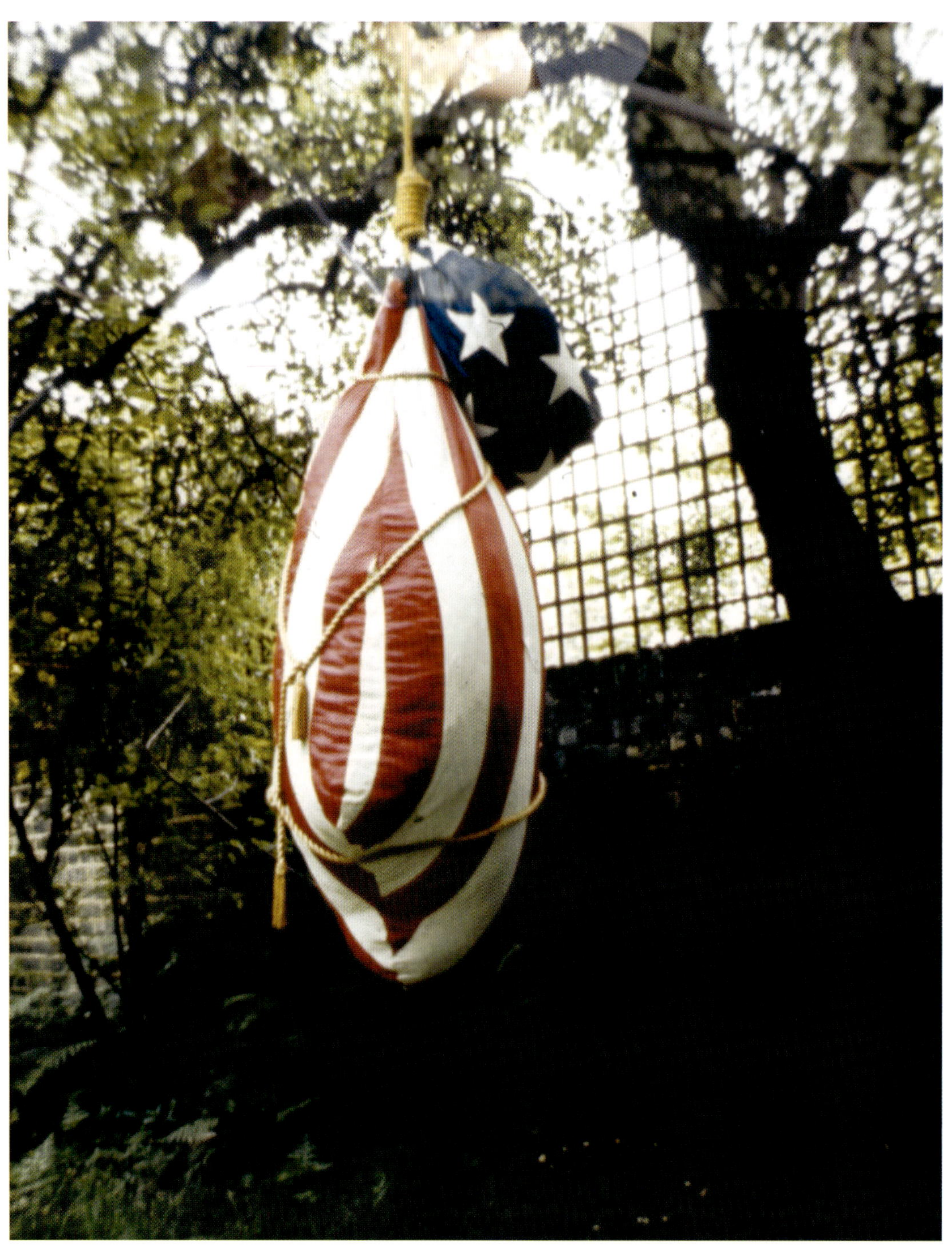

Marc Morrel, *Hanging Flag*, American flag, rope, braided cord, foam and pulley, 180 x 90 cm, courtesy of the artist

A number of controversial art exhibits have been at the heart of recent debates regarding the sanctity of the flag. In 1966, in the midst of the Vietnam War, former Marine Marc Morrel exhibited several flag sculptures in a New York gallery. As a result, the gallery owner, Stephen Radich, was charged with 'casting contempt' and fined $500, and the trials and appeals went on for several years. He was eventually vindicated, but not without the trials going all the way to the Supreme Court. In 1970, as if in response to Morrel's works and Radich's woes, Faith Ringgold, Jon Hendricks, and Jean Toche organised *The People's Flag Show* at Judson Memorial Church in New York City, in which artists were invited to create works in response to the flag. Over two hundred works were displayed, a flag was burned, a symposium held, and the three organisers were arrested, convicted, and sentenced to a fine of $100. Not much in relation to the floggings and assassinations of other artists convicted of blasphemy, but telling nonetheless.

Two decades later, when Dread Scott's installation, *What is the Proper Way to Display a U.S. Flag?* was exhibited at the School of the Art Institute of Chicago in 1989, more protests and congressional debates began. President George HW Bush called it "disgraceful", but more importantly it set off a new round of US congressional debate over a constitutional amendment to ban flag desecration. The work consists of a photomontage on the wall composed of various images containing flags – some being burned, some draping over caskets. Below the photo is a register book and a pen on a shelf. Finally, a US flag is spread on the ground in front of the book and image. The idea is for the spectators to become participants by signing and making comments in the book. Of course, to do so, one must *seemingly* (in physical reality, one could have leaned over) stand on the flag. Even those who wanted to protest the display were encouraged to stand on the flag to do so. By laying the flag down on the floor, Scott re-creates the gallery space, separating sacred space from profane: stepping here is permissible, there is not. One space is charged with power, the other is not. Connected with this was an interesting ritual that developed in the display of the flag. As Steven Dubin relates it,

> Veterans developed a protocol which fused artwork and audience into a symbiotic relationship. Each day they entered the gallery, picked up the flag from the floor, ceremoniously folded it, and placed it upon the shelf. This was a remarkable ritualized effort to restore order to a situation where the vets felt a sacred object had been profaned by breaking the customary rules for its display. But the attempt to avert pollution was foiled: just as predictably, gallery personnel or other observers would reposition it on the floor, only for the cycle to repeat again and again.[24]

I shall end this section with Dubin's account of Scott's display, since it touches so well on the various issues that arise from accusations of blasphemy in the context of modern national symbols like the flag. The flag and the rituals surrounding its display are charged with social power that transcends the material realm. These meanings are then contested, re-appropriated and re-ritualised in an ongoing struggle for social stability, and sometimes instability.

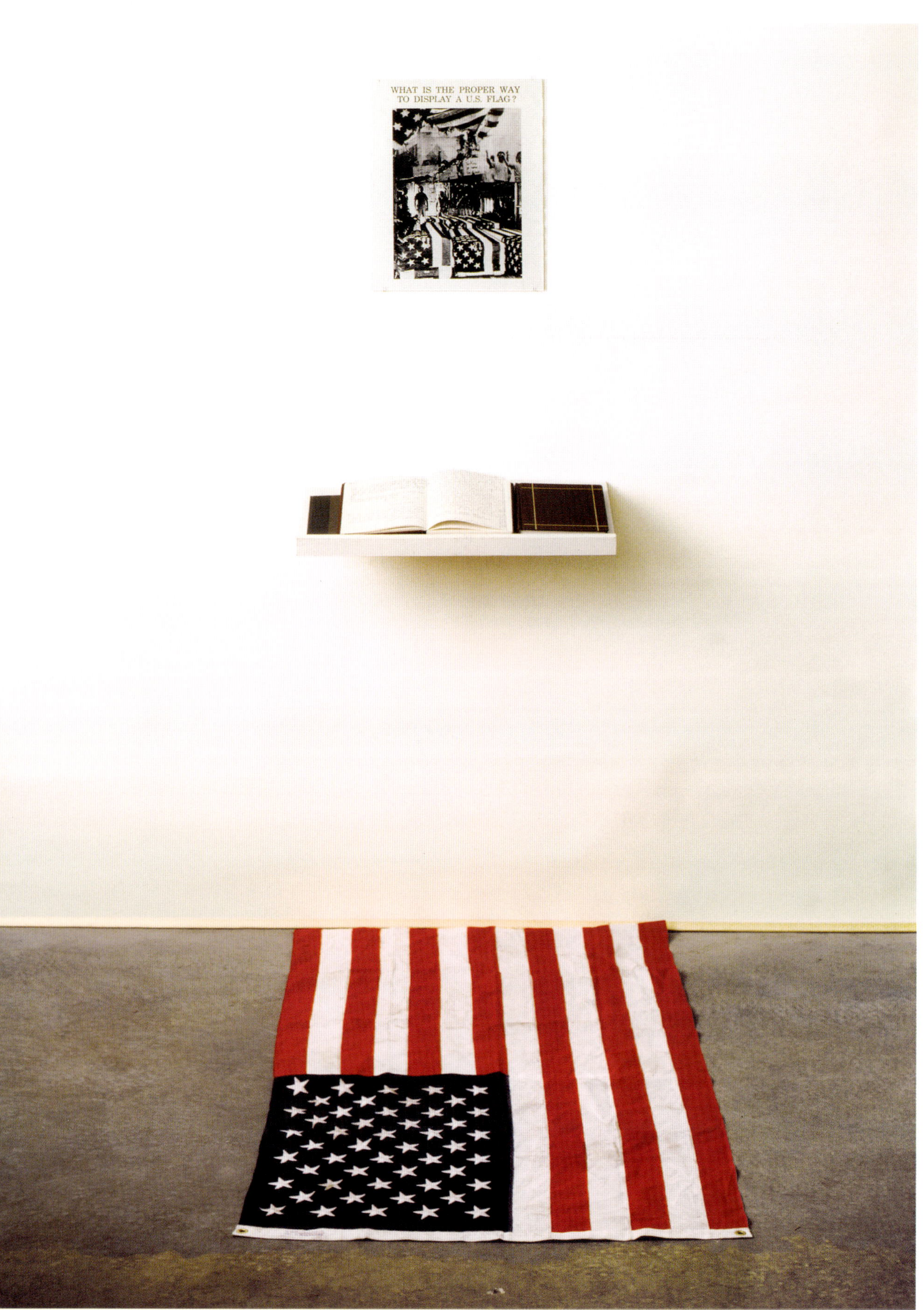
WHAT IS THE PROPER WAY
TO DISPLAY A U.S. FLAG?

WHAT IS THE PROPER WAY
TO DISPLAY A U.S. FLAG?

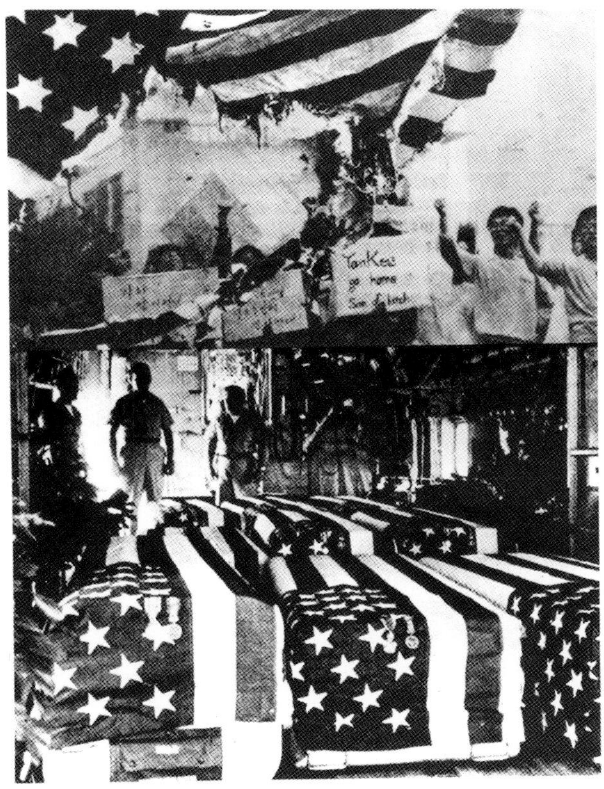

Dread Scott Tyler, *What is the Proper Way to Display a U.S. Flag?*, 1989, installation and detail, courtesy of the artist

The piece is comprised of a photograph depicting images of the American flag, a blank open book on a shelf, and a flag spread out neatly on the floor. This simple composition first appeared in a minority student exhibition in 1989 at the School of The Art Institute of Chicago, and caused so much controversy that an injunction was issued against the school, large protests were held outside and the government cut the funding of the school from $70,000 to $1. The Chicago Police Department declared that any viewer who walked on the flag would be charged with felony.

Freedom of Expression versus Blasphemy?

> In earlier times only heretics and blasphemers had dared challenge traditional claims of authority over expression. The last five centuries have finally established powerful claims of expression against authority.
>
> ARTHUR SCHLESINGER JR, 'Preface' to *Censorship: 500 Years of Conflict*

At the end of this book, we come back to the point from which we began: the Danish cartoon controversy. If the controversy revealed what some Muslims find authoritative and sacred – that is, the Prophet Muhammad and his representation – it also proved what many modernists hold authoritative and sacred – freedom of expression. If Muhammad can be blasphemed against, then, it seems, so can expressive freedom. Modern human rights charters, from the US Declaration of Independence to the European Commission on Human Rights, have authorised individuals to partake in the freedom of expression through speech and religion: to not be coerced or censored by governments or by other social groups. Paradoxically, the individual human now has authority, and taking away the freedom of the individual's expression is tantamount to blaspheming against the religious and political authorities of olden times, in whose place the individual now stands.

The twentieth century feminist author Dame Rebecca West argues against censorship, which prevents the freedom of expression: "There is a point, and it is reached much more easily than is supposed, where interference with freedom of art and literature becomes an attack on the life of society. This freedom is as necessary to the mental survival of a society as a satisfactory sanitary system is to its physical survival."[25] West's comments, however agreeable to the modern mind, must nonetheless be noted for their parallel to the relation between the religious and social dimensions of blasphemy. Recall Justice Hale's comments in the seventeenth century: "Christianity is parcel of the laws of England... therefore to reproach the Christian religion is to speak in subversion of the law." An attack on the *freedom* of artistic expression, in West's view, is an attack on society itself, just as Justice Hale notes that blasphemy against Christian religion is also bad for society. Before modernity and its accompanying liberal, Enlightenment values, blasphemous images were often censored: burned, scratched, painted over, removed from the public eye. In the modern world, it paradoxically also becomes blasphemous to *censor* an image. This does not mean that it used to be one way only and is now the complete opposite. Instead, both responses are now in operation, side-by-side, and this constitutes the current, postmodern dilemma.

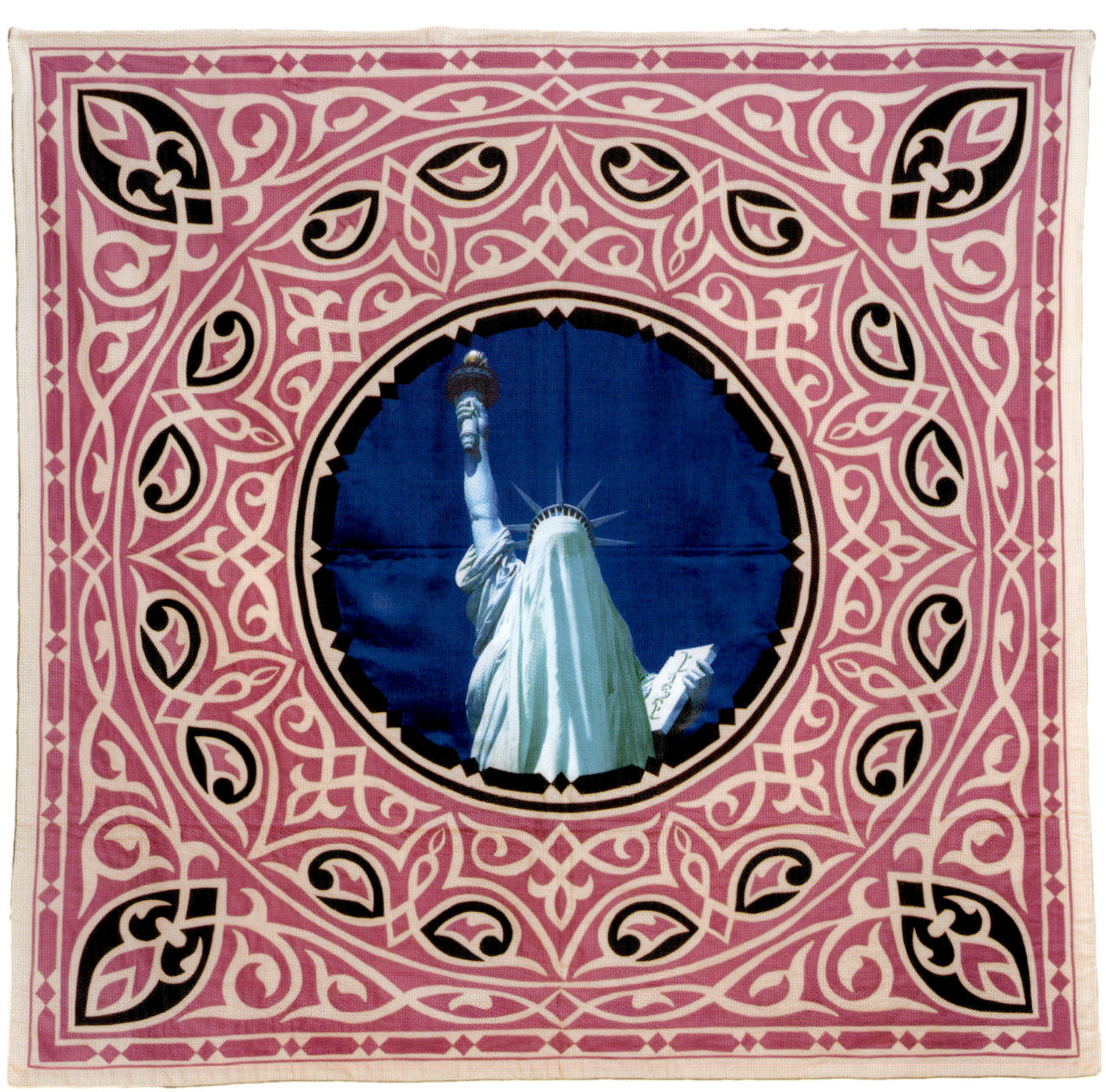

AES art group, from *The Witnesses of the Future: Islamic Project*, 1996, digital image, courtesy of the artists

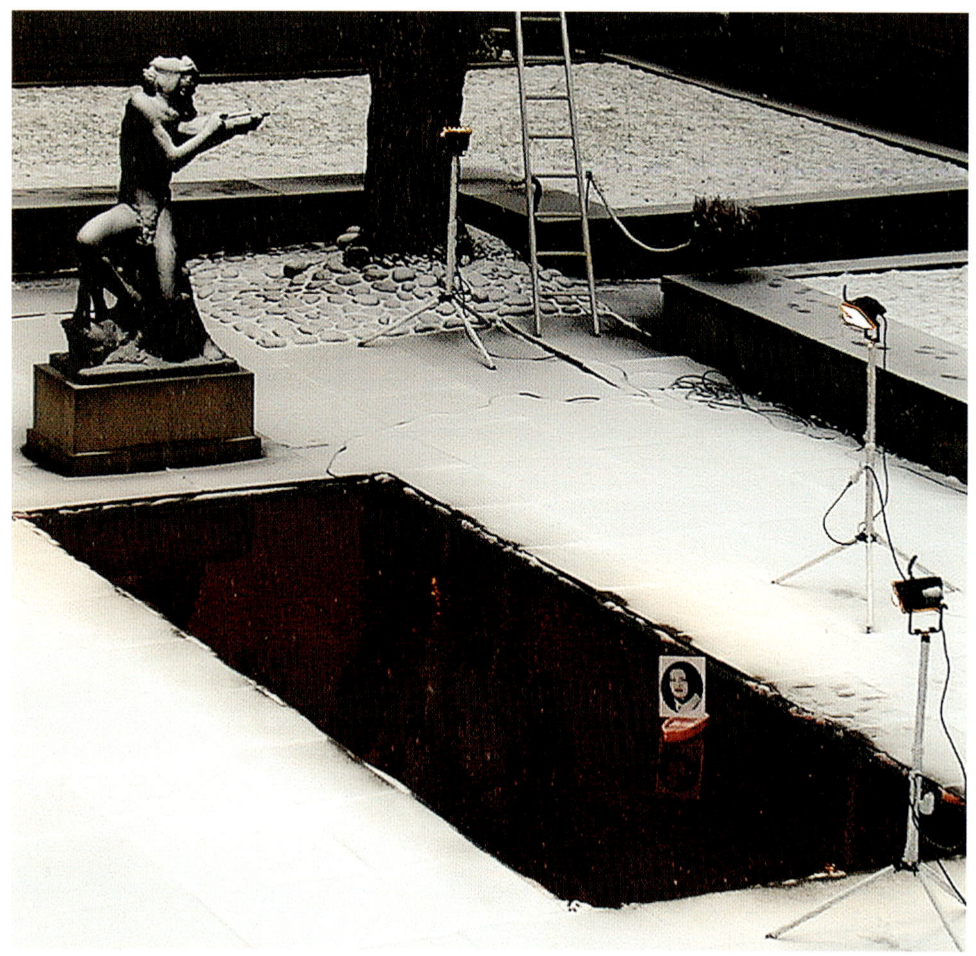

Dror Feiler, *Snow White and the Madness of Truth*, 2004, sound and water installation, outdoors: pond filled with red coloured water, pond size: 700 x 300 cm, boat size: 37 x 16 cm, text collage from documentary and fictive texts, music: JS Bach's *Cantata 199: Mein Hertz schwimmt im Blut* rearranged by Dror Feiler, five aluminium dressed floodlighting, ladder, snow, photography Gunilla Sköld Feiler, courtesy of the artist and photographer, a Feiler2 project, Making Differences, The Museum of National Antiquities, Stockholm

The installation features a portrait of Palestinian suicide bomber, Hanadi Jaradat, floating in a pool of blood coloured water, whilst the sound of Bach's *Mein Herze Schwimmt im Blut* plays in the background. The piece was perceived as anti-Semitic, and caused the Israeli ambassador to Sweden to respond so violently that he vandalised the piece – an event which was filmed and televised. The Israeli government then tried to force the Swedish gallery to take down the piece, but the gallery stood firm. When the piece was re-exhibited later in the year, the curator was attacked by an unidentified man, who tried to throw him down the stairs.

Is freedom really the end of all that we seek to 'spread' to all nations?

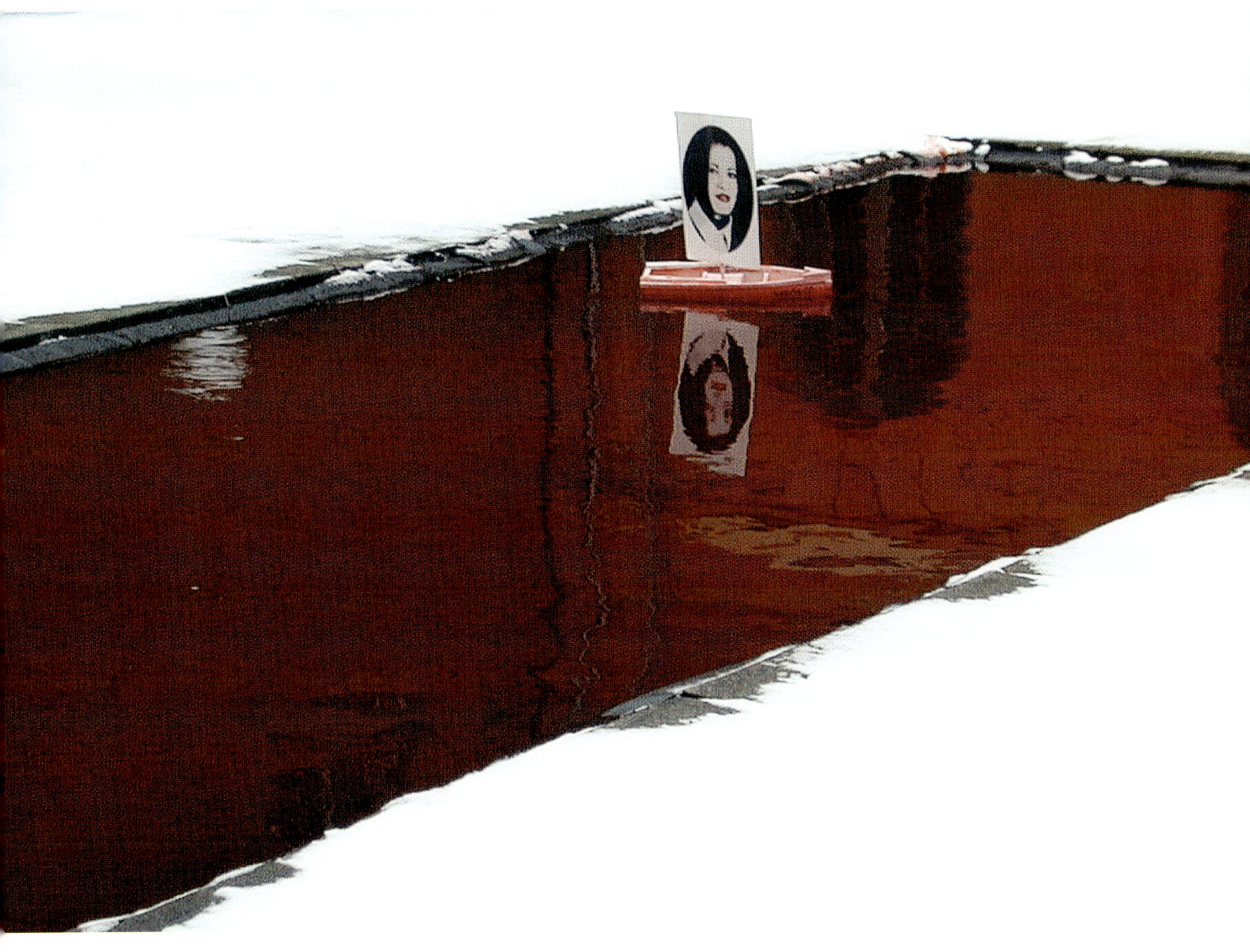

Criticising the extremities to which freedom of expression has gone in the postmodern world, Stanley Fish, law professor and cultural critic, suggests that the journalists and editors of *Jyllands-Posten*, and most journalists for that matter, see themselves as objective reporters, neutral in regard to religion. And yet, Fish continues, they adhere to "the religion we call liberalism". In that religion are basic tenets, the first is that everything "is to be permitted, but nothing is to be taken seriously"; respect all manner of belief, just don't take it seriously enough to be bothered, changed, or moved by it. In other words, everyone should have their own religion, as long as it is a matter of the heart, of private, internal beliefs. But when these are manifested in the public realm, in ongoing dialogue, then one must tread lightly, not talking too loudly, since others might take offence. To the contrary, Fish concludes, "a firm adherent of a comprehensive religion doesn't want dialogue about his beliefs; he wants those beliefs to prevail. Dialogue is not a tenet in his creed, and invoking it is unlikely to do anything but further persuade him that you have missed the point – as, indeed, you are pledged to do, so long as liberalism is the name of your faith."[26] Historian Arthur Schlesinger agrees that "The true believer is always an incipient censor." But Schlesinger, a truer liberal than Fish, opines by quickly equating such firm belief with "fanaticism" and concludes that "we fortunate ones on this side of the moon" must celebrate those who "affirm the rights of expression against the tyranny of authority."[27] Implicit on both accounts is the fact that, as long as there are true believers/firm adherents, and as long as there are authorities, there will always be charges of blasphemy, and activities of iconoclasm and censorship.

"Imagine there's no heaven", "nothing to kill or die for". John Lennon summed up many liberal ideals. But if there really is nothing worth living or dying for, then where are we? Is nothing special, sacred, held above others? If there is no authority, then can the human individual mean anything? If everything is on a level playing field, then we say good-bye to religion, but also to art, government, and civilisation in general. And if we do think freedom is worth killing and dying for, as contemporary nations embroiled in wars on Middle Eastern countries proclaim (even if many of us don't believe it), are we not at the same place as religious fanaticism? So, is freedom really the end of all that we seek to 'spread' to all nations?

I am not suggesting definitive answers here and, in the end, blasphemy *will* continue, because societies will continue to hold certain values, objects, and ideas sacred (or, hold them as 'self-evident truths'). This book has attempted to demonstrate some of the myriad ways in which words, ideas, and especially images have broken a particular society's established boundary between the sacred and the profane, and challenged people to rethink their supposedly universally-held beliefs and practices. If 'we' imagine that it is 'they' (whoever that may be) who are still hung up on issues of blasphemy, then perhaps 'we' need to rethink what it is we continue to hold dear and sacred beyond reproach, even if we must go beyond the traditional religious authoritative structures.

Alexander Kosolapov, *Icon-Caviar*, 1989, courtesy of the artist

REFERENCES AND RESOURCES

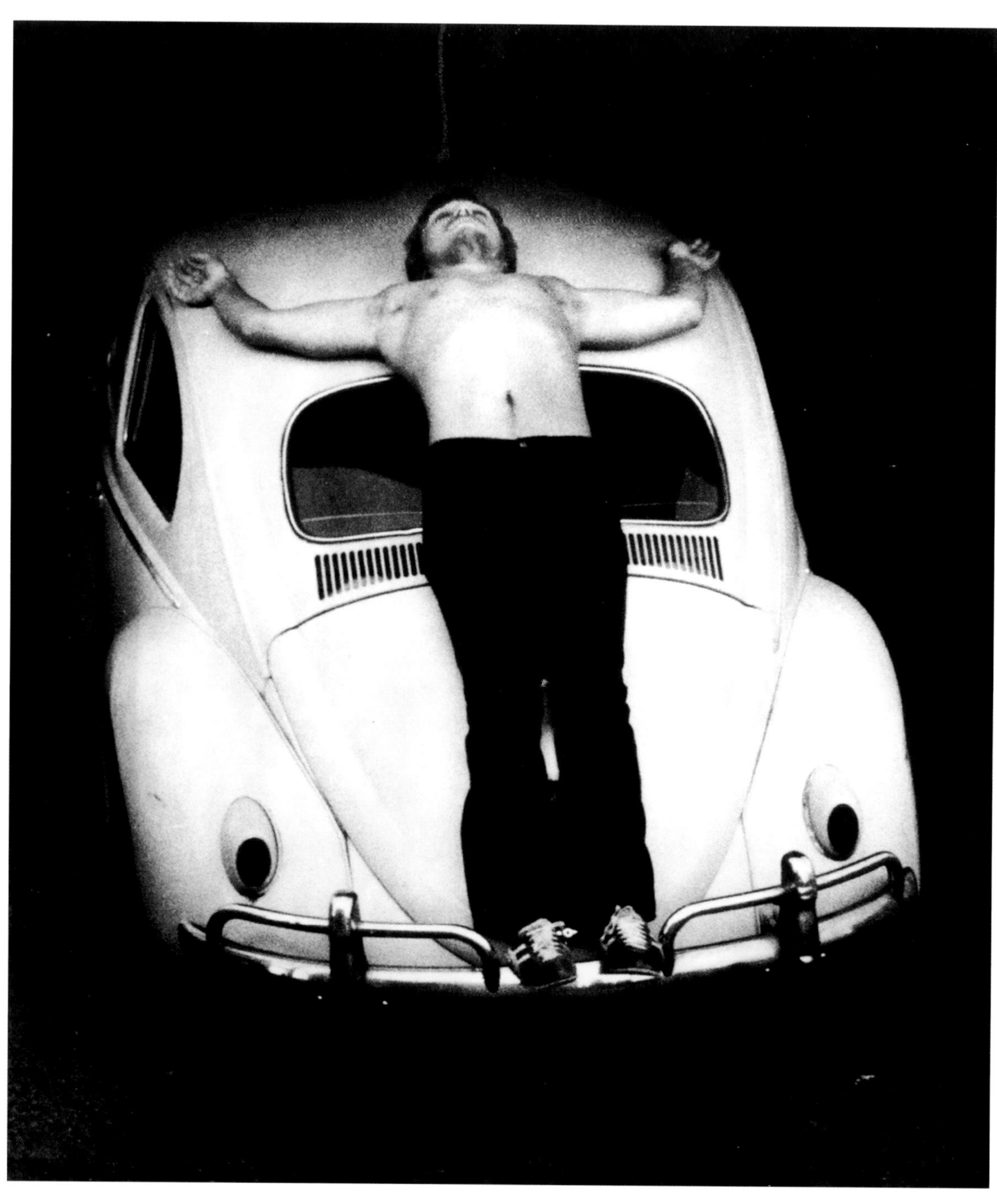

Chris Burden, *Trans-Fixed*, 1974, Volkswagen and nails, courtesy of the artist

NOTES

THE POWER OF OFFENSIVE IMAGES

Introduction

1_Kimmelman, Michael, "A Startling New Lesson in the Power of Imagery", *The New York Times*, 8 February, 2006. • 2_Freedberg, David, *The Power of Images*, Chicago: University of Chicago Press, 1989, p. 1. Freedberg's book is influential on all that is contained in my present book, even if I do not cite him directly throughout. • 3_Levy, Leonard, *Treason Against God*, New York: Schocken, 1981, p. xiii. I am greatly indebted to Levy's historical research, even as my own take here has attempted to shift his analysis into an investigation of the visual arts. Levy offers more of a legal analysis and history. • 4_Eliot, TS, *After Strange Gods*, London: Faber and Faber, 1934, p. 52. I will return to Eliot's essay in the final chapter.

DEFINING AND DELIMITING BLASPHEMY

Chapter One

1_*Burstyn v. Wilson*, 343 U.S. 495, 1952, pp. 533-540. • 2_*The New York Times*, col. 4, 31 December, 1950, p. 23. • 3_*Burstyn v. Wilson*, pp. 504-505. • 4_*Treason Against God*, New York: Schocken, 1981, is the title of Leonard Levy's first book on the subject. His second and much more expansive work, *Blasphemy: Verbal Offense Against the Sacred, from Moses to Salman Rushdie*, New York: Knopf, 1993, provides much of the historical background for my work. • 5_In the introduction to my *Religion, Art, and Visual Culture*, New York: Palgrave, 2002, I have gone into detail on the controversy surrounding Chris Ofili's *Holy Virgin Mary*, indicating the more prominent status of elephant dung in certain African cultures. • 6_See Gehl, Paul, "Texts and Textures: Dirty Pictures and Other Things in Medieval Manuscripts", *Corona* 3, 1983, pp. 68–77. • 7_Histories of blasphemy in Judaism can be found in Levy's *Blasphemy*; Habertal, Moshe and Avishai Margalit, *Idolatry*, trans. by Naomi Goldblum, Cambridge, MA: Harvard University Press, 1992; and Daniel J Lasker, "Blasphemy: Jewish Concept", in *Encyclopedia of Religion*, ed. Lindsay Jones, vol. 2, 2nd ed., Detroit: Macmillan Reference, 2005, pp. 968-971. • 8_Most prominent is Ernst Renan's, *The Life of Jesus*, New York: The Modern Library, 1927. • 9_Levy, *Blasphemy*, p. 61. See also Antónia Szabari's intriguing essay on Luther's speech-acts in "The Scandal of Religion: Luther and Public Speech", in *Political Theologies: Public Religions in a Post-Secular World*, ed. Hent de Vries and Lawrence E Sullivan, New York: Fordham University Press, 2006. • 10_Islamic issues of blasphemy can be found in Carl Ernst, "Blasphemy: Islamic Concept", in *Encyclopedia of Religion*, ed. Lindsay Jones. Vol.2. 2nd ed., Detroit: Macmillan Reference USA, 2005, pp. 974-977; and Ernst, *Words of Ecstasy*, Albany: State University of New York Press, 1985. • 11_For general works on Sufism, with attention to the issue of heresy, see Carl Ernst's works: *Words of Ecstasy in Islam*, Albany, NY: SUNY Press, 1985; and *Sufism*, Boston: Shambhala, 1997. • 12_See Walter Benjamin, *The Origin of German Tragic Drama*, trans. John Osborne, London: Verso, 1977, 37ff.

1_Belting, Hans, *Likeness and Presence*, trans. Edmund Jephcott, Chicago: University of Chicago Press, 1994, p. 1. • 2_See Luke Harding, "How the Buddha got his wounds", *The Guardian*, March 3, 2001. Accessed at: http://www.guardian.co.uk/Archive/Article/0,4273,4145138,00.html • 3_Particularly important here are the works by Kalman P Bland, *The Artless Jew*, Princeton: Princeton University Press, 2000; Erwin Goodenough, *Jewish Symbols in the Greco-Roman Period*, Princeton: Princeton University Press, 1988; Moshe Halbertal and Avishai Margalit, *Idolatry*, trans. by Naomi Goldblum, Cambridge, MA: Harvard University Press, 1992; Richard Cohen, *Jewish Icons*, Berkeley: University of California Press, 1998; and the essays in Catherine M Soussloff, ed., *Jewish Identity in Modern Art History*, Berkeley: University of California Press, 1999, and Margaret Olin, *The Nation Without Art*, Lincoln NE: University of Nebraska Press, 2001. Also important are the collected readings by Vivian B Mann in *Jewish Texts on the Visual Arts*, Cambridge: Cambridge University Press, 2000. • 4_Chagall, Marc, "On Jewish Art—Leaves from my Notebook", [1922] in *Marc Chagall: On Art and Culture*, Benjamin Harshav, ed., Stanford: Stanford University Press, 2003, p. 40. • 5_See the comprehensive study by Marvin Perry and Frederick Schweitzer, *Anti-Semitism: Myth and Hate from Antiquity to the Present*, New York: Palgrave Macmillan, 2002. • 6_John of Damascus, *On the Divine Images: Three Apologies Against Those Who Attack the Divine Images*, David Anderson, trans., Crestwood, N.Y.: 1980, p. 16. Quoted in Moshe Barasch *Icon*, New York: New York University Press, 1992, p. 209. • 7_See Leo Steinberg's *The Sexuality of Christ in Renaissance Art and in Modern Oblivion*. 2nd ed., Chicago: University of Chicago Press, 1996. • 8_For more on Islam and images, see Finbarr Barry Flood, "Between Cult and Culture: Bamiyan, Islamic Iconoclasm, and the Museum" *Art Bulletin* 84.4, December 2002: pp. 641-659; Marshall G.S. Hodgson, "Islam and Image," History of Religions 3,1969: 220-60; Oleg Grabar's *The Formation of Islamic Art*, New Haven, CT: Yale University Press, 1987; G.R. Hawting, *The Idea of Idolatry and the Emergence of Islam*, Cambridge: Cambridge University Press, 1999 and Oliver Leaman, *Islamic Aesthetics*, Notre Dame, IN: University of Notre Dame Press, 2004. • 9_Flood, "Between Cult and Culture," pp. 646-7. • 10_Burton, Sir Richard Francis, *Personal Narrative of a Pilgrimage to Al-Madinah and Meccah*, New York: G.P. Putnam, 1856, p.p. 369-70. • 11_Kifner, John, "Images of Muhammad, Gone for Good," *The New York Times* 12 February 2006. Accessed 15 May, at: http://www.nytimes.com/2006/02/12/weekinreview/12kifner.html?ex=1297400400&en=b69003cbf685f0fe&ei=5090&partner=rssuserland&emc=rss . Interestingly enough, there is a bas-relief of Muhammad (and Moses and many others) in the U.S. Supreme Court building in Washington. In 1997, Muslim groups protested and asked that it be removed, but the Court refused. • 12_The quotes are taken from John Renard, *Seven Doors to Islam*, Berkeley: University of California Press, 1996, 125ff. For some general works on Islamic calligraphy, see Nabil Safwat, *The Art of the Pen: Calligraphy of the 14th to 20th Centuries*, New York: Azimuth Editions/Oxford University Press, 1996; Annemarie Schimmel, *Calligraphy and Islamic Culture*, New York: New York University Press, 1984, and *Islamic Calligraphy*, New York: Metropolitan Museum of Art, 1992; and Manijeh Bayani, Anna Contadini, and Tim Stanley *The Decorated Word: Qurans of the 17th to 19th centuries*, New York: Azimuth Editions/ Oxford University Press, 1999. • 13_See the Amnesty International report, *Pakistan: Use and Abuse of the Blasphemy Laws*, Amnesty International, 1994. • 14_A dictum by Rabbi Hamnuna, from the Babylonian treatise Gittin 45. Quoted in R. Travers Herford, *Christianity in Talmud and Midrash*, New York: KTAV, 1903, p. 160. • 15_Herford, *Christianity in Talmud and Midrash*, pp. 155-161. • 16_Villa-Flores, Javier, "'To Lose One's Soul': Blasphemy and Slavery in New Spain, 1596–1669," *Hispanic American Historical Review* 82.3 (2002): p. 438. See also, Kathryn Joy McKnight, "Blasphemy as Resistance: An African Slave Woman Before the Inquisition," in *Women in the Inquisition*, Mary E. Giles, ed., Baltimore: Johns Hopkins University Press, 1999, p.p. 229-253. • 17_See the excellent website at Jewish Theological Seminary's library: http://www.jtslibrarytreasures.org/

Chapter Three

I_Eliot, TS, *After Strange Gods*, London: Faber and Faber, 1934, p. 52. • 2_Bacon, Francis, *The Advancement of Learning*, ed., Arthur Johnston, Oxford: Clarendon Press, 1974, p. 15 [I. II. §9]. • 3_Hamerton, Philip G, *The Intellectual Life*, New York: John B. Alden, 1885, p.p. 376 – 377. • 4_See notes on "Modern" in the *American Heritage Dictionary*, 4th edition, Boston: Houghton Mifflin, 2000. • 5_Llobera, Josep R, *The God of Modernity: The Development of Nationalism in Western Europe*, Oxford: Berg, 1994, p. 143. Also key here are the works Benedict Anderson, *Imagined Communities*, rev. ed., London: Verson, 1991, and Eric Hobsbawm's *Nations and Nationalism Since 1780*, Cambridge: Cambridge University Press, 1990. • 6_Julius, Anthony, *Transgressions: The Offences of Art*, Chicago: University of Chicago Press, 2002, p. 53. • 7_Claiming cloning as blasphemy was quite widespread. One Christian publication called *Bible Class* went so far to make a link between Dolly the sheep and the two-horned lamb of Revelation 13, going on to say that cloning was the "ultimate blasphemy". Accessed at: http://www.ensignmessage.com/archives/bang.html • 8_"Human Cloning Goes Too Far", Op-Ed, Montreal *Gazette*, 14 January 1998, B2. • 9_Spiegelman, Art, "Drawing Blood: Outrageous Cartoons and the Art of Outrage", *Harpers Magazine*, June 2006, p. 45. • 10_See Shaila Dewan, "Lady Liberty Trades in Some Trappings", *The New York Times*, 5 July 2006. Accessed online, 5 July 2006, at: http://www.nytimes.com/2006/07/05/us/05liberty.html?_r=1&oref=slogin. • 11_Quoted in Levy, *Treason Against God*, pp. 313–314. • 12_Quoted in J Hoberman, "Socialist Realism: from Stalin to Sots. (Joseph Stalin)", *Artforum International* 32.2, Oct 1993: 72(8). *Expanded Academic ASAP*, Thomson Gale. Accessed 6 July 2006. • 13_Quoted in Hoberman, "Socialist Realism". • 14_Quoted in David Elliott, "Sots Art", *Grove Art Online*, Oxford University Press, accessed 7 July 2006, at: http://www.groveart.com.ezproxy.tcu.edu/ • 15_Hoberman, "Socialist Realism". • 16_"Introduction," *Soviet Dissident Artists*, Renee Baigell and Matthew Baigell, eds., New Brunswick, NJ: Rutgers University Press, 1995, p. 5. • 17_Julius, Anthony, *Idolizing Pictures*, London: Thames and Hudson, 2000, p. 23. Many ideas for this section come from Julius' book. • 18_Bulatov, Erik, quoted in the "Introduction", *Soviet Dissident Artists*, p. 11. • 19_Kosolapov, Alexander, in Soviet Dissident Artists, pp. 261 261. • 20_Ortner, Sherry B, "On Key Symbols," in *A Reader in the Anthropology of Religion*, ed., Michael Lambek, Oxford: Blackwell, 2002, p. 161. • 21_This is the title of David Morgan's chapter on the topic in *The Sacred Gaze*, Berkeley: University of California Press, 2005. He notes the iconic status of the flag alongside the bible and the cross. • 22_From a report to the Daughters of the American Revolution Flag Committee, printed in *American Monthly Magazine*, April 1899, p. 903; reprinted in Robert Justin Goldstein, ed., *Desecrating the American Flag*, Syracuse, NY: Syracuse University Presss, 1996, p. 21. Quoted in Morgan, *Sacred Gaze*, p. 237. • 23_Whelan, David, "Wrapped in the Flag: How Can Brands Respond to America's Resurgent Patriotism?", *American Demographics*, December, 2001, p. 37. • 24_Dubin, Steven, *Arresting Images*, London: Routledge, 1992, p. 109. In his chapter in this book, "Rally 'Round the Flag," Dubin provides a much more detailed and cogent account of the Dread Scott case than I can provide here. • 25_West, Rebecca, preface to Bernard Causton and G Gordon Young, *Keeping it dark; Or, The Censor's Handbook*, London, Mandrake Press, Ltd., 1930, p. 7. • 26_Fish, Stanley, "Our Faith in Letting It All Hang Out", *The New York Times*, Op-Ed, 12 February 2006. • 27_Schlesinger, Arthur, "Preface", *Censorship: 500 Years of Conflict*, New York: Oxford University Press, 1994, pp. 7 and 8.

BIBLIOGRAPHY

- Anderson, Benedict, *Imagined Communities: Reflections on the Origin and Spread of Nationalism*, London: New Left Books, 1983.
- Apostolos-Cappadona, Diane, *Dictionary of Christian Art*, New York: Continuum, 1994.
- Atkins, Robert and Svetlana Mintcheva, eds., *Censoring Culture: Contemporary Threats to Free Expression*, New York; London: New Press, 2006.
- Baker, K, "Making Arts Brings Federal Charges", in *San Francisco Chronicle*, August 23, 2005.
- Barasch, Moshe, *Icon*, New York: New York University Press, 1992.
- Barron, Stephanie, *Degenerate Art: Fate of the Avant-garde in Nazi Germany*, New York: Harry N Abrams, Inc., March 1991.
- Bassols, Miguel, 'On Blasphemy: Religion and Psychological Structure', in *Lacanian Theory of Discourse*, Mark Bracher, ed., New York: New York University Press, 1994.
- Belting, Hans, *Likeness and Presence*, Edmund Jephcott, trans., Chicago: University of Chicago Press, 1994.
- Besant, A W, *Blasphemy*, London: Printed by A Besant and C Bradlaugh, 1882.
- Bland, Kalman P, *The Artless Jew*, Princeton: Princeton University Press, 2000.
- *Blasphemy and Film Censorhip: Submission into the European Court of Human Rights in Respect of Nigel Wingrove Versus the United Kingdom*, Article 19, 1995.
- Bevan, E, *Holy Images: An Inquiry into Idolatry and Image-Worship in Ancient Paganism and in Christianity*, London: G. Allen & Unwin, 1940.
- Cabantous, Alain, *Blasphemy: Impious Speech in the West from the Seventeenth to the Nineteenth Century*, New York: Columbia University Press, 2002.
- Camille, Michael, *The Gothic Idol: Ideology and Image-making in Medieval Art*, Cambridge: Cambridge University Press, 1989.
- Carmilly-Weinberger, Moshe, *Fear of Art: Censorship and Freedom of Expression in Art*, New York: Bowker, 1986.
- Clapp, Jane, *Art Censorship: A Chronology of Proscribed and Prescribed Art*, Metuchen, New Jersey: Scarecrow Press 1972.
- Clare, Janet, *Art Made Tongue-tied by Authority: Elizabethan and Jacobean Dramatic Censorship*, Manchester: Manchester University Press, 1990.
- Cohen, Richard I, *Jewish Icons: Art and Society in Modern Europe*, Berkeley: University of California Press, 1998.
- Coleman, Peter, *Obscenity, Blasphemy, Sedition: 100 Years of Censorship in Australia*, Jacaranda Press: Brisbane, 1962.
- Conolly, L W, *The Censorship of British Drama, 1737-1824*, San Marino: Huntington Library; Folkestone: (Distributed by) Dawson, 1976.
- Cossman, Brenda, *Censorship and the Arts: Law, Controversy, Debate, Facts*, Toronto: Ontario Association for Art Galleries, 1995.
- Crowder, Colin, 'Blasphemy', in *Dictionary of Ethics, Theology and Society*, Paul Barry Clarke and Andrew Linzey, eds., London: Routledge, 1996.
- De Grazia, Edward, *Girls Lean Back Everywhere: The Law of Obscenity and the Assault on Genius*, New York: Vintage, 1992.
- Doty, Gene, 'Blasphemy and the Recovery of the Sacred', in *Violence, Utopia, and the Kingdom of God: Fantasy and Ideology in the Bible*, George Aichele and Tina Pippin, eds., New York: Routledge, 1998.
- Dubin, Steven C, *Arresting Images: Impolitic Art and Uncivil Actions*, London: Routledge, 1992.
- Duggan, L, "Censorship in the Name of Feminism", in Ellis, K et al, eds., *Caught Looking: Feminism, Pornography and Censorship*, East Haven Conn: Long River Books, 1992.
- Dyrness, William A, *Reformed Theology and Visual Culture: The Protestant Imagination from Calvin to Edwards*, New York: Cambridge University Press, 2004.
- Eagerton Jr, S Y, *Pictures and Punishment: Art and Criminal Prosecution during the Florentine Renaissance*, Ithaca: Cornell University Press, 1985.
- Eire, Carlos MN, *War Against the Idols: The Reformation of Worship from Erasmus to Calvin*, Cambridge: Cambridge University Press, 1986.
- Eliot, TS, *After Strange Gods*, London: Faber and Faber, 1934.
- Elkins, James, *On the Strange Place of Religion in Contemporary Art*, New York: Routledge, 2005.
- Ellis, A, "Censorship and the Media", in Kieran, M, ed., *Media Ethics*, London: Routledge, 1998.

- Ernst, Carl W, 'Blasphemy: Islamic Concept', in *Encyclopedia of Religion*, vol. 2., Lindsay Jones, ed., 2nd ed., Detroit: Macmillan Reference USA, 2005, pp. 974–977.
- Ernst, Carl W, *Following Muhammad: Rethinking Islam in the Contemporary World*, Chapel Hill, North Carolina: University of North Carolina Press, 2003.
- Ernst, Carl W, *Words of Ecstasy in Islam*, Albany, New York: State University of New York Press, 1985.
- Evans, GR, *A Brief History of Heresy*, Oxford: Blackwell, 2003.
- Freedberg, D, "Johannes Molanus on Provocative Paintings" in *Journal of the Warburg and Courtauld Institutes*, vol. 34, 1971, pp. 229–245.
- Flood, Finbarr Barry, 'Between Cult and Culture: Bamiyan, Islamic Iconoclasm, and the Museum', *Art Bulletin* 84.4, December 2002, pp. 641–659.
- Freedberg, David, *The Power of Images: Studies in the History and Theory of Response*, Chicago: University of Chicago Press, 1989.
- Friedman, Jerome, *Blasphemy, Immorality, and Anarchy: The Ranters and the English Revolution*, Athens, Ohio: Ohio University Press, 1987.
- Galsworthy, John, *Censorship and Art*, RA Kessinger Publishing Company, June 2004.
- Gamboni, Dario, *The Destruction of Art*, New Haven, Connecticut: Yale University Press, 1997.
- Gehl, Paul, 'Texts and Textures: Dirty Pictures and Other Things in Medieval Manuscripts', *Corona* 3, 1983, pp. 68–77.
- Goodenough, Erwin, *Jewish Symbols in the Greco-Roman Period*, Princeton: Princeton University Press, 1988.
- Grabar, Oleg, *The Formation of Islamic Art*, New Haven, Connecticut: Yale University Press, 1987.
- Greenaway, Peter, 'Blasphemy in Cinema', in *Peter Greenaway: Interviews*, Jackson, Mississippi: University Press of Mississippi, 2000.
- Gruzinski, Serge, *Images at War: Mexico from Columbus to Blade Runner (1492–2019)*, Heather MacLean, trans., Durham, North Carolina: Duke University Press, 2001.
- Gurstein, Rochelle, *The Repeal of Reticence: A History of America's Cultural and Legal Struggles over Free Speech, Obscenity, Sexual Liberation, and Modern Art*, New York: Hill & Wang, 1998.
- Habertal, Moshe and Avishai Margalit, *Idolatry*, Naomi Goldblum, trans., Cambridge, Massachusettss: Harvard University Press, 1992.
- Harris, N, "Reluctant Alliance: 'American Art, American Religion", in Arthurs, A and Wallach, G, eds., *Crossroads: Art and Religion in American Life*, New York: The New York Press, 2001.
- Hauptman, W, "The Suppression of Art in the McCarthy Decade", in *Artforum*, vol. 12, no. 2, 1973, pp. 48–52.
- Hawthorn, Matt, *The Degenerate Art Book*, Arnolfini Live, May 2001.
- Hawting, GR, *The Idea of Idolatry and the Emergence of Islam*, Cambridge: Cambridge University Press, 1999.
- Heins, Majorie, *Sex, Sin and Blasphemy: A Guide to America's Censorship Wars*, New York: New Press, 1993.
- Hewett, Bob, *The Book of Blasphemy*, Hertford: Authors Online, 2002.
- Heartney, Eleanor, *Postmodern Heretics: The Catholic Imagination in Contemporary Art*, New York: Midmarch Arts, 2004.
- Hocks, Mary E, and Michelle R Kendrick, *Eloquent Images: Word and Image in the Age of New Media*, Cambridge, Mass.: MIT Press, 2003.
- Hodgson, Marshall GS, 'Islam and Image', *History of Religions* 3, 1969, pp. 220–260.
- Houser, Craig, Leslie C Jones, Simon Taylor, Jack Ben-Levi, *Abject Art: Repulsion and Desire in American Art*, New York: Whitney Museum, 1993.
- Jacobsen, C, "Redefining Censorship: A Feminist View", *Art Journal*, vol. 50, No. 4, 1991, pp. 42–55.
- Julius, Anthony, *Idolizing Pictures: Idolatry, Iconoclasm, and Jewish Art*, New York: Thames & Hudson, 2001.
- Julius Anthony, *Transgressions: The Offences of Art*, Chicago: University of Chicago Press, 2003.
- Julius, A, *Transgressions: The Offence of Art*, London: Thames and Hudson, 2002.
- Kleeblatt, Norman L, ed., *Mirroring Evil: Nazi Imagery/Recent Art*, New York: The Jewish Museum; New Brunswick, New Jersey: Rutgers University Press, 2001.
- Kosuth, Joseph, *The Play of the Unmentionable: An Installation by Joseph Kosuth at the Brooklyn Museum*, New York: New Press in Association with the Brooklyn Museum, 1992.
- Lasker, Daniel, 'Blasphemy: Jewish Concept' in *Encyclopedia of Religion*, Lindsay Jones, ed., vol. 2, 2nd ed., Detroit: Macmillan Reference, 2005, pp. 968–971.
- Lawton, David, *Blasphemy*, Philadelphia: University of Pennsylvania Press, 1993.

- Leaman, Oliver, *Islamic Aesthetics*, Notre Dame, Indiana: University of Notre Dame Press, 2004.
- Levy, Leonard Williams, *Blasphemy: Verbal Offense Against the Sacred, From Moses to Salman Rushdie*, New York: Knopf, 1993.
- Levy, Leonard Williams, *Treason Against God: A History of the Offense of Blasphemy*, New York: Schocken Books, 1981.
- Lewis, J, *Hollywood v. Hard Core: How the Struggle over Censorship Saved the Modern Film Industry*, New York: NYU Press, 2000.
- Llobera, Josep R, *The God of Modernity: The Development of Nationalism in Western Europe*, Oxford: Berg, 1994.
- Lyons, C, *The New Censors: Movies and the Culture Wars*, Philadelphia: Temple University Press, 1997.
- McKnight, Kathryn Joy, 'Blasphemy as Resistance: An African Slave Woman Before the Inquisition', in *Women in the Inquisition*, Mary E Giles, ed., Baltimore: Johns Hopkins University Press, 1999, pp. 229–253.
- Maitland, Sara, 'Blasphemy and Creativity', in *The Salman Rushdie Controversy in Interreligious Perspective*, Dan Cohn-Sherbok, ed., Edwin Mellen Press, 1990.
- Mellinkoff, Ruth, *The Horned Moses in Medieval Art and Thought*, Berkeley: University of California Press, 1970.
- Meyer, Richard, "Hard Targets: Feminist Art, Male Nudes, and the Force of Censorship" in *Wack! Art and the Feminist Revolution 1965-1980*, Los Angeles: Museum of Contemporary Art, 2006.
- Meyer, Richard, *Outlaw Representation: Censorship and Homosexuality in Twentieth-Century Art*, Oxford: Oxford University Press, 2002.
- Meyer, Richard, *Outlaw Representation: Censorship and Homosexuality in Twentieth-Century American Art*, Boston Massachusetts: Beacon Press, 2004.
- Middleton, Darren JN, ed., *Scandalizing Jesus? Kazantzakis's The Last Temptation of Christ Fifty Years On*, New York: Continuum, 2005.
- Misopappas, Philanax, "Rome's Raities; or the Pope's cabinet unlock'd , and expos'd to view. Being a true and faithful account of the blasphemy, treason massacres...pious frauds, &c. of the Roman Church, etc.," *The Epistle Directory*, London: Printed for James Norris, 1684.
- Mitchell, WJT, *Picture Theory: Essays on Verbal and Visual Representation*, Chicago: University of Chicago Press, 1994.
- Mitchell, WJT, *What Do Pictures Want? The Lives and Loves of Images*, Chicago: University of Chicago Press, 2005.
- Morgan, David, *The Sacred Gaze: Religious Visual Culture in Theory and Practice*, Berkeley: University of California Press, 2005.
- Nash, David S, *Blasphemy in Modern Britain, 1789–present*, London: Ashgate, 1999.
- National Coalition Against Censorship *Censorship Undeterred: A Highly Selective Timeline of Art Controversies 1989-2003*, New York: National Coalition Against Censorship, 2003.
- Paulson, Ronald, *Hogarth's Harlot: Sacred Parody in Enlightenment England*, Baltimore, Maryland; London: Johns Hopkins University Press, 2003.
- Peter, Jennifer A and Crosier, Louis M, eds., *The Cultural Battlefield: Art, Censorship and Public Funding*, Washington, DC: Avocus Publishing, 1995.
- Pidock, David Musa, *Satanic Voices Ancient and Modern: A Surfeit of Blasphemy Including the Rushdie Report: From Edifice Complex to Occult Theory*, Mustaquim, 1992.
- *Planned Attack on Aad Sri Guru Granth Sahib: Academics or Blasphemy*, Chandigarh: International Centre of Sikh Studies, 1994.
- Post, Robert C, *Censorship and Silencing: Practices of Cultural Regulation*, Los Angeles: Getty Research Institute, for the History of Art and the Humanities, 1998.
- *Potentially Harmful: The Art of American Censorship*, Georgia State University, January 2006.
- Pressly, William, *The French Revolution as Blasphemy: Johan Zoffany's Paintings of the Massacre at Paris, August 10, 1792*, Berkeley: University of California Press, 1999.
- Rahmani, A, "A Conversation on Censorship with Carole Schneeman", in M/E/A/N/I/N/G vol. 6, 1989, pp. 3–7.
- *Religion, Body and Gender Early Modern Spain*, San Fransisco: Mellen Research University Press, 1991.
- Renard, John, *Seven Doors to Islam*, Berkeley: University of California Press, 1996.
- Riley, Robin, *Film, Faith, and Cultural Conflict: The Case of Martin Scorsese's The Last Temptation of Christ*, Westport, CT: Praeger, 2003.
- Roberts, Allen F and Mary Nooter Roberts, *A Saint in the City: Sufi Arts of Urban Senegal*, Los Angeles: UCLA Fowler Museum, 2003.

- Rose, B, "Is it Art? Orlan and the Transgressive Act", *Art in America*, vol. 2, 1993, pp. 82–7, 125.
- Sangharakshita, *Buddhism and Blasphemy: Buddhist Reflections on the 1977 Blasphemy Trial*, London: Windhorse Publications, 1978.
- Schimmel, Annemarie, *Islamic Calligraphy*, New York: Metropolitan Museum of Art, 1992.
- Shaw, Gwendolyn DuBois, *Seeing the Unspeakable: The Art of Kara Walker*, Durham, North Carolina: Duke University Press, 2004.
- Soussloff, Catherine M, ed., *Jewish Identity in Modern Art History*, Berkeley: University of California Press, 1999.
- Sova, Dawn B, *Forbidden Films: Censorship Histories of 125 Motion Pictures*, New York: Checkmark Books, 2001.
- Steinberg, Leo, *The Sexuality of Christ in Renaissance Art and in Modern Oblivion*, 2nd ed., University of Chicago Press, 1996.
- *Suspended License: Censorship and the Visual Arts*, Seattle; London: University of Washington Press, 1997.
- Szabari, Antónia, 'The Scandal of Religion: Luther and Public Speech', in *Political Theologies: Public Religions in a Post-Secular World*, ed. Hent de Vries and Lawrence E Sullivan, New York: Fordham University Press, 2006.
- Tedford, Thomas L, *Freedom of Speech in the United States* (5th ed.), State College, Pennsylvania: Strata Publications, 2005.
- Tedford, TL, "Religio-Moral Heresy: From Blasphemy to Obscenity", in Tedford, TL and DA Herbeck, eds.), *Freedom of Speech in the United States*, New York: Random House, 1985.
- Truex, Jerry Duane, *The Problem of Blasphemy: The Fourth Gospel and Early Jewish Understandings*, University of Durham, 2001.
- Villa-Flores, Javier, '"To Lose One's Soul": Blasphemy and Slavery in New Spain, 1596–1669', *Hispanic American Historical Review* 82:3, 2002, pp. 435–468.
- Walter, Nicholas, *Blasphemy Ancient and Modern*, London: Rationalist Press, 1990.
- Webster, Richard, *A Brief History of Blasphemy: Liberalism, Censorship and "The Satanic Verses"*, Southwold: Orwell Press, 1990.
- White, Garrett, ed., *Forbidden Art: The Postwar Russian Avant-Garde*, New York: Distributed Art Publishers, 1998.
- Williams, B, *The Williams Report: Report of the Committee on Obscenity and Film Censorship*, London, 1979.
- Williams, Jerry M, *Censorship and Art in Pre-Enlightenment Lima*, Scripta Humanistica, January 2004.
- Zerzel, William, ed., *Censorship: 500 Years of Conflict*, New York: Oxford University Press, 1984.

INDEX

People

Works of Art and Exhibitions

Films and Television Programmes

Texts and Publications

Political and Religious Concepts, Practices, Places, Events and Groups

Institutions and Organisations

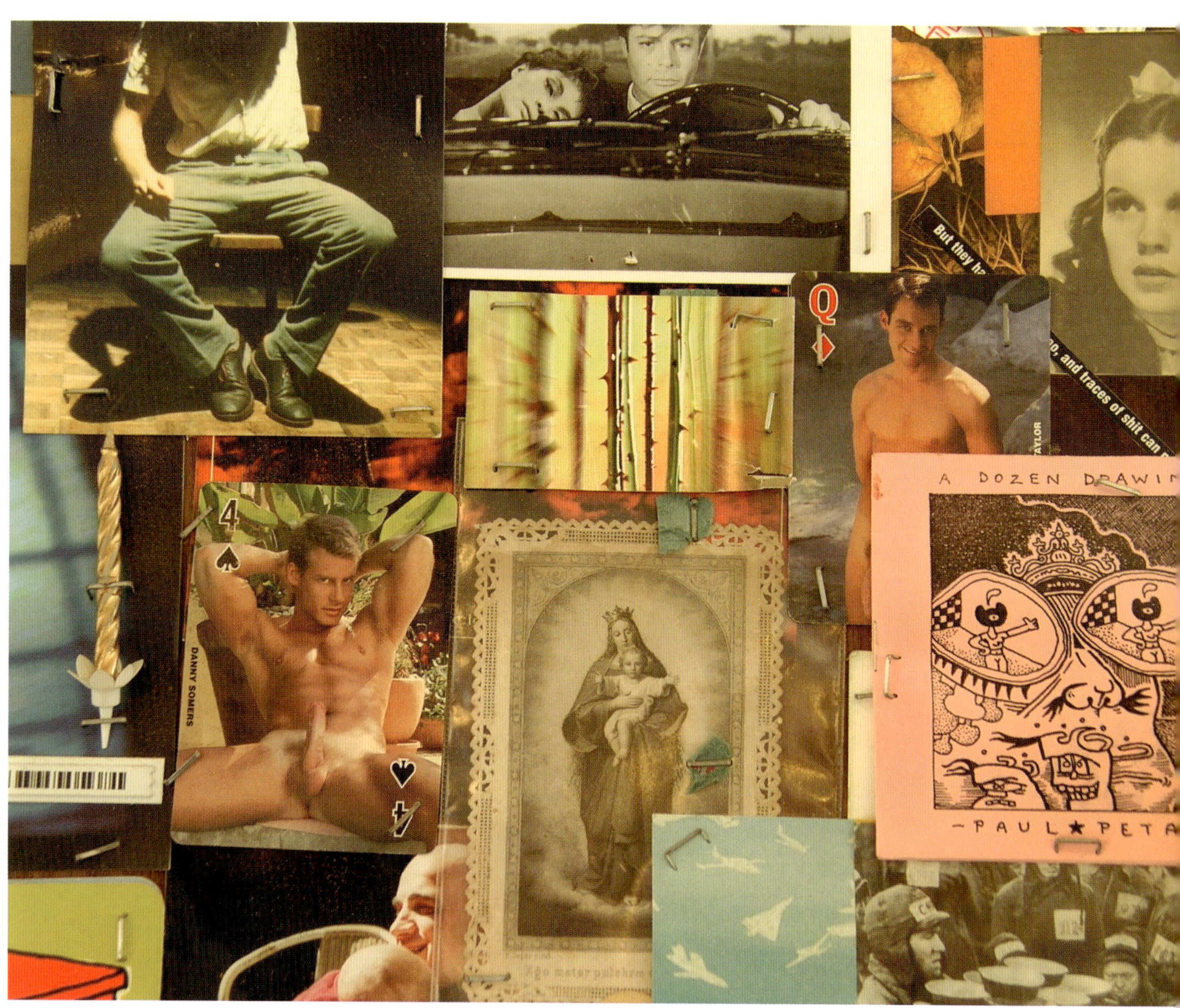

Franko B, *Untitled*, detail, nd, private collection

Written by S Brent Plate

Black Dog Publishing Limited
Unit 4.4 Tea Building
56 Shoreditch High Street
London
EI 6JJ

Tel: +44 (0)20 7613 1922
Fax: +44 (0)20 7613 1944
Email: info@bdp.demon.co.uk

British Library Cataloguing-in-Publication Data.

A CIP record for this book is available from the British Library.

ISBN10 1 904772 53 6
ISBN13 978 1 904772 53 8

architecture art design
fashion history photography
theory and things

www.bdpworld.com

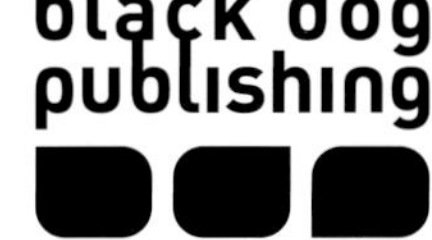